UNIX®
in Plain English

Third Edition

UNIX®
in Plain English

Third Edition

Kevin Reichard
Eric Foster-Johnson

M&T Books
An imprint of IDG Books Worldwide, Inc.

Foster City, CA • Chicago, IL • Indianapolis, IN • New York, NY

UNIX® in Plain English, Third Edition

Published by
M&T Books
An imprint of IDG Books Worldwide, Inc.
919 E. Hillsdale Blvd., Suite 400
Foster City, CA 94404
www.idgbooks.com (IDG Books Worldwide Web site)

Library of Congress Catalog Card Number: 98-75376

ISBN: 0-7645-7011-0

Printed in the United States of America

10 9 8 7 6 5 4 3 2 1

1P/ST/RS/ZY/FC

Distributed in the United States by IDG Books Worldwide, Inc.

Distributed by Macmillan Canada for Canada; by Transworld Publishers Limited in the United Kingdom; by IDG Norge Books for Norway; by IDG Sweden Books for Sweden; by Woodslane Pty. Ltd. for Australia; by Woodslane (NZ) Ltd. for New Zealand; by Addison Wesley Longman Singapore Pte Ltd. for Singapore, Malaysia, Thailand, Indonesia, and Korea; by Norma Comunicaciones S.A. for Colombia; by Intersoft for South Africa; by International Thomson Publishing for Germany, Austria, and Switzerland; by Toppan Company Ltd. for Japan; by Distribuidora Cuspide for Argentina; by Livraria Cultura for Brazil; by Ediciencia S.A. for Ecuador; by Ediciones ZETA S.C.R. Ltda. for Peru; by WS Computer Publishing Corporation, Inc., for the Philippines; by Unalis Corporation for Taiwan; by Contemporanea de Ediciones for Venezuela; by Computer Book & Magazine Store for Puerto Rico; by Express Computer Distributors for the Caribbean and West Indies. Authorized Sales Agent: Anthony Rudkin Associates for the Middle East and North Africa.

For general information on IDG Books Worldwide's books in the U.S., please call our Consumer Customer Service department at 800-762-2974. For reseller information, including discounts and premium sales, please call our Reseller Customer Service department at 800-434-3422.

For information on where to purchase IDG Books Worldwide's books outside the U.S., please contact our International Sales department at 650-655-3200 or fax 650-655-3297.

For consumer information on foreign language translations, please contact our Customer Service department at 1-800-434-3422, fax 317-596-5692, or e-mail rights@idgbooks.com.

For information on licensing foreign or domestic rights, please phone +1-650-655-3109.

For sales inquiries and special prices for bulk quantities, please contact our Sales department at 650-655-3200 or write to the address above.

For information on using IDG Books Worldwide's books in the classroom or for ordering examination copies, please contact our Educational Sales department at 800-434-2086 or fax 317-596-5499.

For press review copies, author interviews, or other publicity information, please contact our Public Relations department at 650-655-3000 or fax 650-655-3299.

For authorization to photocopy items for corporate, personal, or educational use, please contact Copyright Clearance Center, 222 Rosewood Drive, Danvers, MA 01923, or fax 978-750-4470.

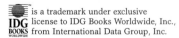

ABOUT IDG BOOKS WORLDWIDE

Welcome to the world of IDG Books Worldwide.

IDG Books Worldwide, Inc., is a subsidiary of International Data Group, the world's largest publisher of computer-related information and the leading global provider of information services on information technology. IDG was founded more than 30 years ago by Patrick J. McGovern and now employs more than 9,000 people worldwide. IDG publishes more than 290 computer publications in over 75 countries. More than 90 million people read one or more IDG publications each month.

Launched in 1990, IDG Books Worldwide is today the #1 publisher of best-selling computer books in the United States. We are proud to have received eight awards from the Computer Press Association in recognition of editorial excellence and three from Computer Currents' First Annual Readers' Choice Awards. Our best-selling *...For Dummies®* series has more than 50 million copies in print with translations in 31 languages. IDG Books Worldwide, through a joint venture with IDG's Hi-Tech Beijing, became the first U.S. publisher to publish a computer book in the People's Republic of China. In record time, IDG Books Worldwide has become the first choice for millions of readers around the world who want to learn how to better manage their businesses.

Our mission is simple: Every one of our books is designed to bring extra value and skill-building instructions to the reader. Our books are written by experts who understand and care about our readers. The knowledge base of our editorial staff comes from years of experience in publishing, education, and journalism — experience we use to produce books to carry us into the new millennium. In short, we care about books, so we attract the best people. We devote special attention to details such as audience, interior design, use of icons, and illustrations. And because we use an efficient process of authoring, editing, and desktop publishing our books electronically, we can spend more time ensuring superior content and less time on the technicalities of making books.

You can count on our commitment to deliver high-quality books at competitive prices on topics you want to read about. At IDG Books Worldwide, we continue in the IDG tradition of delivering quality for more than 30 years. You'll find no better book on a subject than one from IDG Books Worldwide.

IDG BOOKS WORLDWIDE

John Kilcullen
Chairman and CEO
IDG Books Worldwide, Inc.

Steven Berkowitz
President and Publisher
IDG Books Worldwide, Inc.

VIII WINNER — *Eighth Annual Computer Press Awards 1992*

IX WINNER — *Ninth Annual Computer Press Awards 1993*

X WINNER — *Tenth Annual Computer Press Awards 1994*

XI WINNER — *Eleventh Annual Computer Press Awards 1995*

IDG is the world's leading IT media, research and exposition company. Founded, in 1964, IDG had 1997 revenues of $2.05 billion and has more than 9,000 employees worldwide. IDG offers the widest range of media options that reach IT buyers in 75 countries representing 95% of worldwide IT spending. IDG's diverse product and services portfolio spans six key areas including print publishing, online publishing, expositions and conferences, market research, education and training, and global marketing services. More than 90 million people read one or more of IDG's 290 magazines and newspapers, including IDG's leading global brands — Computerworld, PC World, Network World, Macworld and the Channel World family of publications. IDG Books Worldwide is one of the fastest-growing computer book publishers in the world, with more than 700 titles in 36 languages. The "...For Dummies®" series alone has more than 50 million copies in print. IDG offers online users the largest network of technology-specific Web sites around the world through IDG.net (http://www.idg.net), which comprises more than 225 targeted Web sites in 55 countries worldwide. International Data Corporation (IDC) is the world's largest provider of information technology data, analysis and consulting, with research centers in over 41 countries and more than 400 research analysts worldwide. IDG World Expo is a leading producer of more than 168 globally branded conferences and expositions in 35 countries including E3 (Electronic Entertainment Expo), Macworld Expo, ComNet, Windows World Expo, ICE (Internet Commerce Expo), Agenda, DEMO, and Spotlight. IDG's training subsidiary, ExecuTrain, is the world's largest computer training company, with more than 230 locations worldwide and 785 training courses. IDG Marketing Services helps industry-leading IT companies build international brand recognition by developing global integrated marketing programs via IDG's print, online and exposition products worldwide. Further information about the company can be found at www.idg.com. 10/8/98

Credits

Acquisitions Editor
Laura Lewin

Development Editor
Matthew E. Lusher

Technical Editor
William Rousseau

Copy Editor
Barry Childs-Helton

Project Coordinator
Tom Debolski

Book Designer
London Road Design

Graphics and Production Specialists
Linda Marousek
Hector Mendoza
E. A. Pauw
Christopher Pimentel

Quality Control Specialists
Mick Arellano
Mark Schumann

Proofing & Indexing
York Production Services

About the Authors

Kevin Reichard and **Eric Foster-Johnson** are UNIX and Internet experts, as well as veteran computer book authors. They have written top-selling books on UNIX and Linux. Reichard has also authored such top-sellers as *Linux in Plain English* and *UNIX Fundamentals*. Foster-Johnson, also a programming expert, has paved the way for many an Internet programmer with his *Cross-Platform Perl* and *Graphical Applications with Tcl and Tk*.

As always, for Sean — Kevin

To Katya — Eric

Preface

Welcome to *UNIX in Plain English!* This reference work is designed to give you instant access to the UNIX and X Window System commands and concepts you'll use in your everyday work. In essence, we organized the many handwritten notes sitting next to our terminals and the Post-It notes attached to our monitors, and presented them in a fashion that benefits both beginning and advanced UNIX users. We, too, have tired of flipping through disorganized notes and reference books that end up being more complex than the documentation.

Why do you need a reference work like this, when you have manuals upon manuals lining your bookshelves (in addition to an online help system)?

To be honest, finding information on UNIX systems can be an onerous chore. UNIX documentation tends to be on the weak side when it comes to looking up anything quickly: The manuals provide a wealth of advanced technical information, but they assume a certain level of familiarity with computing in general and the UNIX operating system in particular. Yes, most UNIX systems have online manual pages that cover the entire command set. But in order to use the manual page, you first need to know the name of the command. Because most of us don't know exactly what we want until we find it, often the **man** pages aren't really much help when we're looking for easy-to-grasp information about specific commands, let alone basic UNIX concepts. Plus, UNIX is definitely geared for the educated user. Once you understand the basic mechanisms, commands, and structures, you'll do reasonably well in your everyday work.

That's where this edition of *UNIX in Plain English* comes in. We've assembled lists of the UNIX and X Window command sets in alphabetical order, by type, and cross-referenced with DOS commands. We've also added a reference, "UNIX in Plain English," that lists common computer tasks and then offers the necessary UNIX commands, working backward from the usual reference format.

This book is also designed as a companion to *Teach Yourself UNIX*, fourth edition (IDG Books, 1999). Although we wrote *Teach Yourself UNIX* purely as a beginners' tutorial, we did include a reference section at the end of the book, which we used on a regular basis ourselves. Accordingly, we intend *UNIX in Plain English* as an extension of that reference section.

Although we list all the command-line options for all UNIX commands in this work, you can find fuller explanations of the major UNIX commands in *Teach Yourself UNIX*. If you're looking for more information about some lesser-known UNIX commands, you can either rush out and buy yet another UNIX text (we list some essential works in the Bibliography) or check your system documentation.

How This Book Is Organized

We have found that when we search for information on UNIX commands in real-world situations, several possibilities occur:

- We know exactly what we're looking for, and all we need is the information about a specific command. (As you might expect, this option occurs least often.)
- We're not quite sure what we're looking for, but we know exactly what we want to do. (Another unlikely occurrence because we rarely know exactly what we want to do.)
- We have a vague idea of what we want to do. (This occurs more frequently in real life than in computing.)

- We're not quite sure what we want to do, but we know it's similar to something that we know how to do.
- We're totally lost and want to browse through our options. (Bingo!)

In response to these real-world needs, we've decided to organize UNIX and X Window commands in several different ways. Most UNIX/X reference works list all the commands in alphabetical order, assuming that you know exactly what you're looking for and therefore can look it up in a mondo listing of commands. (Yeah, right.) Although we included an alphabetical listing of the commands we cover in this book ("UNIX from A to Z"), we've also included several other references that present UNIX commands in slightly different formats. A "UNIX in Plain English" section presents a whole slew of common computing tasks, along with the corresponding UNIX and/or X command. For DOS users, we've organized a list of all DOS commands ("UNIX/DOS Cross-Reference") and their counterparts in UNIX. Finally, the heart of the book (Chapters 2-10) divides UNIX commands into broad categories (printing, text processing, and so on).

Chapters 2 through 10 also contain extended explanations of UNIX commands. We've organized these explanations into what we feel is an easy-to-use format: The commands are displayed in large type at the top of the page, followed by sections on usage, examples, options, arguments, related commands, and any other relevant information. We've purposely left a lot of space around these command listings; if you're like us, you'll soon be making notes for yourself in the margins.

Conventions Used in This Book

All commands can be found in **boldface** throughout the book. Commands that are to be typed directly into the system are displayed in a `monospaced` typeface.

In addition, you should be aware of some of the references still used in the UNIX operating system:

- **Bell**. Back in the old days of teletype data entry, the machines featured a bell, much like the typewriters of that era. Because there was often little feedback between a user and the computer, the computer would ring a bell to attract the attention of the user, who more than likely was across the room staring out the window. Today, of course, computers don't have bells, they have speakers. A reference to a bell usually means a beep emanating from the speaker.

- **Case**. In UNIX, uppercase and lowercase characters matter when you're dealing with files. For instance, **Kevin.report** is different from **kevin.report** and **kevin.Report** and **Kevin.Report**. You'll need to worry about case when you enter commands into a system. The only information within this book that is designed to be entered directly into a computer is noted with the `monospaced` font.
- **Keys**. Not every UNIX keyboard features the same set of keys. In fact, keyboards have historically differed quite a bit; vendors such as Sun Microsystems, Hewlett-Packard, DEC, and IBM have introduced variations on the standard keyboard. These days, the PC-style keyboard is becoming ubiquitous in the UNIX world. However, for the purposes of this book, we're not going to get into a discussion of differing keyboards, and for the most part the keys mentioned within this book should be present on all keyboards. That said, there are two things you should note: The **Enter** and the **Return** keys are the same (in this book, we'll use **Enter** because that seems to be the trend in modern UNIX usage), and the backspace key is usually labeled **Backspace** or **BkSp**.

A Word of Warning

Even though this is a comprehensive reference work about the UNIX operating system, you should be aware that we have not included every single option for every single command. In fact, we're not even listing every single command. To be honest, many UNIX commands are so obscure that you're unlikely to come close to using them; other, more venerable UNIX commands have been superseded by newer, more effective commands.

Why not list these commands? Because this book was written with the KISS principle in mind: **Keep It Simple, Stupid**. We focus on the commands that most beginning and intermediate UNIX users need to access most of the time.

Thus we're not covering commands such as (for example) **ar** (**archive**), because it's highly unlikely that the vast majority of UNIX users will ever need it—or that they'll notice its absence.

UNIX Variants

A book like this must confront the inevitable issue of how much of the UNIX operating system to cover and which UNIX variants to cover.

Throughout much of its history, UNIX was developed by a group within AT&T, which AT&T later sold to Novell. Other early UNIX work was done at the University of California at Berkeley, which lead to BSD UNIX (Berkeley Software Distribution). Most major UNIX vendors took what they thought was the best of the AT&T UNIX, mixed in BSD features, and added their own extensions to the pot. The result: many similar, but slightly different, versions of UNIX.

Currently UNIX is a veritable Tower of Babel, with differing versions from Sun Microsystems (SunOS, Solaris), Hewlett-Packard (HP-UX), IBM (AIX), SCO (SCO UNIX), as well as various Intel-based versions (BSD, Linux).

Although vendors are working to eliminate many of these differences, don't be surprised if your system doesn't support all the commands and all the options listed in this book. We've tried to flag the most obvious instances of commands and options that are not found on every system. We tested the commands and options in this book on several systems, but as in life, nothing is guaranteed.

How to Reach the Authors

We welcome your feedback. You can reach us via electronic mail at `reichard@mr.net` or `erc@pconline.com`.

Acknowledgments

We'd like to thanks Laura Lewin, our long-suffering editor, for all her assistance on this and all our other titles. Also, we'd like to thank Matt Lusher for making this as friction-free a process as possible.

Brief Contents

Contents

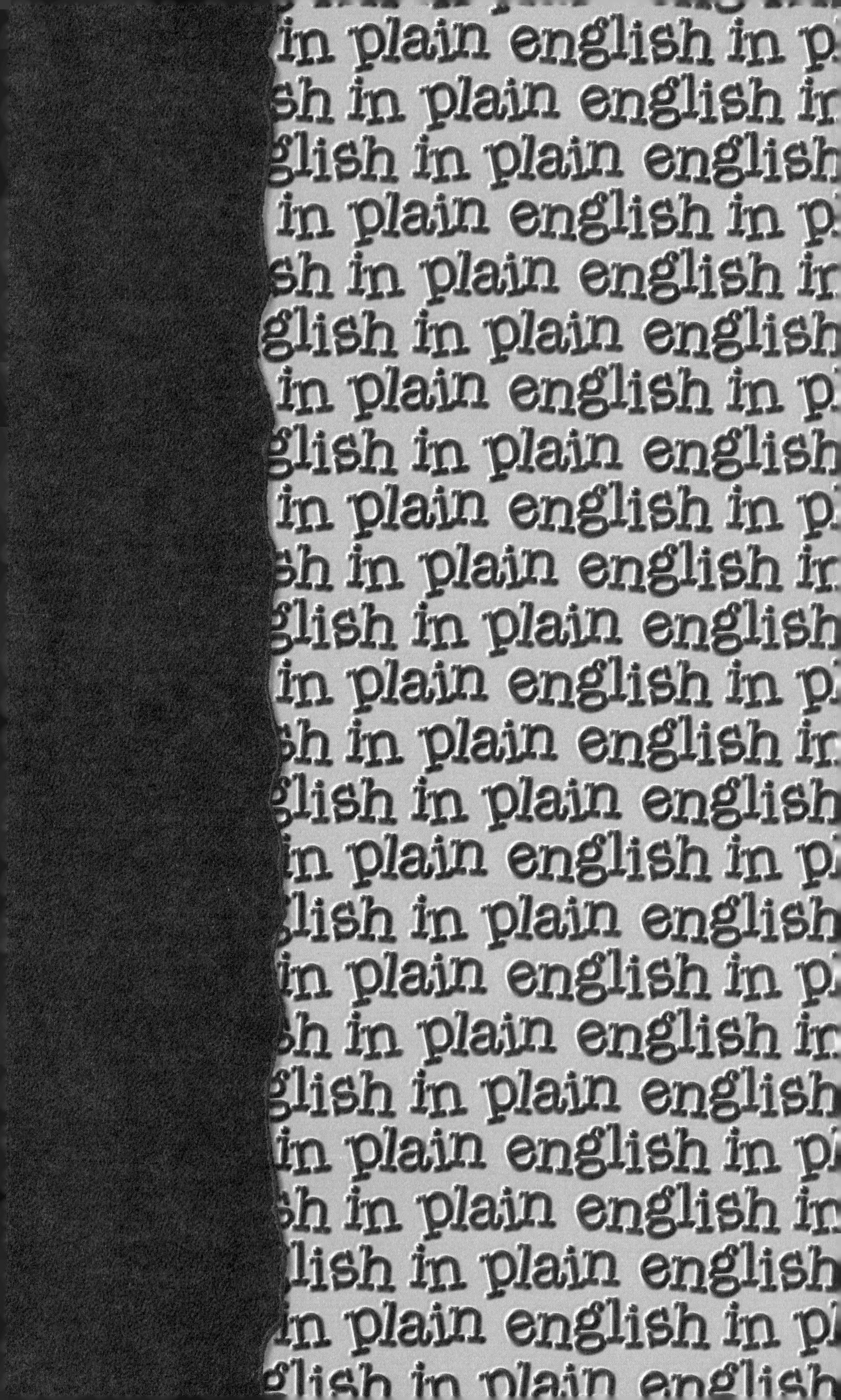
in plain english in p
sh in plain english in
glish in plain english
in plain english in p
sh in plain english in
glish in plain english
in plain english in p
glish in plain english
in plain english in p
sh in plain english in
glish in plain english
in plain english in p
sh in plain english in
glish in plain english
in plain english in p
glish in plain english
in plain english in p
sh in plain english in
glish in plain english
in plain english in p
sh in plain english in
glish in plain english
in plain english in p

1

Understanding UNIX: Commands and Structures

On the surface, UNIX seems unnecessarily complex — witness the large number of commands listed later in this book. But underneath the surface lie the roots of a simple, elegant operating system. The details may be complex, but the mechanisms favor simplicity.

A good example of this simplicity is the way you tell the computer exactly what you want it to do. If you weren't familiar with UNIX, you might be intimidated by this cryptic symbol on your screen:

```
$
```

This **prompt** tells you the system is waiting for you to enter a command. Of course, if you had no background in UNIX, you'd already be confused. Think of the **$** prompt, however, as the system's way of requesting a command from you, the all-powerful user; then UNIX may not seem quite so intimidating. (Several symbols denote prompts in UNIX, depending on which shell you're using. The Korn, Bourne, and **bash** shells use **$** as the prompt; the C shell uses %. But we're getting ahead of ourselves here; more about shells later.)

1

CAUTION

Remember that when you see a prompt in an example, do *not* type the prompt symbol when you enter a command line. The prompt is on the page only to show you where to start.

Understanding Commands

You may feel more enlightened when you first learn how to interact with the computer. Remember at all times: *The computer is not smarter than you are.* It may be faster, but it's a lot dumber. Without instructions — called *commands* — from you, the computer can do little more than sit there and run up an electric bill. It does exactly as you instruct. The secret is to make sure that what you tell the computer to do is actually what you want done.

With that in mind, you can confidently stride up to your terminal and enter a command. At the prompt, you type a command (or multiple commands) as well as more specific instructions (arguments and options, which we'll get to in a moment); the combination is called a *command line*. No matter what you want to do in UNIX — run a program, list the files in a directory, run a text editor—you get UNIX to do it by issuing a command.

As you know if you've peeked ahead, UNIX recognizes hundreds of commands. Some are used frequently in UNIX systems; for instance, text editors summoned by commands such as **vi** or **ed** are handy for creating short files or memos. Some commands are specific to certain versions of UNIX; others crop up in virtually every UNIX variant. This book focuses on commands you can find almost everywhere. A typical command line looks something like this:

```
$ ls -1
```

After entering the information as a command line, you'd press the Enter or Return key to send the command line to the system. The **-1** (*one*, not *ell*) in this command line is called an *option*. Options and arguments modify a command in some way, usually by narrowing the terms of the command. For instance, one of the many options associated with the **ls** command (which lists the contents — the files — of a directory) tells the computer to display the output in a single column instead of the multiple columns it would use *by default* (that is, normally).

TIP

As you've probably figured out, the example given here happens when you type the command line shown just after the previous paragraph.

Options exist for nearly every UNIX command. Mastering these options simplifies your use of UNIX.

CROSS-REFERENCE

Chapters 2–8, which summarize most of the UNIX commands, emphasize options in the Examples sections.

When you run the **ls** command line, your terminal displays something similiar to the following:

```
$ ls -1                personnel
data                   misc
financials             newdata
```

These filenames are typical, but not imporatnt for our discussion; for the moment, note that the command has produced a list of files in a single column. Without the **-1** option, the output from the **ls** command would look more like this:

```
$ ls
data        figures          newdata        personnel
misc       expenses      financials
```

This example of an option is relatively minor. Most UNIX options have more far-reaching results, as you'll find out when you start using them daily.

Fathoming Files

Commands aren't worth a whole lot if you don't tell them what to work on; normally you'd use a *filename* to do that. (The few UNIX commands that don't use filenames — as you might expect — don't do much, unless all you want to do is find the current date and time with the **date** command.) UNIX sees everything the system acts upon as a file — *everything*. For example, a directory is merely a file that represents a grouping of other files; a printer, a tape drive, or any other device in the system, looks like a file to UNIX.

UNIX manages printing, for example, by setting up a printer as a file. Thus, when you issue a command to print a document, in fact, you are directing the output of the command to a file that represents the printer.

On the surface, this way of looking at the system seems enormously simple: Commands work (mostly) on files. The catch: It's up to you to keep track of what the files represent, which can be a tad more difficult. Understanding the files themselves can help.

A *file* is a distinct electronic "place," an electronic structure that the computer uses to store information in a format it can use: *bits.* A bit is either 0 or 1. Strung together, these bits are the basic stuff of all information managed by the computer. A file is simply a way to organize these bits into a consistent logical format; otherwise, they'd be scattered around the hard disk with no reasonable method of retrieving them.

TIP

It's worth remembering: Everything that UNIX works on is a file, and everything it uses must reside in a file.

Some files contain commands that tell the system what to do, other files let the system work on them. When you run a text editor like **vi** (for example), you're referencing a special file that executes a command. When you edit a text file within **vi**, you're working with a file that simply contains text. When you use the **lp** command to print the file you've just edited, you're sending your edited file to yet another file (in this case, one that represents a printer). As you save the edited file in a subdirectory, UNIX stores a reference to your file in still another file (this one representing the subdirectory).

Sound confusing? It can be, but don't worry; the more you work with UNIX, the more this file-juggling makes sense. For the moment, consider these four types of files:

- Ordinary files
- Directories
- Special device files
- Links

Each type has subtypes and other important details:

- **Ordinary files** can be *text files* (containing only text characters), *data files* (for instance, a database file may contain characters other than ASCII characters), *command text files* (which provide commands to your system), and *executable files* (programs).

- **Directories** contain information about other files. We'll cover directories in more depth later in this chapter.
- **Special device files** control certain physical aspects of the computer system. For instance, when you use the **tar** command to create a tape archive, you're writing files to a special device file (usually **/dev/rmt0**) that represents the actual tape drive (which it tells how to archive your work).
- **Links** give you access to a file to under different names in different locations. This is one feature of UNIX that marks it as a multiuser operating system. If several users must use a particular file, storing duplicate files for all those users is a waste of a precious resource: disk space. It makes better sense to create links that all refer to the same file.

Demonstrating Directories

Whenever you work with files, you need a place to put them. *Directories* organize your files and provide consistent locations for them. Without directories, daily UNIX usage would quickly become a nightmare — particularly on a large system where hundreds of users may be trying to keep track of thousands of files.

As you saw earlier in this chapter, a directory is simply a file that references other files, like a manila folder that might hold files and other folders (called *subdirectories*), which in turn can contain files and directories of their own. Every directory is actually a subdirectory of some other directory — except one, designated by a slash (/), called the *root directory*.

If you want to find any file in a UNIX system, you have to start at the root; which is why a full (or, in UNIX parlance, *absolute*) filename *always* begins with a slash. An absolute filename indicates the position of a file within the directory tree. The top of the tree begins with the root directory (/), and then shows one of the other subdirectories that the root contains (common examples include **users**, **etc**, **usr**, and **tmp**). Next (provided your friendly system administrator has assigned you one of these) is a *home directory*, the starting point from which you begin every UNIX session. Customarily, this home directory is a subdirectory of **users** (which is, in turn, a subdirectory of the root); the larger the system you're on, the more important it is to know where you are.

UNIX gives you many commands for creating, deleting, and managing directories. As you get comfortable with UNIX, you'll probably want to create directories of your own, naming them to match your tasks. For instance, you may want to designate a **reports** directory to contain reports for your boss — and for the moment, keeping your directory names that simple can't hurt. Dealing with directories can be confusing when a lot of commands are involved — which is why this book's bibliography recommends selected books and tutorials on more advanced UNIX usage.

Mastering Standard Input/Output

If files and commands represent Square One in UNIX, you're now on Square Two: learning to use them.

The simple prompt is more versatile than it appears; for example, you can issue more than one command at a time from there. It's not uncommon to see a command prompt begin with an actual command, qualified by an option, followed by an instruction to send the command's output to yet another command. UNIXdom calls this stringing-together of commands *standard input and output (I/O)* or *redirection*.

To illustrate, consider **cat**. (No, it's not a reading lesson; it's a common UNIX command.) Running the **cat** command with no options looks like this:

```
$ cat
```

So far, all you can do with this command is enter keystrokes; when you hit the Enter key, your input will be repeated on the monitor. The keystrokes have not been saved to disk; once you display them on the screen, they're gone forever and you have to make more to get anything else to happen.

Like most UNIX commands, **cat** assumes that standard input means someone is typing at the keyboard, and standard output means display on the terminal. That's why using **cat** by itself, without options or filenames, merely displays your keystrokes on the terminal screen. Not much use, unless you enjoy having a computer mimic your typing.

The **cat** command wakes up and becomes useful when you add a filename to the command line. To display the contents of an existing report file on screen, for example, you could use **cat** like this:

```
$ cat kevin.report
Because of declining sales, I recommend that
we halt production of the 1190–AAA widget
immediately.
```

By entering a filename, you've negated **cat**'s assumption that input will come from the keyboard, telling it instead that input will come from a specific file. Therefore, instead of your keystrokes, **cat** displays the contents of the file after you press Enter.

Using input/output commands, you can direct **cat** to perform many additional functions. For example, suppose you want to save your keystrokes to an ASCII file. The following command tells **cat** to send standard input — your keystrokes — to a file named **report.1999**:

```
$ cat > report.1999
```

In this instance, **cat** becomes a rudimentary text editor. You enter text one line at a time; when you're finished, press Ctrl–D to end input.

TIP

Generally speaking, Ctrl–D ends input for any UNIX command that requires input.

If you type the command a little differently, you can use **cat** to copy the contents of a file to a new file:

```
$ cat report.1998 > report.1999
```

This command line specifies both input (**report.1998**) and output (**report.1999**). The file **report.1998** remains intact; the command copies its contents into a new file, **report.1999**.

Finally, you can append your keystrokes (or an existing file) to the end of another existing file by typing the command this way:

```
$ cat report.1999 > report.1998
```

Here you would be copying the contents of **report.1999** to the end of the file **report.1998**. If you want to add information directly to the end of the file **report.1998**, use the following:

```
$ cat > report.1998
```

Table 1–1 reviews the input/output commands we've looked at here.

Table 1–1 *Input/Output Commands*

Symbol	Usage	Result
>	*command>filename*	Sends output of *command* to *filename.*
<	*command<filename*	*Command* uses input from *filename.*
>	*command> filename*	Appends the output of *command* to *filename.*
|	*command1|command2*	Runs *command1* and sends its output to *command2.*

Sharp-eyed readers will notice that the < symbol listed in Table 1–1 performs the equivalent of the following command (covered earlier):

```
$ cat kevin.report
```

This command achieves the same result as

```
$ cat < kevin.report
```

What's different is how the UNIX shell treats the two commands. In the first instance, the shell treats the filename, **kevin.report**, as an *argument* to the **cat** command — additional information that changes the way the command acts. In the second instance, the shell treats **kevin.report** as input for the **cat** command.

You can use more than one input/output command in a single command line. For example, many UNIX commands — especially if they're working with shell scripts — look like this:

```
$ command <infile > outfile
```

This command line combines two commands: (1) use input from *infile* and (2) send the output to *outfile*.

Pondering Pipes

To move a step beyond standard input/output, you can get to know another powerful UNIX tool: *pipes*. A pipe is like a shortcut; it uses the output of one command as input for a second command. It looks like this:

```
$ command1 | command2
```

This type of command line is a *pipeline*. For instance, if you wanted to sort a file before printing it, normally you'd use the **sort** command to sort the file, and then send the output to the **lp** command to print the sorted file. If you combined those two commands into a pipeline, the resulting command line would look like this:

```
$ sort textfile | lp
```

Adding one command to make a pipeline is a convenient illustration, but you don't have to stop there. You can enter multiple pipes on a command line. Here's an example of a longer pipeline:

```
$ ls *.1999 | grep profits | lp
```

This command line searches for all files ending in **1999** in the current directory, and then sends the output of that **ls** command to the **grep** command. **Grep** searches the listed files for the string **profits**. and then sends any lines containing the **profits** string to the **lp** command, which prints out the lines. Not bad for one command line.

Pipelines offer a glimpse of what you can do with the UNIX operating system; you'll see more as you go through the chapters ahead. Remember, however, that this book's main purpose is to list and describe UNIX commands; for a general primer on the UNIX operating system, Appendix A is the best place to start.

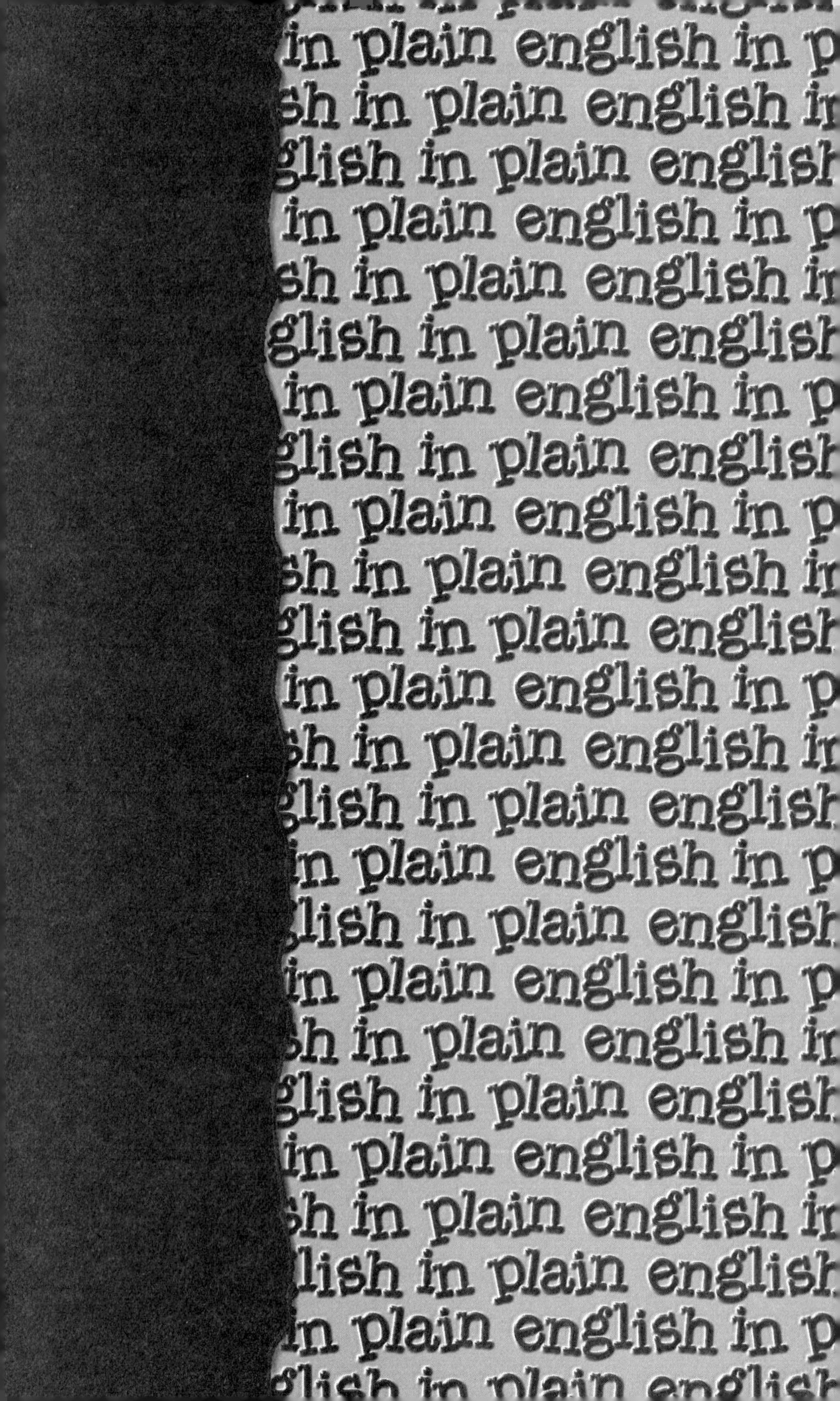
in plain english

UNIX in Plain English

Most of us know what we want to do when we sit down in front of a terminal. The challenge, then, is figuring out how to tell the operating system exactly what we want to do. Unfortunately, the operating system doesn't make it any easier; it's not very forgiving if your command doesn't quite match your goal.

This reference is for those who know exactly what they want to do and need a lead on the corresponding UNIX command. We've listed common computing tasks in the left column (the italicized keywords are in alphabetic order); the conforming UNIX commands appear in the right column. Most commands are listed a few different ways; for instance, you can find the common **ls** command under both **list** and **file**.

If you want to...	Use this command
look up Internet **addresses** for hostnames	**nslookup**
append other files to an existing file	**cat**
track **appointments** and schedule meetings	**cm**, **dtcm**
create a tape **archive**	**tar**, **cpio**
search for **ASCII** strings within binary files	**strings**
search for and replace **ASCII** characters	**tr**
create a tape **backup**	**tar**, **cpio**
print a 10-character **banner**	**banner**
start the **Bourne** shell	**sh**
start the **C** shell	**csh**
calculate your mortgage payments	**calctool**, **dtcalc**, **xcalc**
perform math **calculations**	**bc**, **dc**
display current month in **calendar** form	**cal**, **cm**, **dtcm**
display a **calendar**	**cm**, **dtcm**
call another terminal	**ct**
call another UNIX system	**cu**
cancel jobs scheduled with the **at** command	**atrm**
cancel print job	**cancel**
capture a screen image	**xv**, **xwd**
chat with another user on the network	**talk**
calculate a file's **checksum**	**sum**
clear the screen	**clear**
display a **column** from a sorted file	**cut**
strip **column**-formatting commands	**col**
combine presorted files with a common field	**join**
combine several files into a new file	**cat**
run **command** at specific time	**at**
enter UNIX **commands** in a graphical environment	**xterm**, **dtterm**, **shelltool**
run a series of **commands**	**batch**
time a **command**	**time**, **timex**
compare contents of two directories	**dircmp**
compare contents of two presorted files	**comm**
compare three files to see if they are different	**diff3**
compare two files and report on differing lines	**diff**
compare two files and return differing lines	**bdiff**
compare two files to see if they are different	**cmp**
compare two files and report differences	**sdiff**

If you want to...	Use this command
compare two files and commonalities	**sdiff**
compile C programs	**cc**
compress a file	**compress**, **pack**
query and **configure** network interfaces	**ifconfig**
verify **connection** to remote host	**ping**
copy a file	**cat**, **cp**, **filemgr**, **dtfile**
copy files to and from networked remote systems	**rcp**
copy files to and from remote UNIX system	**uucp**
count the number of words in text file	**wc**
create a new text file	**cat**, **dtpad**, **textedit**, **xedit**
change **current** directory	**cd**
stop a **current** process	**kill**
display **date** and time	**date**
change a file's **date** to the current date	**touch**
decode file after communications	**uudecode**
delete a file	**rm**, **filemgr**, **dtfile**
create a **directory**	**mkdir**, **filemgr**, **dtfile**
display disk space used by a **directory**	**du**
generate a **directory** listing	**ls**
change current working **directory**	**cd**
remove a **directory**	**rmdir**, **filemgr**, **dtfile**
return current working **directory**	**pwd**
compare the contents of two **directories**	**dircmp**
display free or total **disk space**	**df**
display **disk space** used by a directory	**du**
display a file	**cat**, **page**, **dtpad**, **textedit**, **xedit**
display a file one screen at a time	**more**
display first ten lines of a file	**head**
display last ten lines of a file	**tail**
display packed files	**pcat**
edit a text file	**vi**, **ed**, **dtpad**, **textedit**, **xedit**
send **electronic mail**	**mailx**, **dtmail**, **mailtool**
send return **electronic mail** when you're on vacation	**vacation**
notify you when **electronic mail** arrives	**notify**, **xbiff**

If you want to...	Use this command
encode file before communications	**uuencode**
encrypt a file	**crypt**
display or set **environment variables**	**env**
format **equations**	**eqn**, **neqn**
erase a file	**rm**
exit	**exit**
copy a **file**	**cat**, **cp**, **filemgr**, **dtfile**
create a new text **file**	**cat**, **dtpad**, **textedit**, **xedit**
change a **file**'s date to the current date	**touch**
display a **file**	**cat**, **page**
display a **file** one screen at a time	**more**
display first ten lines of a **file**	**head**
display last ten lines of a **file**	**tail**
edit a **file**	**vi**, **ed**, **dtpad**, **textedit**, **xedit**
encrypt a **file**	**crypt**
erase a **file**	**rm**
find a **file**	**find**
format a structured **file**	**awk**, **nawk**
send output to **file** as well as to screen	**tee**
change ownership of **file**	**chown**
move a **file** or multiple **files**	**mv**
display a column from a sorted **file**	**cut**
sort a **file**	**sort**
sort a structured **file**	**awk**, **nawk**
search a structured **file**	**awk**, **nawk**, **grep**
split a **file** into smaller **files**	**csplit**, **split**
determine **file** type	**file**
change **file-access** permissions	**chmod**
create or determine default **file-access** permissions	**umask**
append other **files** to an existing file	**cat**
combine presorted **files** with a common field	**join**
combine several **files** into a new **file**	**cat**
compare contents of two presorted **files**	**comm**
compare two **files** and report on differing lines	**diff**
compare two **files** and return differing lines	**bdiff**

If you want to...	Use this command
compare two **files** to detect differences	**cmp**
compare three **files** to detect differences	**diff3**
display packed **files**	**pcat**
merge **files** side by side	**paste**
change ownership of a group of **files**	**chgrp**
list **files**	**ls**
list network statistics	**netstat**
link **files**	**ln**
search for ASCII strings within binary **files**	**strings**
remove **files**	**rm**
find a file	**find**
display a **font**	**xfd**, **xfontsel**
list available **fonts**	**xlsfonts**
format equations	**eqn**, **neqn**
format images for laser printer	**xdpr**, **xpr**
format tables	**tbl**
format text file	**newform, pr**
format a structured file	**awk**, **nawk**
format text for laser printer	**troff**
format text for line printer	**nroff**
format text (right-justify)	**fmt**
format text to specific width	**fold**
enter UNIX commands in a **graphical** environment	**xterm**, **dtterm**, **shelltool**
log in new **group**	**newgrp**
find out what **groups** a user belongs to	**groups**
get **help**	**man**, **apropos**, **whatis**, **xman**
verify connection to remote **host**	**ping**
look up Internet addresses for **hostnames**	**nslookup**
display user **ID**	**id**
report **I/O** statistics	**iostat**
capture a screen **image**	**xv**, **xwd**
display a screen **image**	**xv**, **xwud**
format **images** for laser printer	**xdpr**, **xpr**
query and configure network **interfaces**	**ifconfig**
look up **Internet** addresses for hostnames	**nslookup**
start **Korn** shell	**ksh**

If you want to...	Use this command
insert **line** numbers into a text file	**nl**
link files	**ln**
list files	**ls**
save a **log** of your current computing session	**script**
log in as another user	**su**
log in a new group	**newgrp**
log in to a remote system	**rlogin**, **telnet**
log in to a system	**login**
print your **login** name	**logname**
track **logins** to other remote systems	**uulog**
log off (or **log out** from) system	**exit**
run a command even after you **log off** (or **log out**)	**nohup**
show who is **logged in** to the system	**who**, **rwho**
run a command at a **low priority**	**nice**
send electronic **mail**	**mailx**, **dtmail**, **mailtool**
send return electronic **mail** when you're on vacation	**vacation**
notify you when **mail** arrives	**notify**
view **manual pages**	**man**, **xman**
perform **math** calculations	**bc**, **dc**
reports virtual **memory** statistics	**vmstat**
merge files side by side	**paste**
send **message** to all users logged in to a system	**wall**
turn on/off the ability to receive **messages** from other users	**mesg**
calculate your **mortgage** payments	**calctool**, **dtcalc**, **xcalc**
move a file or multiple files	**mv**
query and configure **network** interfaces	**ifconfig**
display system **news**	**news**
show status of all machines on **network**	**ruptime**
list **network** statistics	**netstat**
run a command **nicely** (at a lower priority)	**nice**
send **output** to file as well as to screen	**tee**
change **ownership** of file	**chown**
change **ownership** of a group of files	**chgrp**
pack a file	**compress**, **pack**
display **packed** files	**pcat**

If you want to...	Use this command
set your **password**	**passwd**
pause before executing a command	**sleep**
print	**lp**, **lpr**, **dtlp**
prepare a file for **printing**	**pr**
print a 10-character banner	**banner**
cancel **print** job	**cancel**
print jobs scheduled with at command	**atq**
show status of **print** requests	**lpstat**
start **print** spooler	**lpsched**
stop **print** spooler	**lpshut**
stop a current **process**	**kill**
show current **processes**	**ps**
query and configure network interfaces	**ifconfig**
quit	**exit**
schedule **recurring** tasks	**crontab**
verify connection to **remote** host	**ping**
start a **remote** shell on a remote system	**rsh**
copy files to and from **remote** system	**rcp**, **uucp**, **ftp**
log in to a **remote** system	**telnet**, **rlogin**
start a **remote** shell on a **remote** system	**rsh**
run a UNIX command on a **remote** system	**rsh, remsh, uux,**
track logins to other **remote** systems	**uulog**
remove a directory	**rmdir**, **dtfile**, **filemgr**
remove files	**rm**, **dtfile**, **filemgr**
run a UNIX command on a remote system	**uux**
schedule personal events	**calendar**, **cm**, **dtcm**
schedule recurring tasks	**at, crontab,**
capture a **screen** image	**xv**, **xwd**
search a structured file	**awk**, **grep**, **nawk**
search for text string	**egrep**, **fgrep**, **grep**
search and replace ASCII characters	**tr**
sort a file	**sort**
sort a structured file	**awk**, **nawk**
check **spelling** in text file	**spell**
split a file into smaller files	**csplit**, **split**
display to **standard output**	**echo**
list network **statistics**	**netstat**

If you want to...	Use this command
get a report of virtual memory **statistics**	**vmstat**
show **status** of all machines on the network	**ruptime**
search for a text **string**	**egrep**, **fgrep**, **grep**
strip column-formatting commands	**col**
strip formatting commands	**deroff**
return UNIX **system name**	**uname**
display **system news**	**news**
list **systems** that you can communicate with	**uuname**
format **tables**	**tbl**
set **tabs**	**tabs**
create a **tape** backup	**tar**, **cpio**
display **terminal** information	**tput**
display **terminal** options	**tty**
set **terminal** configuration	**stty**
check spelling in **text** file	**spell**
edit **text** file	**vi**, **ed**, **dtpad**, **textedit**, **xedit**
format **text** file	**newform**
format **text** for laser printer	**troff**
format **text** for line printer	**nroff**
format **text** (right-justify)	**fmt**
format **text** to specific width	**fold**
insert line numbers into a **text** file	**nl**
create a new **text** file	**cat**, **dtpad**, **textedit**, **xedit**
search for **text** string	**egrep**, **fgrep**, **grep**
display date and **time**	**date**
run a command at a specific **time**	**at**
time a command	**time**, **timex**
determine file **type**	**file**
uncompress a file	**uncompress**
unpack a file	**unpack**
report **up** time	**uptime**
display **user** ID	**id**
list **users**	**listusers**
display information about other **users** on the system	**who**
find information about other **users** on the system	**finger**

If you want to...	Use this command
show status of **uucp** requests	**uustat**
send return mail when you're on **vacation**	**vacation**
verify connection to remote host	**ping**
report **virtual** memory statistics	vmstat
force shell to **wait**	**wait**
count the number of **words** in text file	**wc**
return current **working** directory	**pwd**
write message to another user on the network	**write**

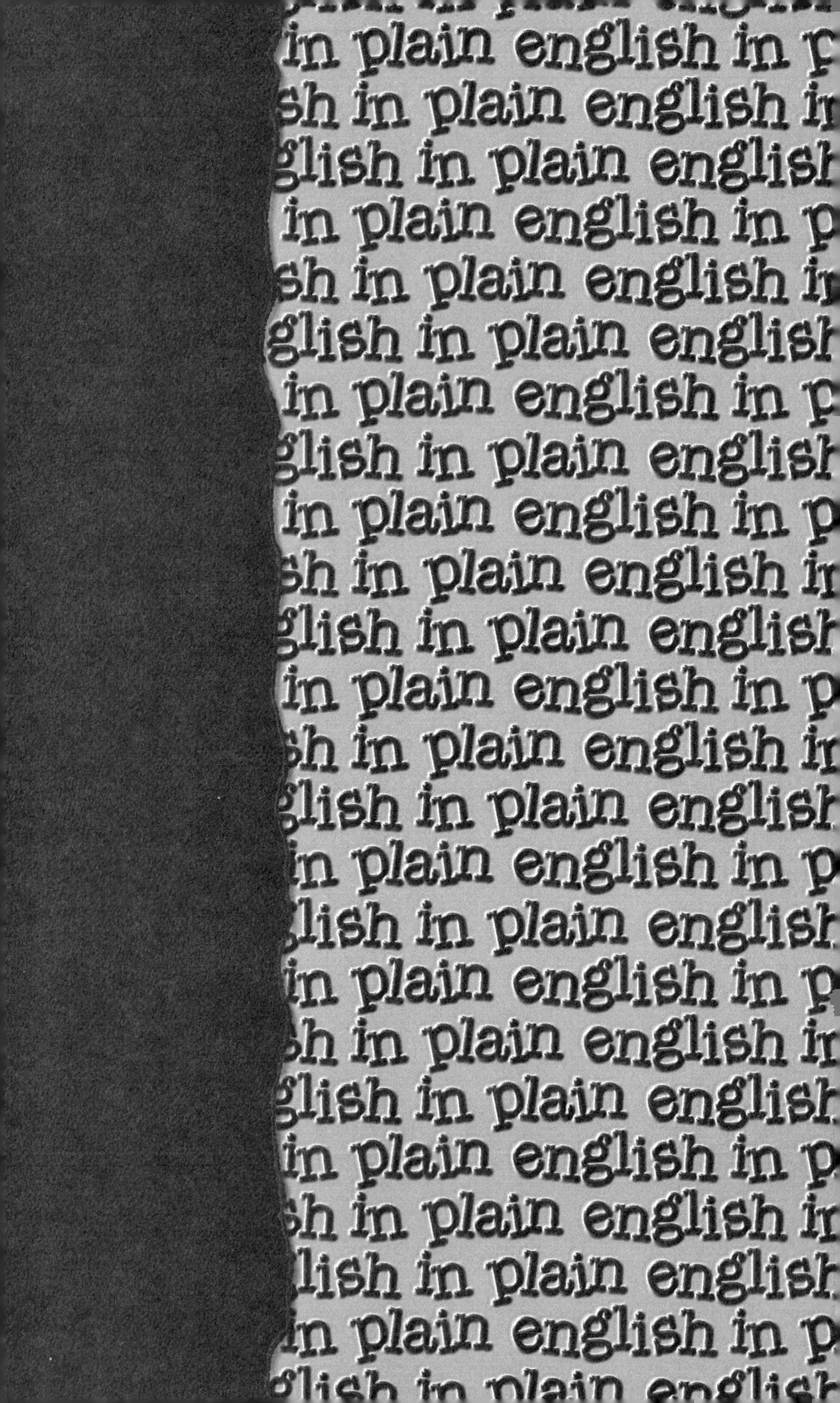
in plain english

UNIX/DOS Cross-Reference

Oldtime UNIX hacks may think it heresy to include a DOS cross reference in a UNIX reference text — after all, isn't UNIX the greatest operating system ever created? We do have a few good reasons to include this section:

- Most computer users, whether they are using UNIX or not, are somewhat familiar with DOS, whether running DOS itself or by accessing DOS commands under Windows 3.1, Windows 95, Windows NT, or Windows 98. In our experience, even computer users who use one operating system at work — say, a proprietary mainframe operating system or something like VMS — probably use a PC clone and Windows/DOS at home. The personal computer made personal computing affordable for the masses, and after all, Windows/DOS is one of the most popular operating systems on the face of the earth.

- Many UNIX users will be moving up from DOS and Windows. This is an unalterable fact of UNIX life. Many corporations are finding that DOS-based networks simply can't handle the large-scale computing chores handled rather effortlessly by UNIX-based networks.
- DOS has its roots in UNIX. The originators of DOS (not Microsoft, incidentally) patterned DOS after CP/M, which was itself patterned after UNIX and used many of the same commands (such as cd and echo) while maintaining the same file structure and philosophy (standard input/output plays a large role in DOS computing). Of course, this was many, many years ago, and both DOS and UNIX have changed quite a bit in response to different computing needs. For instance, DOS is heavy on disk utilities, such as **CHKDSK** and **DISKCOPY**; UNIX is heavy on networking, text-editing, and text-manipulation commands. Each system evolved to accommodate the needs of folks who ended up using it: DOS is the system of choice for single, standalone PC users, while UNIX has always dominated the multiuser corporate and academic worlds.

Don't worry if you're a DOS or Windows user and don't recognize all of the DOS commands in this list. Like UNIX, some older DOS commands have managed to hang in there despite their relative obscurity. It's safe to say that 99 percent of all DOS users have never even heard of the **CTTY** command, much less used it. And because this listing of DOS commands is current as of MS-DOS 6.0, many new commands (such as **MSAV**, which concerns an anti-virus utility) may be unfamiliar.

Not all DOS commands have a UNIX analog, obviously. Similarly, some UNIX commands have no parallel in the DOS world. We note cases in which there is no UNIX equivalent. And not all of the commands are perfectly matched; in some cases, we've listed the rough equivalent.

DOS Command	UNIX Command
APPEND	None
ASSIGN	None
ATTRIB	chmod
BACKUP	cpio, tar
BREAK	None
CALL	exec
CD	cd
CHCP	None
CHDIR	cd
CHKDSK	None
CHOICE	None
CLS	clear
COMMAND	csh, sh
COMP	bdiff, cmp, diff, diff3, sdiff
COPY	cp
CTTY	stty
DATE	date
DBLSPACE	None
DEFRAG	None
DEL	rm
DELTREE	rm -r
DIR	ls
DISKCOMP	None
DISKCOPY	None
DOSKEY	**history** (Korn and Bourne shells)
DOSSHELL	None
ECHO	echo
EDIT	vi
EXIT	None
EXPAND	uncompress, unpack
FASTHELP	apropos, man, whatis
FASTOPEN	None

DOS Command	UNIX Command
FC	**bdiff**, **cmp**, **diff**, **diff3**, **sdiff**
FDISK	**None**
FIND	**find**
FOR	**for** (shell command)
FORMAT	**None**
GOTO	**goto** (C shell)
GRAFTABL	**None**
GRAPHICS	**None**
HELP	**apropos**, **man**, **whatis**
IF	**if** (shell command)
INTERLNK	**None**
INTERSVR	**None**
JOIN	**None**
KEYB	**None**
LABEL	**None**
LOADFIX	**None**
LOADHIGH	**None** (thankfully)
MEM	**None**
MEMMAKER	**None**
MIRROR	**None**
MKDIR	**mkdir**
MODE	**stty**, **tty**
MORE	**more**, **pg**
MOVE	**mv**
MSAV	**None**
MSBACKUP	**cpio**, **tar**
MSD	**None**
NLSFUNC	**None**
PATH	**setenv PATH** (C shell), **setpath** (Bourne shell)
PAUSE	**sleep**
POWER	**None**
PRINT	**lp**
PROMPT	**PS1**
RECOVER	**None**
REM	**#**
RENAME	**mv**

DOS Command	UNIX Command
REPLACE	None
RESTORE	cpio, tar
RMDIR	rmdir
SET	env
SETVER	None
SHARE	None
SHIFT	None
SMARTDRV	None
SORT	sort
SUBST	None
SYS	None
TIME	date
TREE	None
TYPE	cat, more, page, pg]
UNDELETE	None (unfortunately)
UNFORMAT	None
VER	uname
VERIFY	None
VOL	None
VSAFE	None
XCOPY	cp
XTREE	mkdir

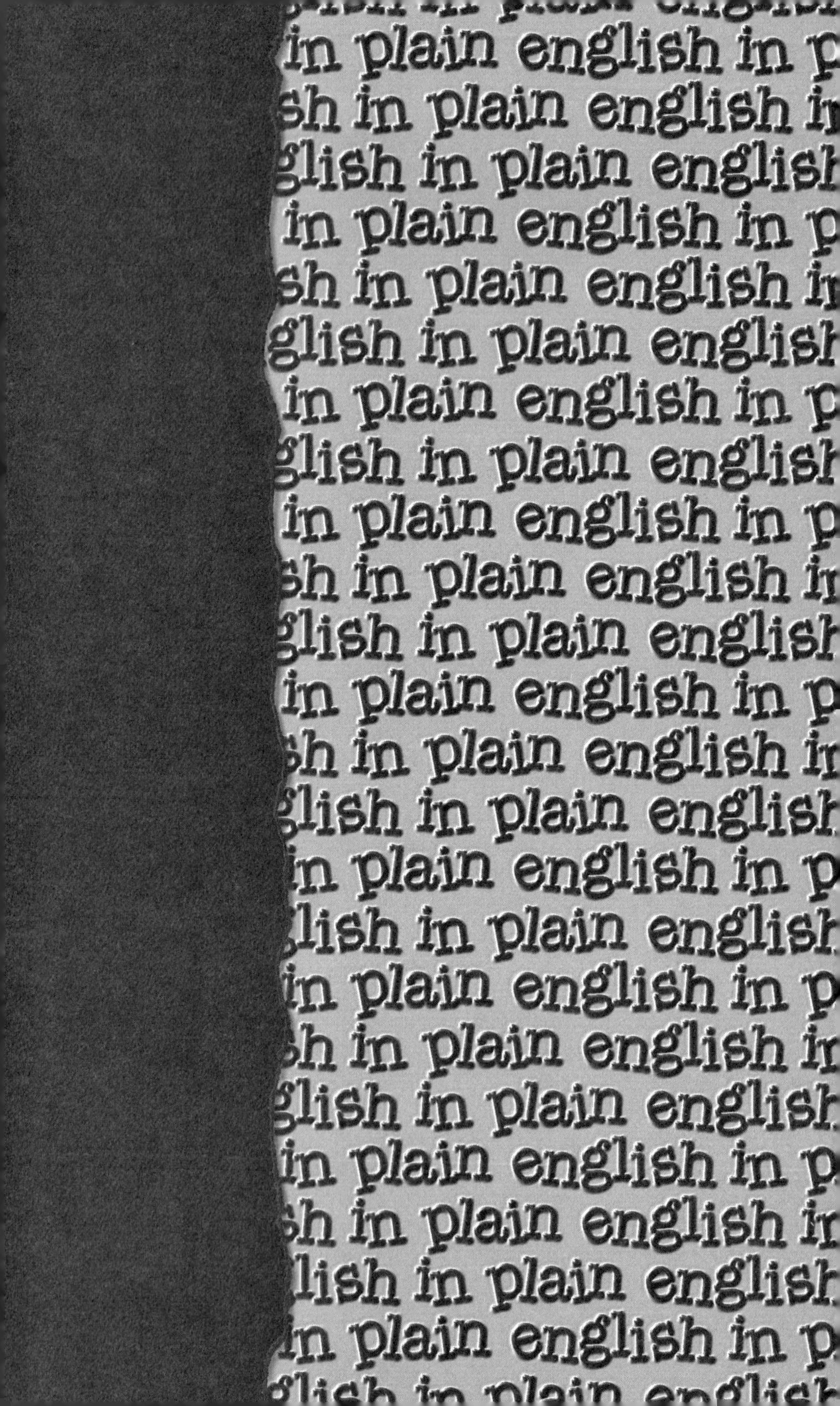
in plain english

UNIX Commands A–Z

Here is an alphabetical listing of the commands covered in Chapters 2 (General-Purpose Commands), 3 (File-Manipulation Commands), 4 (Text-Processing Commands), 5 (Printing Commands), 6 (Networking Communications Commands), 7 (FTP Commands), 8 (Graphics Commands), 9 (Programming Commands), and 10 (System-Administration Commands). Quite aside from the shell commands and variables in Chapter 12, this list certainly does not exhaust every available UNIX command—life's too short, and we're too young, to try to compile such a list. Most UNIX users won't need to use all the commands listed here, much less an additional set of commands whose obscurity is rivaled only by their lack of usefulness in everyday computing chores.

This list is offered to the majority of UNIX users who want to get on with their work without having the operating system interfere with their chores. To that end, this list represents the UNIX commands most users are most likely to use.

Command	Chapter
apropos	General-Purpose Commands (Chapter 2)
at	System-Administration Commands (Chapter 10)
atq	System-Administration Commands (Chapter 10)
atrm	System-Administration Commands (Chapter 10)
awk	General-Purpose Commands (Chapter 2)
banner	Printing Commands (Chapter 5)
basename	General-Purpose Commands (Chapter 2)
batch	System-Administration Commands (Chapter 10)
bc	General-Purpose Commands (Chapter 2)
bdftopcf	Graphics Commands (Chapter 8)
bdiff	File-Manipulation Commands (Chapter 3)
bitmap	Graphics Commands (Chapter 8)
cal	General-Purpose Commands (Chapter 2)
calctool	Graphics Commands (Chapter 8)
calendar	General-Purpose Commands (Chapter 2)
cancel	Printing Commands (Chapter 5)
cat	File-Manipulation Commands (Chapter 3)
cc	General-Purpose Commands (Chapter 2)
cd	File-Manipulation Commands (Chapter 3)
chgrp	System-Administration Commands (Chapter 10)
chmod	General-Purpose Commands (Chapter 2)
chown	File-Manipulation Commands (Chapter 3)
clear	General-Purpose Commands (Chapter 2)
clock	Graphics Commands (Chapter 8)
cm	Graphics Commands (Chapter 8)
cmdtool	Graphics Commands (Chapter 8)
cmp	File-Manipulation Commands (Chapter 3)
col	Text-Processing Commands (Chapter 6)
comm	File-Manipulation Commands (Chapter 3)
compress	File-Manipulation Commands (Chapter 3)
cpio	System-Administration Commands (Chapter 10)
crontab	System-Administration Commands (Chapter 10)
crypt	File-Manipulation Commands (Chapter 3)
csh	General-Purpose Commands (Chapter 2)
csplit	File-Manipulation Commands (Chapter 3)
ct	Networking Communications Commands (Chapter 6)
cu	Networking Communications Commands (Chapter 6)

Command	Chapter
cut	Text-Processing Commands (Chapter 6)
date	General-Purpose Commands (Chapter 2)
dc	General-Purpose Commands (Chapter 2)
deroff	Text-Processing Commands (Chapter 6)
diff	File-Manipulation Commands (Chapter 3)
diff3	File-Manipulation Commands (Chapter 3)
dircmp	File-Manipulation Commands (Chapter 3)
df	General-Purpose Commands (Chapter 2)
dtcalc	Graphics Commands (Chapter 8)
dtcm	Graphics Commands (Chapter 8)
dtfile	Graphics Commands (Chapter 8)
dthelpview	Graphics Commands (Chapter 8)
dticon	Graphics Commands (Chapter 8)
dtksh	Graphics Commands (Chapter 8)
dtlp	Graphics Commands (Chapter 8)
dtmail	Graphics Commands (Chapter 8)
dtpad	Graphics Commands (Chapter 8)
dtstyle	Graphics Commands (Chapter 8)
dtterm	Graphics Commands (Chapter 8)
dtwm	Graphics Commands (Chapter 8)
du	General-Purpose Commands (Chapter 2)
echo	General-Purpose Commands (Chapter 2)
ed	Text-Processing Commands (Chapter 6)
egrep	File-Manipulation Commands (Chapter 3)
env	General-Purpose Commands (Chapter 2)
eqn	Text-Processing Commands (Chapter 6)
exit	General-Purpose Commands (Chapter 2)
fgrep	File-Manipulation Commands (Chapter 3)
file	File-Manipulation Commands (Chapter 3)
filemgr	Graphics Commands (Chapter 8)
finger	Networking Communications Commands (Chapter 6)
fmt	Text-Processing Commands (Chapter 6)
fold	Text-Processing Commands (Chapter 6)
fsinfo	Graphics Commands (Chapter 8)
fslsfonts	Graphics Commands (Chapter 8)
fstobdf	Graphics Commands (Chapter 8)
ftp	FTP Commands (Chapter 7)

Command	Chapter
ghostview	Graphics Commands (Chapter 8)
grep	File-Manipulation Commands (Chapter 3)
groups	General-Purpose Commands (Chapter 2)
head	File-Manipulation Commands (Chapter 3)
iconedit	Graphics Commands (Chapter 8)
id	General-Purpose Commands (Chapter 2)
ifconfig	Networking Communications Commands (Chapter 6)
iostat	System-Administration Commands (Chapter 10)
join	File-Manipulation Commands (Chapter 3)
kill	General-Purpose Commands (Chapter 2)
ksh	General-Purpose Commands (Chapter 2)
listusers	General-Purpose Commands (Chapter 2)
ln	File-Manipulation Commands (Chapter 3)
login	System-Administration Commands (Chapter 10)
logname	Networking Communications Commands (Chapter 6)
lp	Printing Commands (Chapter 5)
lpsched	Printing Commands (Chapter 5)
lpshut	Printing Commands (Chapter 5)
lpstat	Printing Commands (Chapter 5)
ls	File-Manipulation Commands (Chapter 3)
mailtool	Graphics Commands (Chapter 8)
mailx	Networking Communications Commands (Chapter 6)
man	General-Purpose Commands (Chapter 2)
mesg	Networking Communications Commands (Chapter 6)
mkdir	File-Manipulation Commands (Chapter 3)
mkfontdir	Graphics Commands (Chapter 8)
more	File-Manipulation Commands (Chapter 3)
mv	File-Manipulation Commands (Chapter 3)
mwm	Graphics Commands (Chapter 8)
nawk	General-Purpose Commands (Chapter 2)
neqn	Text-Processing Commands (Chapter 6)
netstat	Networking Communications Commands (Chapter 6)
newform	Text-Processing Commands (Chapter 6)
newgrp	System-Administration Commands (Chapter 10)
news	General-Purpose Commands (Chapter 2)
nice	General-Purpose Commands (Chapter 2)
nl	Text-Processing Commands (Chapter 6)

Command	Chapter
nohup	General-Purpose Commands (Chapter 2)
notify	Networking Communications Commands (Chapter 6)
nroff	Text-Processing Commands (Chapter 6)
nslookup	Networking Communications Commands (Chapter 6)
oclock	Graphics Commands (Chapter 8)
olwm	Graphics Commands (Chapter 8)
openwin	Graphics Commands (Chapter 8)
pack	File-Manipulation Commands (Chapter 3)
page	File-Manipulation Commands (Chapter 3)
passwd	General-Purpose Commands (Chapter 2)
paste	Text-Processing Commands (Chapter 6)
pcat	File-Manipulation Commands (Chapter 3)
ping	Networking Communications Commands (Chapter 6)
pr	Printing Commands (Chapter 5)
ps	General-Purpose Commands (Chapter 2)
pwd	General-Purpose Commands (Chapter 2)
rcp	Networking Communications Commands (Chapter 6)
rlogin	Networking Communications Commands (Chapter 6)
rm	File-Manipulation Commands (Chapter 3)
rmdir	File-Manipulation Commands (Chapter 3)
rsh	Networking Communications Commands (Chapter 6)
ruptime	Networking Communications Commands (Chapter 6)
rwho	Networking Communications Commands (Chapter 6)
script	General-Purpose Commands (Chapter 2)
sdiff	File-Manipulation Commands (Chapter 3)
sh	General-Purpose Commands (Chapter 2)
shelltool	Graphics Commands (Chapter 8)
shutdown	System-Administration Commands (Chapter 10)
sleep	General-Purpose Commands (Chapter 2)
sort	Text-Processing Commands (Chapter 6)
spell	Text-Processing Commands (Chapter 6)
split	File-Manipulation Commands (Chapter 3)
startx	Graphics Commands (Chapter 8)
strings	File-Manipulation Commands (Chapter 3)
stty	System-Administration Commands (Chapter 10)
su	General-Purpose Commands (Chapter 2)
sum	Networking Communications Commands (Chapter 6)

Command	Chapter
tabs	Text-Processing Commands (Chapter 6)
tail	File-Manipulation Commands (Chapter 3)
talk	Networking Communications Commands (Chapter 6)
tapetool	Graphics Commands (Chapter 8)
tar	File-Manipulation Commands (Chapter 3)
tbl	Text-Processing Commands (Chapter 6)
tee	General-Purpose Commands (Chapter 2)
telnet	Networking Communications Commands (Chapter 6)
textedit	Graphics Commands (Chapter 8)
time	General-Purpose Commands (Chapter 2)
timex	General-Purpose Commands (Chapter 2)
toolwait	Graphics Commands (Chapter 8)
touch	File-Manipulation Commands (Chapter 3)
tput	System-Administration Commands (Chapter 10)
tr	Text-Processing Commands (Chapter 6)
troff	Text-Processing Commands (Chapter 6)
tty	System-Administration Commands (Chapter 10)
twm	Graphics Commands (Chapter 8)
umask	General-Purpose Commands (Chapter 2)
uname	General-Purpose Commands (Chapter 2)
uncompress	File-Manipulation Commands (Chapter 3)
uniq	Text-Processing Commands (Chapter 6)
unpack	File-Manipulation Commands (Chapter 3)
uptime	System-Administration Commands (Chapter 10)
uucp	Networking Communications Commands (Chapter 6)
uudecode	Networking Communications Commands (Chapter 6)
uuencode	Networking Communications Commands (Chapter 6)
uulog	Networking Communications Commands (Chapter 6)
uuname	Networking Communications Commands (Chapter 6)
uustat	Networking Communications Commands (Chapter 6)
uux	Networking Communications Commands (Chapter 6)
vacation	Networking Communications Commands (Chapter 6)
vi	Text-Processing Commands (Chapter 6)
vmstat	System-Administration Commands (Chapter 10)
wait	General-Purpose Commands (Chapter 2)
wall	Networking Communications Commands (Chapter 6)
wc	Text-Processing Commands (Chapter 6)

Command	Chapter
whatis	General-Purpose Commands (Chapter 2)
who	Networking Communications Commands (Chapter 6)
write	Networking Communications Commands (Chapter 6)
X	Graphics Commands (Chapter 8)
xauth	Graphics Commands (Chapter 8)
xbiff	Graphics Commands (Chapter 8)
xcalc	Graphics Commands (Chapter 8)
xclipboard	Graphics Commands (Chapter 8)
xclock	Graphics Commands (Chapter 8)
xcmap	Graphics Commands (Chapter 8)
xconsole	Graphics Commands (Chapter 8)
xditview	Graphics Commands (Chapter 8)
xdm	Graphics Commands (Chapter 8)
xdpr	Graphics Commands (Chapter 8)
xdpyinfo	Graphics Commands (Chapter 8)
xdvi	Graphics Commands (Chapter 8)
xedit	Graphics Commands (Chapter 8)
xfd	Graphics Commands (Chapter 8)
xfontsel	Graphics Commands (Chapter 8)
xfs	Graphics Commands (Chapter 8)
xhost	Graphics Commands (Chapter 8)
xinit	Graphics Commands (Chapter 8)
xkill	Graphics Commands (Chapter 8)
xload	Graphics Commands (Chapter 8)
xlock	Graphics Commands (Chapter 8)
xlogo	Graphics Commands (Chapter 8)
xlsfonts	Graphics Commands (Chapter 8)
xmag	Graphics Commands (Chapter 8)
xman	Graphics Commands (Chapter 8)
xpr	Graphics Commands (Chapter 8)
xprop	Graphics Commands (Chapter 8)
xrdb	Graphics Commands (Chapter 8)
xv	Graphics Commands (Chapter 8)
xwd	Graphics Commands (Chapter 8)
xwininfo	Graphics Commands (Chapter 8)
xwud	Graphics Commands (Chapter 8)

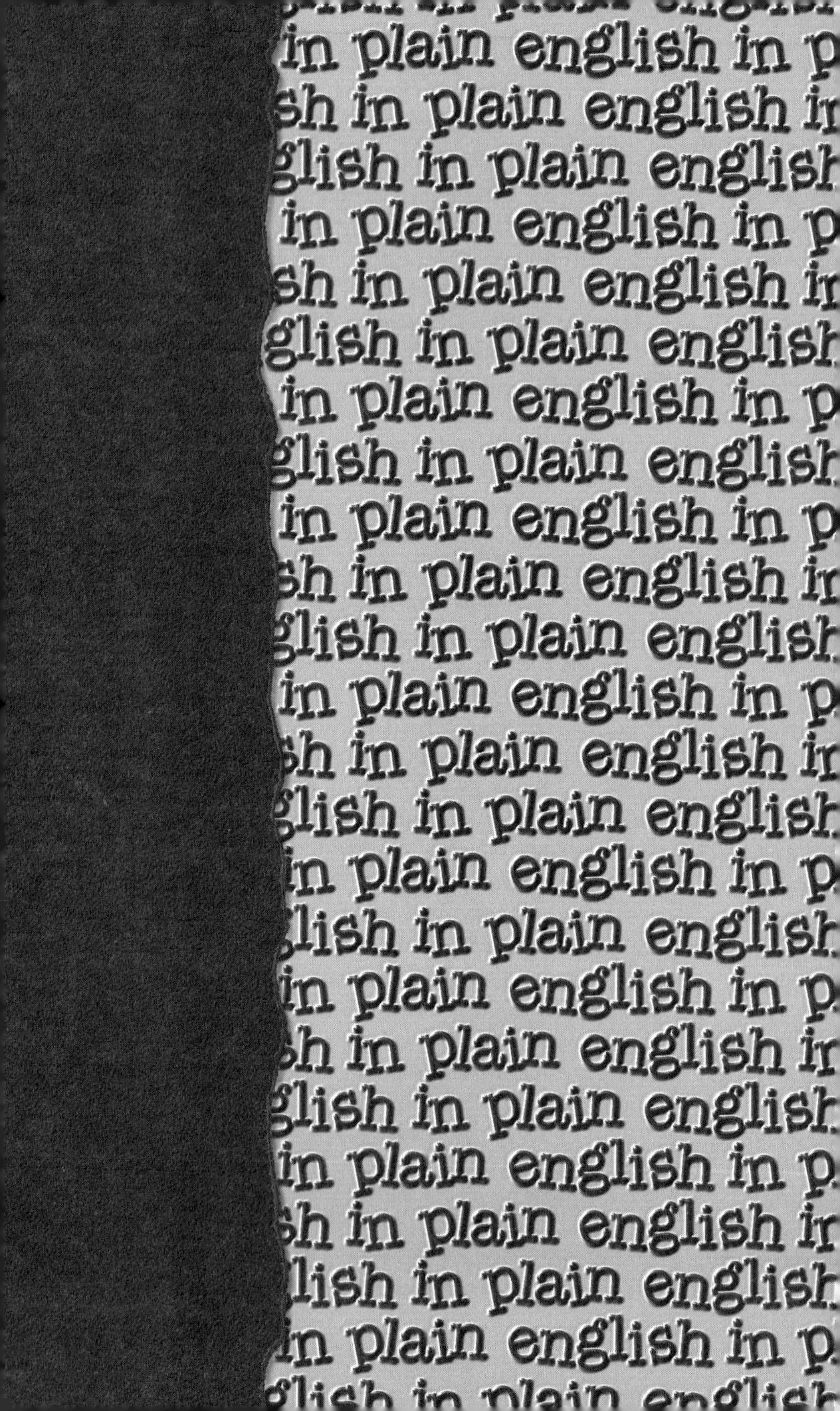
in plain english

2

General-Purpose UNIX Commands

These general-purpose commands cover a wide variety of everyday UNIX tasks. Most UNIX users find them indispensable.

apropos — Online Help

2

apropos *keyword(s)*

Purpose

Returns information about the specified keyword(s) from the online manual pages. Not available on all systems.

Example

```
$ apropos shell
```

Options

None.

Related Commands

man	Returns information from online-manual pages.
whatis	Returns information from online-manual pages.
xman	Returns information from online-manual pages under the X Window System.

basename — Actual Filename

basename *pathname suffix*

Purpose

Returns only the actual filename when presented with a pathname. Specifying a suffix removes any previous suffix. Generally, **basename** is used in shell scripts and in other situations calling for command substitution.

Example

```
$ basename /usr/users/kevin/files/1997/stuff
stuff
```

Options

None.

bc — Calculator

bc *options files*

Purpose

This calculator command supports a wide range of commands and conditions. The **bc** command incorporates a language very similar to the C programming language. Running **bc** makes the command prompt disappear, after which you can enter keywords, symbols, and operations directly.

The **bc** command is a complex tool with its own set of specialized commands that are worthy of further study; for now, consider the short example listed here. For further study, see the Bibliography for a list of UNIX tutorials.

Example

```
$ bc
scale=5
sqrt((66*6)/55)
2.6832
quit
```

Options

-c Sends the command line to standard output, not to the **dc** command (which normally does the back-end processing for **bc**).

-l Makes the math library available. (**Note**: When you invoke this option, you automatically set the scale to 20.)

Common Instructions

+	Addition.
-	Subtraction.
/	Division.
*	Multiplication.
%	Remainder.

^	Exponentiation.
sqrt(n)	Square root.
scale = *n*	Sets scale to *n* (after decimal point).
ibase = *n*	Sets input base to *n* (default is 10).
obase = *x*	Sets output base to *x* (default is 10).
define *a*(*b*)	Defines the function *a* with the argument *b*.
for, **if**, **while**	Statement keywords.

Other Operators and Symbols

assignment	=+ =- =* =/ =^ =
relational	< <= > >= == !=
unary	- ++ --

Other Symbols

/* */	Comment lines.
{ }	Brackets statements.
[ ]	Array index.
*_text_*	Prints *text*.

Math-Library Functions

s	sine.
c	cosine.
a	arctangent.
e	exponential; base *e*

cal — Month/Year Calendar Display

cal *option*

Purpose

Displays the current month in calendar form. If a year is specified, the command prints a 12-month calendar. If a month and year are specified, that specific month is printed.

NOTE

Don't confuse the **cal** command with the **calendar** command.

NOTE

The command **cal 94** displays the calendar for the year A.D. 94, not 1994. Also, the calendar is based on British/American convention. Try **cal 1752** to see the jump to the Gregorian calendar.

Examples

```
cal 11 1994
   November 1994
Su Mo Tu We Th Fr Sa
       1  2  3  4  5
 6  7  8  9 10 11 12
13 14 15 16 17 18 19
20 21 22 23 24 25 26
27 28 29 30

cal 1997
                               1997

       January               February               March
Su Mo Tu We Th Fr Sa  Su Mo Tu We Th Fr Sa  Su Mo Tu We Th Fr Sa
          1  2  3  4                     1                     1
 5  6  7  8  9 10 11   2  3  4  5  6  7  8   2  3  4  5  6  7  8
12 13 14 15 16 17 18   9 10 11 12 13 14 15   9 10 11 12 13 14 15
19 20 21 22 23 24 25  16 17 18 19 20 21 22  16 17 18 19 20 21 22
26 27 28 29 30 31     23 24 25 26 27 28     23 24 25 26 27 28 29
                                            30 31
        April                  May                  June
Su Mo Tu We Th Fr Sa  Su Mo Tu We Th Fr Sa  Su Mo Tu We Th Fr Sa
       1  2  3  4  5               1  2  3   1  2  3  4  5  6  7
 6  7  8  9 10 11 12   4  5  6  7  8  9 10   8  9 10 11 12 13 14
13 14 15 16 17 18 19  11 12 13 14 15 16 17  15 16 17 18 19 20 21
20 21 22 23 24 25 26  18 19 20 21 22 23 24  22 23 24 25 26 27 28
27 28 29 30           25 26 27 28 29 30 31  29 30
```

Options

month Specific month, in numerical form.

year Specific year.

Related Commands

calendar Sets up a personal calendar.

date Displays current date and time.

calendar — Personal Calendar

calendar *option*

Purpose

This rudimentary personal organizer allows you to store events in a file named **calendar**. On the current day, the **calendar** command scans the **calendar** file for all events occurring on that day. (Many users place **calendar** commands in their startup files.)

Events must be listed on one line, with the date in one of three formats:

11/12

Nov. 12

November 12

Examples

```
11/12  drinks with Eric
11/15  drinks with Eric
11/18  drinks with Eric
```

If this were your **calendar** file, you'd be reminded of these important engagements when you ran the **calendar** command on November 12, November 15, and November 18.

Option

Privileged users can use this option to scan the system for files named **calendar** in login directories, automatically sending corresponding events from each file to the appropriate user.

Related Commands

cal	Returns a monthly or yearly calendar.
cm	Manages appointments.
date	Displays current date and time.
dtcm	Manages appointments.

chmod — Change Mode

chmod *option mode filename(s)*

Purpose

Changes the file-access permissions on a given file, on several files, or on the contents of an entire subdirectory. Only the owner of the file or a privileged user can change the mode of a file.

UNIX provides two ways to change permissions: through symbolic or numeric form. The *numeric form* sets absolute permission values; the *symbolic form* sets values relative to the current value.

To get the current permissions, use the **ls** command, which is covered in Chapter 3.

Example Using Numeric Form

```
$ chmod 744 kevin.report
```

This example uses the **chmod** command on the file **kevin.report** to set a permission status where the owner can read, write, and execute a file; the file's specified group (and all other users) can read the file but cannot execute the file or write to it.

The value 744 comes from adding together the mode values found in the next section, "Modes." The lowest possible value is 000 — which means no one can read, write to, or execute the file — and the highest possible value is 777, which allows everyone to read, write to, and execute the file. Here's the exact arithmetic used to arrive at 744:

Number	Meaning
400	Owner has read permission.
200	Owner has write permission.
100	Owner has execute permission.
040	Group has read permission.
004	World has read permission.
744	

The next time you run an **ls** command (using the long form, of course) on the file **kevin.report**, the permissions would be set this way:

```
rwxr—r—
```

2

Modes

The *mode* is an octal number in the following format:

Number	Meaning
400	Owner has read permission.
200	Owner has write permission.
100	Owner has execute permission.
040	Group has read permission.
020	Group has write permission.
010	Group has execute permission.
004	World has read permission.
002	World has write permission.
001	World has execute permission.

When you add the numbers of the permissions you want to grant, their total corresponds to your particular set of permissions. For example, **423** means that you, the user, can read the file, users in your group can write to the file, and the rest of the world can write to and execute the file. (Note that you usually need read permission to execute a file.)

Symbolic Form

When you set permissions in this manner, the modes are entered in symbolic form but the structure of the command remains the same. Instead of using numerals in the mode field, you'd use one of the following symbols to set permissions:

Symbol	Meaning
u	User (who actually owns the file).
g	Group.
o	Other.
a	All (this is the default).

Symbol	Meaning
+	Adds a permission to the current permissions.
-	Removes a permission from the current permissions.
=	Assigns an absolute permission irrespective of the current permission.
r	Read.
w	Write.
x	Execute.
l	Mandatory lock during access.

You can set more than one mode at a time, but be sure to separate the settings with commas (leave no spaces on either side of such commas). In addition, you can set permissions for more than one set of users in the same mode statement, as shown in the following examples.

Examples Using Symbolic Form

```
$ chmod u+x kevin.report
```

This command line allows the owner of the file **kevin.report** to execute the file.

```
$ chmod u-x kevin.report
```

This command line removes permission from the owner of the file **kevin.report** to execute the file.

```
$ chmod u+x,go-w file.report
```

This command line allows the owner of the file **kevin.report** to execute the file, while removing the permissions of the group and all other users to write to the file.

Option

-R	Recursively changes through subdirectories and files.

Related Commands

chgrp	Changes group membership.
chown	Changes file ownership.
newgrp	Changes to a new working group.

clear — Clear Screen

clear

Purpose

Clears the screen.

Example

```
$ clear
```

csh — C Shell

csh

Purpose

Starts the C shell, one of many UNIX command-line interfaces. (See Chapter 11 for more information.)

date — Current Date

date *option +format*
date *option string* **(for privileged users)**

Purpose

Displays current date in a wide variety of formats (as the list of options indicates). Or, for those with privileged status, the date command can be used to set the system date and time.

Examples

```
$ date
```

This command returns the current date and time.

```
$ date -u
```

This command line returns the date and time in universal time, or Greenwich Mean Time.

```
$ date +%A
```

This command line returns the date and time with the day of the week spelled out.

```
$ date 1115063099
```

This command line sets the date and time to November 15, 6:30 a.m., 1999. Only privileged users can change the system date and time.

Option

-u	Returns the date and time in universal time, or Greenwich Mean Time (GMT).

Options (Privileged Users)

-**a**[-]s,f	Adjusts the time by seconds (s) or fractions of seconds (f). The default is to adjust the time forward; use - to adjust the time backward.
[*MMdd*]*hhmm*[*yy*]]	Changes the date and time (using month, day, hour, minute, and year).

Formats

%**a**	Day of the week abbreviated (Sun, Mon, and so on).
%**A**	Day of the week spelled out (Sunday, Monday, and so on).
%**b**	Month abbreviated (Jan, Feb, and so on; same as %**h**).
%**B**	Month spelled out (January, February, and so on).
%**c**	Date and time for a particular country's time zone.
%**d**	Day of the month in two digits (01–31).
%**D**	Date returned in *mm*/*dd*/*yy* format.
%**e**	Day of the month as numeral (1–31).
%**h**	Month abbreviated (Jan, Feb, and so on; same as %**b**).
%**H**	Hours returned in military time (00–23).

2

%I	Hours returned in nonmilitary time (0–12).
%j	Day returned in Julian date (001–365).
%m	Month returned as a number (01 for January, 02 for February, and so on).
%M	Minutes (0–59).
%n	Insert a newline.
%p	Time of day indicated (as AM or PM).
%S	Seconds (0–59).
%t	Inserts a tab.
%T	Time in *hh:mm:ss* format.
%U	Week returned as a number (0–51), with week starting on Sunday.
%w	Day of the week as a number (0 for Sunday, 1 for Monday, and so on).
%W	Week returned as a number (0–51), with week starting on a Monday.
%x	Country-specific time format.
%X	Country-specific date format.
%y	Year returned in two digits (99).
%Y	Year returned in four digits (1999).
%Z	Time zone

dc — Desk Calculator

dc *file*

Purpose

This command performs arbtrary-precision integer arithmetic, either from commands contained in a file or from keyboard input. Normally **dc** is not used by itself; it works as a reverse calculator — commands and operators follow the numbers they affect — and most people prefer not to use this format. The more straightforward **bc** command acts as a friendly front end for the **dc** command.

2

Examples

```
$ dc
7 10 * p
70
```

This command multiplies 7 by 10 and then prints the result.

```
$ 27-p
```

This command subtracts 27 from the previous number.

Commands

+	Adds last number to previous number.
-	Subtracts last number from previous number.
*	Multiplies last number from previous number.
/	Divides last number from previous number.
c	Clears all values.
i	Changes input base.
k	Sets scale factor (number of digits after decimal).
o	Changes output base.
p	Prints current result.
q	Quits **dc**.
v	Finds square root.

Related Command

bc Calculator

dfdfdf — Disk Free

df *options system_name*

Purpose

Displays information about the amount of free disk space on a file system or a file system specified by *system_name*. By selecting from among its options, you can display the total amount of free space (in kilobytes or disk blocks) or the total disk space.

2

Examples

```
$ df
```

This command line returns the amount of free disk space in each directory.

```
$ df -t
```

This command line returns the amount of allocated space, as well as the free disk space.

Options

-b	Displays the amount of free disk space in kilobytes.
-e	Displays the number of free files (not available on all systems).
-F *type*	Used to return information about unmounted file systems, specified by type. (In some versions of UNIX, you can find a list of available types in **/etc/vfstab**.)
-g	Returns the entire **statvfs** structure for all unmounted file systems.
-k	Prints the amount of allocation in kilobytes.
-l	Prints information only about local file systems.
-n	Displays the type of file system. Not available on all systems.
-t	Displays free space as well as allocated space. Not available on all systems.

Related Command

du	Displays disk-space usage.

du — Disk Usage

du *options files directories*

Purpose

Displays the amount of disk space used by a directory (and all its subdirectories) in blocks (usually 512 bytes each). The default is the current directory.

Options

-a Displays information about all files (not only directories).

-r Reports on files and directories **du** cannot open.

-s Works in silent mode and displays only totals.

2

Related Command

df Displays disk free-space information.

echo — Echo Input

echo *option string*

Purpose

Echoes text or values to standard output. Technically, **echo** exists in three forms: as a UNIX command (contained in **/bin/echo**), as a C shell command, and as a Bourne shell command. The C shell version does not support the **-n** option, nor does it support escape characters. Customarily, however, the three versions are considered interchangeable despite such small differences.

Examples

```
$ echo "Good morning!"
```

(This command would print the string `Good morning!` to the screen.)

```
$ echo "This is a test" | lp
```

(This command would print the line `This is a test` to the line printer.)

Option

-n Do not end the output with a newline. (The C shell version does not use this option.)

Control Characters

\b Backspace.

\c No newline.

2

\f	Form feed.
\n	Newline.
\r	Carriage return.
\t	Tab.
\v	Vertical tab.
\\	Backslash.
n	ASCII code (any character).

env — Set Environment

env *option* [*variable* = *value*] *command*

Purpose

Displays the current user environment variables with their values or makes changes to environment variables. The term *environment* refers to a variety of variable settings used by the command shell, including the login directory, default shell, login name, terminal type, and command path. When you change these settings, you change the environment.

This command works differently in the C shell. (See Chapter 11 for more information.)

Examples

```
$ env SHELL=/bin/csh
```

This command line sets your default shell to the C shell.

```
$ env HOME=/usr/users/kevin/notes
```

This command line sets the path to your home directory as **/usr/users/kevin/notes**.

Option

– Ignores the current environment variable.

exit — Exit Session

exit

Purpose

Quits the current session. This is actually a shell command, with different options based on the shell version. (See Chapter 11 for more information on shell-specific implementations.)

groups — Groups

groups *user*

Purpose

Returns a list of the groups a user belongs to (the default is a listing of your groups).

Related Commands

chgrp	Changes group.
newgrp	Changes group.

id — User and Group IDs

id *option*

Purpose

Displays your user ID and username, as well as your group ID and groupname.

Option

-a Displays all groups.

Related Commands

lognamc	Displays logname.
who	Displays users.

kill — Kill Program

2

kill *options PID*

Purpose

Kills a current process (as specified by a PID and returned by the **ps** command), provided you own that process or are a privileged user. This command is also built into the Korn, Bourne, and C shells, with slight differences.

The most serious form of this command, **kill -9**, is almost certain to kill any errant process.

Options

-l	Lists the signal names.
-signal	Uses signal information, such as a number (returned by **ps -f**)] or a name (returned by **kill -l**) to kill a process.

Related Command

ps	Process status.

ksh — Korn Shell

ksh

Purpose

Starts the Korn shell, one of UNIX's many command-line interfaces. (See Chapter 11 for more information.)

listusers — List Users

listusers *options*

Purpose

Returns a listing of usernames and IDs. Not available on all systems.

Options

-g *groupname*	Returns members of *groupname.*
-l *login*	Returns list of users with the name *login.*

man — Online Manual

man *command*

Purpose

Displays the online-manual page for a command. This command has many other capabilities that involve either Solaris 2.0 or advanced options geared toward more experienced users. If you want information about the **man** command specific to your system, use the **man man** command.

Related Commands

apropos	Returns information for a specific keyword.
whatis	Returns information from online-manual pages.
xman	Returns online-manual information when you are using the X Window System.

news — Display System Messages

news *options newsitem(s)*

Purpose

Displays all news items distributed systemwide. These items are usually stored in **/usr/news** or **/var/news** and set up by the system administrator.

Options

-a	Displays all of the news items.
-n	Displays the names of all of the news items.
-s	Displays a count of all of the news items.

nice — Run Nicely

nice *option command arguments*

Purpose

Runs a command *nicely* by giving it a very low priority, as with complex commands that can run during a period of reduced activity (such as lunch hour) without causing you inconvenience.

Option

-n Specifies *n* as the decrement in priority. The default is 10.

nohup — No Hangups

nohup *command arguments* **&**

Purpose

Keeps a command running even if you log off the system.

passwd — Password

passwd *options*
passwd *options user* **(privileged users)**

Purpose

Sets the user's password.

Options

-s Displays current password information as follows:

user	Username.
status	Password status: **NP** (no password), **PS** (password), or **LK** (locked).
mm/dd/yy	Date when last changed.

min	Minimum number of days before password must be changed.
max	Maximum number of days before password must be changed.
notice	Number of days before you are given notice that your password must be changed.

Options (Privileged Users)

-a Displays password information for all users.

-d Stops prompting user for password.

-f Forces user to change password.

-l Locks user password.

-n Sets number of days that must pass before user can rechange password.

-w Sets number of days before user is warned that the password expires.

-x Sets number of days before password expires.

Related Command

login Log into the system.

ps — Process Status

ps *options*

Purpose

Returns the status of all current processes. When used by itself, **ps** returns basic information about a process by PID (process ID), TTY, TIME, and COMMAND. A rather long list of options allows you to more effectively find any additional information you might need.

In BSD UNIX, the options are different; for instance, you would use **ps -aux** instead of **ps -ef**.

2

Options

-a	Displays all processes, except group leaders and those not controlled by a terminal.
-c	Displays information about scheduler priorities.
-d	Displays all processes, except group leaders.
-e	Displays information on every process.
-f	Displays full information about processes, including UID, PID, PPID, C, STIME, TTY, TIME, and COMMAND.
-g *list*	Displays processes for *list* of group leader IDs.
-j	Displays session and process group IDs.
-l	Displays a long listing of information, including the priorities set with the **nice** command.
-p *list*	Displays processes whose process IDs are contained in *list*.
-s *list*	Displays processes whose session leaders are contained in *list*.
-t *list*	Displays processes whose terminals are contained in *list*.
-u *list*	Displays processes whose users are contained in *list*.

Related Commands

kill	Kills a process.
nice	Runs command at lower priority.

pwd — Print Working Directory

pwd

Purpose

Returns the current working directory.

Options

None.

Related Command

cd Changes directory.

script — Log Session

script *option filename*

Purpose

Saves a copy of your current computing session. (Actually, this command starts a new session and logs it.) The default storage file is **typescript**; you can specify a different storage file from the command line.

Script saves all characters that appear on your screen, including Control (Ctrl) and Escape (Esc) characters. The recording ends when you type **exit** or **Ctrl-D** to end the session.

Option

-a *filename* Appends output to the new *filename*.

sh — Bourne Shell

sh

Purpose

Starts the Bourne shell. (See Chapter 11 for more information.)

sleep — Suspends Session

sleep *seconds*

Purpose

Suspends the system for a specified number of seconds before running another command. This capability is handy when you are working with shell scripts.

Related Command

wait Waits for the completion of a process.

2

su — Substitute User

su *option user shell_arguments*

Purpose

This command suspends your current shell while logging you in as a substitute user. You can use it to become another user without having to log off and then log on again. The most common use of **su** is to become the superuser temporarily, which enables you to perform privileged administrative commands.

Example

If you wanted to login as **kevin** (which is an experience every person should have in his or her lifetime) while already logged in the system as **erc**, you'd enter the following:

```
$ su kevin
```

The system would then prompt you for the password for user **kevin**.

Option

- Fully become the substitute user by adopting that user's environment.

Related Command

login Log in to the system.

tee — Split Standard Output

tee *options file(s)*

Purpose

Displays standard output on-screen, sending the same output to a specified file at the same time. The **tee** command is the only way to redirect output from a command to both the screen and to a file, or to two separate commands. This command, which is never used on its own, is always part of a longer command line.

Example

```
$ spell textfile | tee badwords
```

This command line runs the **spell** command on the file *textfile*, sending the output to a file named **badwords**.

```
$ ls | tee textfile | wc
```

This command line runs the **ls** command to generate a directory listing, sending the output to **tee**, which writes the listing to the file *textfile* and also sends the listing to the **wc** command, which displays a count of the lines, words, and bytes in the listing.)

Options

-a Appends output to file(s).

-i Ignores system interrupts.

time — Time a Command

time *command*

Purpose

Runs a specified command and reports back on the time it took to run the command (elapsed time, user time, system time) in seconds. An expanded version, **timex**, is available on most UNIX systems.

Example

```
$ time ls
```

This command line runs the **ls** command, which generates a directory listing; **time** then prints the time it took to run **ls**.

2

Options

None.

Related Command

timex Displays time for running a command.

timex — Time a Command

timex *options command*

Purpose

As an expanded version of the **time** command, **timex** runs a specified command and then reports, in seconds, the time needed to run the command (elapsed time, user time, system time). Its options can return the number of blocks read and written, system activity, and other accounting information.

Options

-o	Shows number of blocks used and characters transferred.	
-p	*suboptions*	Returns process activity for the command by using one or more of these suboptions:
	-f	Shows fork/exit flag and exit status.
	-h	Shows "hog" factor: CPU time divided by elapsed time.
	-k	Shows kcore time in minutes.
	-m	Shows mean core size (default).
	-r	Shows CPU use comparisons.
	-t	Shows CPU and system times.
	-s	Returns total system activity while command is running.

Related Command

time Displays time for running a command.

umask — User's File-Permission Mask

umask *values*

Purpose

Creates or returns the current value of the file-creation mask, which determines default values for new files. This value, also known as permissions, determines who has access to files and directories on the system. The **umask** command sets the default permissions for new files; you change the permissions for an existing file with **chmod**. On its own (sans options), **umask** returns the current default value.

This command is the functional opposite of **chmod**. When **ugo** is used with **umask**, permissions are denied for everyone; when **ugo** is used with **chmod**, permissions are granted.

However, **umask** uses a different method of specifying permissions — by numbers rather than symbols:

umask number	file permission	directory permission
0	rw-	rwx
1	rw-	rw-
2	r—	r-x
3	r—	r—
4	-w-	-wx
5	-w-	-w-
6	—	—x
7	—	—

Examples

```
$ umask 137
```

This results in a file permission of -rw-r——-.

Related Command

chmod Changes permissions.

uname — UNIX Name

uname *options*

Purpose

Returns the UNIX system name. On BSD systems, you would use the **hostname** command instead of this one to perform the same function.

CAUTION

Do not confuse the **uname** command with the **uuname** command.

Example

```
$ uname -a
Sun OS eric 5.3 Generic sun4M sparc
```

Options

-a	Reports all information (the sum of all other options).
-m	Returns the hardware name.
-n	Returns the host name.
-p	Returns the processor type.
-r	Returns the operating-system release.
-s	Returns the system name.
-v	Returns the operating-system version.

wait — Wait for Job to Complete

wait *ID*

Purpose

Forces your shell to wait until background processes are completed before starting a new process.

Options

ID	Job-process ID.

Related Commands

ps	Lists job processes.
sleep	Suspends execution.

whatis — Command Summary

whatis *command*

Purpose

Looks up the online-manual page for a command and presents a one-line summary.

Related Commands

apropos	Returns help information about a command.
man	Online-manual pages.
xman	Online-manual pages displayed under the X Window System.

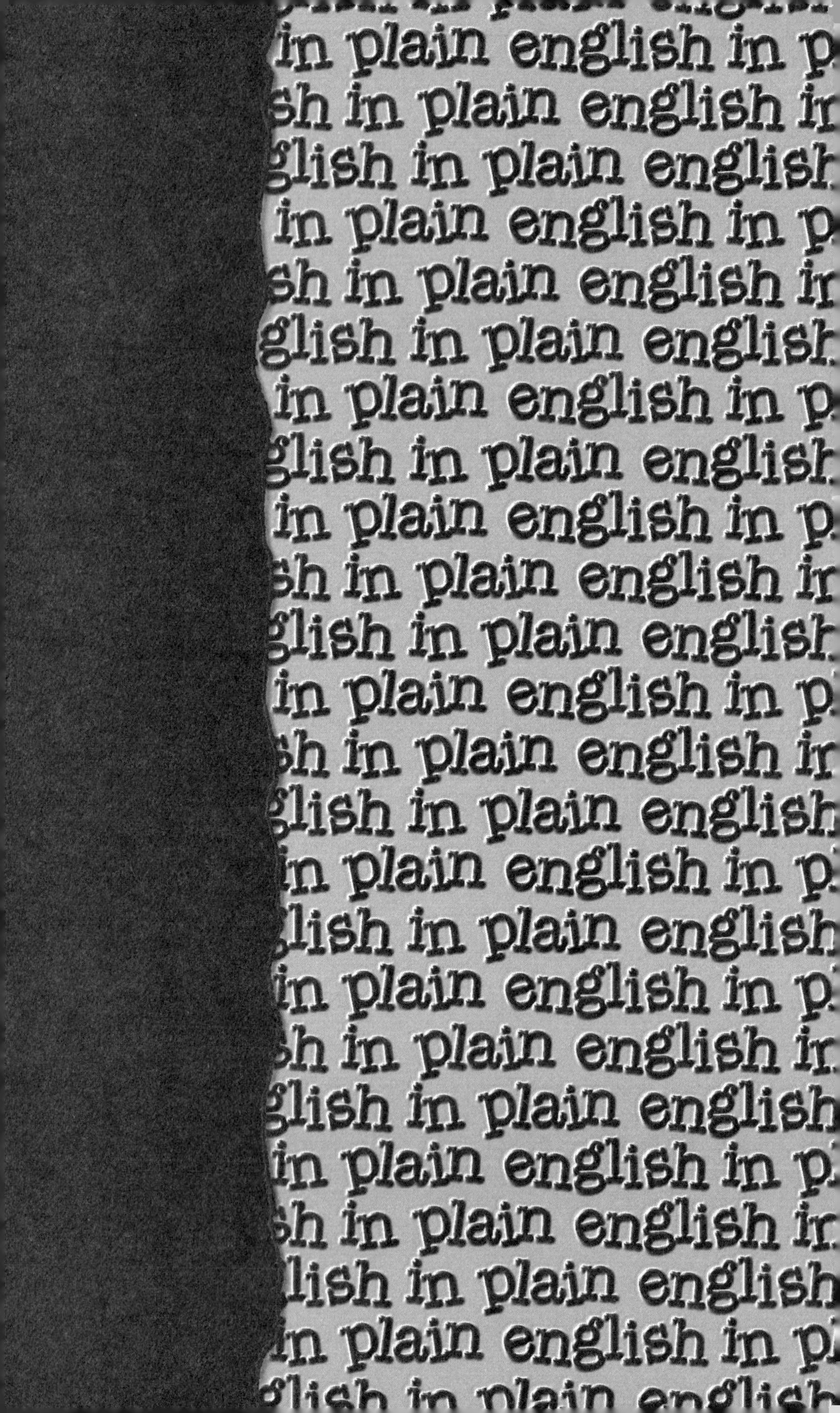

3

File-Manipulation Commands

These commands help you work with UNIX directories and files. By using them, you can compare or create files and directories and manage your creations by deleting or moving them.

bdiff — List Differences in Files

bdiff *file1 file2 options*

Purpose

Compares two files and reports on the differing lines. This command actually invokes the **diff** command after dividing a file into manageable chunks; it works best with text files.

Example

```
$ bdiff kevin.memo kevin.memo.alt
1c1
< Dear Mr. Reichard:
- - -
> Dear Scumbag:
```

Options

N	Divides the files into segments **n** lines long. This affects the values returned regarding specific differing lines, as the example shows.
–s	Suppresses error messages.

Related Commands

cmp	Compares two files and tells you if the files are different.
diff	Compares files and reports *all* differing lines.
diff3	Compares three files.
sdiff	Compares files side by side.

cat — Concatenate Files

cat *options file(s)*

Purpose

This very handy command performs several frequently used chores:

- Combines several files into a new file (using the > operator).
- Appends other files to an existing file (using the > operator).
- Displays a file when no operators are specified.
- Copies a file to a new name (using the > operator).
- Creates a new text file without the fuss of a text editor.

Examples

```
$ cat kevin.report
```

The contents of the file **kevin.report** would be displayed nonstop on the screen.

```
$ cat kevin.report kevin.memo
```

The contents of the files **kevin.report** and **kevin.memo** would be displayed nonstop on the screen.

```
$ cat kevin.report kevin.memo > kevin.words
```

The contents of the files **kevin.report** and **kevin.memo** would be combined into a new file named **kevin.words**, in the order in which they appear on the command line.

```
$ cat kevin.report.old > kevin.report.new
```

The contents of **kevin.report.old** are copied into the new file named **kevin.report.new**.

```
$ cat > kevin.report.1999
```

Cat creates a new file named **kevin.report.1999** and places all keyboard input into that file, halting input when the user types **Ctrl–D**.

```
$ cat kevin.report > kevin.memo
```

The contents of **kevin.report** are appended to the end of the file **kevin.memo**.

```
$ cat - > kevin.report
```

Keyboard input is appended to the end of the file **kevin.report**.

CAUTION

If you're not careful about how you use **cat**, you could overwrite the contents of one file with keyboard entry or the contents of another file. For instance, consider the following command:

```
$ cat - > kevin.report
```

It replaces the current contents of kevin.report with keyboard input.

Options

–	Used as a substitute for a filename, – allows for keyboard entry to be appended to an existing file. Press **Ctrl–D** to end the keyboard entry.
–s (SV)	Works in silent mode; suppresses information about nonexistent files.
–s (BSD)	Removes blank lines from the file.
–u	Output is unbuffered; default is buffered, which means that characters are displayed in blocks.
–v	Prints nonprinting characters, such as control characters, except for tabs, form feeds, and newlines.
–ve	Prints nonprinting characters, such as control characters, except for tabs and form feeds; newlines appear as dollar signs (**$**).
–vt	Prints nonprinting characters, such as control characters, except for newlines; tabs appear as **^I** and form feeds as **^L**.
–vet	Prints all nonprinting characters.

Related Commands

cp	Copies files.
more	Displays files one screen at a time.
page	Displays files one page at a time.
pg	Displays files one page at a time.

cd — Change Directory

cd *directory*

Purpose

Changes current directory to a new directory. This is actually a shell command, but is usually treated as a regular UNIX command.

Examples

```
$ cd
```

This returns you to your home directory.

```
$ cd stuff
```

This changes you to the subdirectory **stuff** and makes it the current directory.

```
$ cd /usr/users/eric/private
```

This changes your current directory to another directory named **/usr/users/eric/private**.

```
$ cd ~/stuff/1997
```

This moves you to a subdirectory within your home directory.

```
$ cd ..
```

This moves your current directory one level up in the directory hierarchy.

Options

None.

Related Command

pwd Prints the name of the current directory.

CROSS-REFERENCE

The **cd** command is also covered in Chapter 11.

chown — Change Ownership

chown *options newowner file(s)*

Purpose

3

Changes the ownership of a given file or files to a new owner. The new owner is either a user ID number or a login name (these can be found in **/etc/passwd**).

The BSD version of this command also allows the group to be changed, although BSD systems may restrict the use of this command to root.

Example

```
$ chown kevin kevin.report
```

(This changes the ownership of the file **kevin.report** to **kevin**.)

Options

-h Changes the ownership of a symbolic link. Not available on all systems.

-R Recursively changes through a subdirectory and symbolic links.

Related Commands

chmod Changes file-access permissions.

chgrp Changes group membership.

newgrp Changes to a new working group.

cmp — Compare Files

cmp *options file1 file2*

Purpose

Compares the contents of two files. If the files are different, **cmp** returns the byte position and line number of the first difference between the two files. If there is no difference in the files, **cmp** returns nothing.

The **cmp** command works on all files, not just text files. Similar commands, such as **diff** and **comm**, work only with text files.

Example

```
$ cmp kevin.report kevin.memo
kevin.report kevin.memo differ: char 31, line 2
```


Options

-l Displays the byte position and the differing characters for *all* differences within the file.

-s Works silently, returning only the exit codes and not the instances of differences. The exit code is one of the following:

- **0** Files are identical.
- **1** Files are different.
- **2** One of the files is unreadable.

Related Commands

comm	Compares files line by line.
diff	Compares files and returns differences.
sdiff	Compares files side by side.

comm — Compare Files

comm *options file1 file2*

Purpose

Compares the contents of two presorted text files. The output is generated in three columns:

Lines found in *file1*	Lines found in *file2*	Lines found in both files

Example

```
$ comm kevin.report kevin.memo
                                     Dear Mr. Jones:
I am happy to    I am sad to
                                     report that your
                                     daughter, Felicia,
was accepted     was rejected
                                      from our fine college.
```

Options

–1	Suppresses the printing of column 1.
–2	Suppresses the printing of column 2.
–3	Suppresses the printing of column 3.
–12	Prints only column 3.
–13	Prints only column 2.
–23	Prints only column 1.

Related Commands

cmp	Compares files byte by byte.
diff	Compares files and returns differences.
sdiff	Compares files side by side.
sort	Sorts files.

compress — Compress Files

compress *options filename(s)*

Purpose

Compresses a file (or files), creating *filename.Z.*

Options

–b*n* Changes the number of bits used in the compression process. The default is 16, and *n* can be set to a numeral between 9 and 16. The lower the setting, the larger the resulting compressed file.

–f Compresses with no feedback; useful in automated shell scripts.

–v Returns information on how much the file was compressed.

Related Commands

uncompress	Uncompresses a compressed file.
pack	Compresses a file or files.
unpack	Uncompresses a compressed file.
zcat	Uncompresses a compressed file.

cp — Copy Files

cp *options sourcefile destinationfile*
cp *options file1 directory*
cp *options directory1 directory2*

Purpose

Copies the contents of one file into another file with a new name, or into another directory, retaining the existing filename. It also copies the contents of one directory into a new directory.

Example

```
$ cp kevin.memo kevin.memo.old
```

This copies the file **kevin.memo** into a new file called **kevin.memo.old**.

```
$ cp kevin.memo /usr/users/kevin/old_junk
```

This copies the file **kevin.memo** into the directory **/usr/users/kevin/old_junk**.

```
$ cp -r /usr/users/kevin/old_junk /usr/users/kevin/backup
```

This copies the contents of the directory **/usr/users/kevin/old_junk** into the new directory **/usr/users/kevin/backup**.

Options

–i	Makes sure you don't overwrite an existing file.
–p	Retains existing permissions. Not available on all systems.
–r	Copies entire directory.

Related Commands

chgrp	Changes group membership.
chmod	Changes file-access permissions.
chown	Changes file ownership.
ln	Links files.
mv	Moves or renames a file or directory.
rm	Removes a file.

crypt — Encrypt Files

crypt *password option* < *file* > *encryptedfile*

Purpose

Stores a text file in a new encrypted file to avoid unauthorized access. The command also enables you to read from an encrypted file.

NOTE

UNIX text editors can read encrypted files.

You need the password not only to encrypt a file, but also to read an encrypted file, although the **–k** option allows you to set the password as an environmental variable, CRYPTKEY. The use of the **–k** option is severely frowned upon; it lessens the security measures afforded by the **crypt** command.

NOTE

The **crypt** command is not supported in versions of UNIX destined for export, in compliance with U.S. security laws.

Example

```
$ crypt < kevin.report > kevin.new.report
```

Options

-k Uses the password set as an environmental variable, CRYPTKEY.

csplit — Split Files

csplit *options arguments*

Purpose

Splits a long file into a series of smaller files. When you set up the command line using **csplit**, you specify whether you want to divide up the file by size or by content — that is, through having **csplit** search for a specific expression.

The resulting files begin with **xx**. For instance, the first filename is **xx00**, the second is **xx01**, and so on. (You're limited to 100 files, so the last file in this sequence would be named **xx99**.)

Example

```
$ csplit -k gone_wind '/^Chapter/' {30}
```

This splits the file **gone_wind** into 30 files, all beginning with the expression "Chapter" at the beginning of the line.

Options

-f*file* Uses *file* instead of *xx* for the beginning of filenames. (For instance, with this option enabled as **-fthis**, the first filename would be **this00**.)

-k Keeps files even though they may not meet command-line criteria.

-s Suppresses printing or displaying character counts.

3

Arguments

/expr/	Creates a file that begins with the current line through the line containing **expr**. You can add a suffix that ends the file a line before **expr** by appending -1 or that ends the file a line after **expr** by appending +1.
%expr%	Same as /expr/, except that no file is created for the text prior to **expr**.
line	Creates a file that begins at the current line and ends one line before line number *line*. (Note: Some documentation refers to this option as *num*. The two names refer to the same option.)
{*n*}	Repeats the previous argument *n* times. Unless you specify *n*, the command line only works once.

Related Command

split Splits a file.

diff — List Differences in Files

diff *options diroptions file1 file2*

Purpose

Compares two files and reports differing lines. The results are clear: The line numbers of the differing lines are noted; the offending line from file1 is marked with < and the offending line from file2 is marked with >. Three hyphens (- - -) separate the contents of the two files. This command works best with text files.

NOTE

Diff cannot process large files; use **bdiff** in those situations.

Example

```
$ diff erc.memo erc.memo.1112
1c1
< Dear Boss:
```

```
---
> Dear Mr. King:
4c4
< This idea should be nuked.
---
> —Eric
```


Options

–b	Ignores blanks at the end of line.
–c	Produces three lines of context for each difference.
–C*n*	Produces *n* lines of context for each difference.
–D *def*	Combines file1 and file2, using C preprocessor controls (**#ifdef**).
–e	Creates a script for the **ed** editor to make file1 the same as file2.
–i	Ignores case.
–t	Expands tabs in output to spaces.
–w	Ignores spaces and tabs.

Diroptions

–l	Long format with pagination by **pr**.
–r	Recursively runs **diff** for files in common subdirectories.
–s	Lists identical files.
–S*file*	Starts directory comparisons with *file*, ignoring files alphabetically listed before *file*.

Related Commands

bdiff	Compares two files and returns the differences.
comm	Compares two files line by line.
cmp	Compares contents of two files.
diff3	Compares three files.
sdiff	Compares files side by side.

diff3 — List Differences in Files

diff3 *options file1 file2 file3*

Purpose

Like **diff**, this command compares three different files and reports the differences. It returns one of the following codes:

====	All three files differ.
====1	file1 is different.
====2	file2 is different.
====3	file3 is different.

Options

–e	Creates an **ed** script that places differences between file2 and file3 into file1. Not available on all systems.
–E	Creates an **ed** script that places differences between file2 and file3 into file1, using brackets to mark any lines that differ in all three files.
–x	Creates an **ed** script that places differences among all three files in another file.
–X	Creates an **ed** script that places differences among all three files into them, using brackets to mark the lines that differ in all three files. Not available on all systems.
–3	Creates an **ed** script that places differences between file1 and file3 in file1.

Related Commands

bdiff	Compares two files and returns the differences.
cmp	Compares contents of two files.
comm	Compares two files line by line.
diff	Compares two files.
sdiff	Compares files side by side.

dircmp — Directory Compare

dircmp *options directory1 directory2*

Purpose

Compares the contents of two directories and returns information on how the directories differ. The information is given in the form of files found in the first directory, files found in the second directory, and files common to both directories.

Options

-d	Compares pairs of common files by using the diff command.
-s	Suppresses information about identical files.
-w*n*	Changes the width of the output line to *n* characters; the default is 72.

Related Commands

bdiff	Compares two files and returns the differences.
diff	Compares two files.
sdiff	Compares files side by side.

egrep — Search Files

egrep *options pattern file(s)*

Purpose

Searches for text (referred to as *patterns* or *expressions*) in a file or multiple files, displaying the results of the search. For instance, you could search for the strings **Spacely Sprockets** and **Jetson Enterprises** in multiple files.

Egrep is related to the commands **grep** and **fgrep**. It is considered the most powerful of the three, as it allows for the searching of multiple strings. In addition, **egrep** allows matching from a file containing a series of expressions. It is also considered to be the fastest of the three commands.

Example

```
$ egrep "Spacely Sprockets|Jetson Enterprises" *
kevin.memo.1112: This proposal from Spacely Sprockets
erc.doc.193: As a representative of Jetson Enterprises
```


This searches all the files in the current directory — as indicated by the wildcard asterisk (*) — for the strings **Spacely Sprockets** and **Jetson Enterprises**.

Options

–b	Returns block number of matched line.
–c	Returns only the number of matches, without quoting the text.
–e *string*	Searches for string beginning with a hyphen (-).
–f *file*	Takes expressions from file *file*.
–h	Returns only matched text with no reference to filenames. (Not available on all systems.)
–i	Ignores case.
–l	Returns only filenames containing a match, without quoting the text.
–n	Returns line number of matched text, as well as the text itself.
–v	Returns lines that do *not* match the text.

Related Commands

diff	Compares two files.
fgrep	Searches for text in files.
grep	Searches for text in files.
sdiff	Compares files side by side.

fgrep — Fast Grep

fgrep *options pattern file(s)*

Purpose

Searches for text (referred to as *patterns*) in a file or multiple files, displaying the results of the search. For instance, you could search for the strings **Spacely Sprockets** and **Jetson Enterprises** in multiple files. **Fgrep** searches only for literal text strings. It will not search for expressions. **Fgrep** is related to the commands **grep** and **egrep**.

3

Example

```
$ fgrep "Spacely Sprockets|Jetson Enterprises" *
kevin.memo.1112: This proposal from Spacely Sprockets
is
erc.doc.193: As a representative of Jetson Enterprises
```

This searches all the files in the current directory — as indicated by the wildcard asterisk * — for the strings **Spacely Sprockets** and **Jetson Enterprises**.

Options

–b	Returns block number of matched line.
–c	Returns only the number of matches, without quoting the text.
–e *string*	Used to search for string *string* beginning with a hyphen (-).
–f *file*	Takes expressions from file *file*.
–h	Returns only matched text with no reference to filenames.
–i	Ignores case.
–l	Returns only filenames containing a match, without quoting the text.
–n	Returns line number of matched text, as well as the text itself.
–v	Returns lines that do not match the text.
–x	Returns a line only if the string matches an entire line.

Related Commands

diff	Compares two files.
egrep	Searches for text in files.
grep	Searches for text in files.
sdiff	Compares files side by side.

file — Determine File Type

file *options filename*

Purpose

Describes file type of the given file. If needed, **file** will check the magic file (/**etc**/**magic**) for file types.

CAUTION

The information returned by **file** is not always correct. However, **file** is best at detecting text files, shell scripts, PostScript files, and UNIX commands.

Options

–c	Checks the magic file.
–f*list*	Runs the file command on the filenames contained in the file *list*.
–h	Ignores symbolic links.
–m*file*	Uses *file* as the magic file, not /**etc**/**magic**.

find — Find Files

find *pathname(s) condition(s)*

Purpose

Finds a file. Of course, it's not *quite* that simple—you can enter as many conditions as you want (relating to when the file was created, when it was last accessed, what links are present, and so on), as you'll see when you review the available conditions.

Examples

```
$ find / -ctime -2 -print
```

This returns all the files on the entire file system that have been changed fewer than two days ago.

```
$ file $HOME -name '*memo' -print
```

This returns all the files in your home directory that end with the string **memo**.

Options

–atime *days*	Finds files that were accessed: +*d* more than *d* days ago. *d* exactly *d* days ago. –*d* fewer than *d* days ago.
–ctime *days*	Finds files that were changed: +*d* more than *d* days ago. *d* exactly *d* days ago. –*d* fewer than *d* days ago.
–exec *command* { } \;	Runs UNIX command after a file is found.
–follow	Follows symbolic links and the associated directories.
–fstype *type*	Finds files of a specific file *type*.
–group *group*	Finds files belonging to group *group*, which can be a name or ID.
–inum *num*	Finds a file with an inode number of *num*.
–links *links*	Finds files with the following: +*l* more than *l* links. *l* exactly 1 link. –*l* fewer than *l* links.
–local	Searches for files on the local file system.
–mtime *days*	Finds files that were modified: +*d* more than *d* days ago. *d* exactly *d* days ago. –*d* fewer than *d* days ago.

–name *file*	Finds a file named *file*.
–newer *filename*	Returns all files that have been modified more recently than *filename*.
–nogroup	Finds files owned by a group not listed in **/etc/group**.
–nouser	Finds files owned by a user not listed in **/etc/passwd**.
–ok *command* { } \;	Runs UNIX command after a file is found, verifying the action with the user.
–perms *nnn*	Matches specified file permissions (such as **rwx**).
–print	Prints the results of the search to the screen. This option is mandatory if you want to see the results of your search. (Not mandatory when using Linux.)
–size *blocks* [*chars*]	Finds a file that is blocks *blocks* large, or *chars* characters large.
–type *t*	Returns names of files of type *t*. Type *t* can be *b* (block special file), *c* (character special file), *d* (directory), *f* (plain file), *l* (symbolic link), or *p* (pipe).
–user *user*	Matches files belonging to a user, as specified by name or ID.
–xdev	Searches for files on the same filesystem as the specified pathname. (Only for BSD systems.)

Logical Selectors

–a	and
–o	or
\!	not
\(...\)	group together

grep — Search Files

grep *options pattern file(s)*

Purpose

Searches for text (referred to as patterns or expressions) in a file or multiple files, displaying the results of the search. For instance, you could search for the string **Spacely Sprockets** in multiple files.

Grep is related to the commands **fgrep** and **egrep**. Of the three, **grep** supports the fewest options — for instance, **grep** will not accept input from a text file — and is considered to be the slowest.

Examples

```
$ grep "Spacely Sprockets" *
kevin.memo.1112: This proposal from Spacely Sprockets is
```

This searches all the files in the current directory — as indicated by the wildcard asterisk * — for the string **Spacely Sprockets**.)

Options

–b Returns block number of matched line. Not available on all systems.

–c Returns only the number of matches, without quoting the text.

–h Returns only matched text with no reference to filenames. Not available on all systems.

–i Ignores case.

–l Returns only filenames containing a match, without quoting the text.

–n Returns line number of matched text, as well as the text itself.

–s Suppresses error messages.

–v Returns lines that do *not* match the text.

Related Commands

diff	Compares two files.
egrep	Searches for text in files.
fgrep	Searches for text in files.
sdiff	Compares files side by side.

head — Display Top of File

head *option file(s)*

Purpose

Displays the beginning of a file. The default is 10 lines.

Option

-n Specifies the number of lines to display. The default is 10 lines.

Related Command

tail Displays end of file.

join — Join Files

join *options file1 file2*

Purpose

Joins together two presorted files that have a common key field. Only lines containing the key field will be joined.

Example

```
$ cat workers
Eric     286  erc
Geisha   280  geisha
Kevin    279  kevin
```

```
$ cat workers.1
Eric      8    555-6674
Geisha    10   555-4221
Kevin     2    555-1112

$ join workers workers.1 > workers.2

$ cat workers.2
Eric      286  erc       8    555-6674
Geisha    280  geisha    10   555-4221
Kevin     279  kevin     2    555-1112
```


Options

–a*filename*	Lists lines in *filename* that cannot be joined. If *filename* is now specified, unjoinable lines from both files will be listed.
–e *string*	Replaces empty fields in output with *string*.
–j*filename m*	Joins on the *m*th field of file filename (or both if filename is not specified).
–o *file.field*	Output contains fields specified by field number *field*.
–t*char*	*Char* will be used as a field separator, instead of the default.

Related Commands

awk	Text-processing language.
comm	Compares files line by line.
cut	Cuts fields.
sort	Sorts files.

3

ln — Link Files

ln *options originalfile linkfile*
ln *options file(s) directory*

Purpose

Links two or more files. In essence, this allows the same file to be accessed under different names. No matter how many names exist, there's still only one file. The **ln** command also creates linked files with the same name in different directories.

You may want to create symbolic links, since these links can occur across file systems and are easier to keep track of with the **ls** command.

CAUTION

Don't reverse the file order with this command, or you can inadvertently trash good files. Remember: the first file is the original. The second file names the link. The link then points back at the original file.

Examples

```
$ ln kevin eric
```

This creates a link named **eric** to the file **kevin**.

```
$ ln kevin /usr/users/kevin/misc
```

This creates a link to **kevin** in **/usr/users/kevin/misc**. The linked file will also be named **kevin**.

Options

–f	Forces linking — that is, does not ask for confirmations.
–n	Does not overwrite an existing file.
–s	Creates a symbolic link.

Related Commands

chmod	Changes file-access permissions.
chown	Changes file ownership.
cp	Copies files.

ls Lists files.

mv Moves files.

ls List Files

ls *options names*

Purpose

Lists the contents of the specified directory. If no directory is specified, the contents of the current directory are listed.

This is both one of the simplest (conceptually, there's nothing more simple than returning the contents of a directory) and the most complex (witness the presence of 23 options!) commands within the UNIX operating system. Of course, not all 23 options are equal; you'll use **–F** and **–l** quite a bit; chances are you won't find much use for **–u** or **–c**.

Examples

```
$ ls
data      figures     misc    newdata    personnel
expenses  financials
```

This returns a listing of the files in the current directory.

```
$ ls newdata
newdata
```

This confirms that the file *newdata* is contained in the current directory.

```
$ ls god
god not found
```

This searches for a specific file, which is not in the current directory.

```
$ ls -a
. .. .mailrc   .profile  data   financials   misc
newdata        personnel
```

This lists all files, including hidden files, which begin with a period (.).

3

Options

–1	Lists one item per line.
–a	Lists all contents, including hidden files.
–b	Shows invisible characters in octal.
–c	Lists by creation/modification time.
–C	Lists in column (the default).
–d	Lists only the name of the directory, not the contents.
–f	Assumes that names are directories, not files.
–F	Flags executable filenames with an asterisk (*), directories with a slash (/), and symbolic links with an @.
–g	Lists in long form, omitting the owner of the file.
–i	Lists the inode for each file.
–l	Lists the contents of a directory in long form.
–L	Lists the true files for symbolic links.
–m	Lists the contents across the screen, separated by commas.
–n	Same as **–l**, except it uses numbers instead of names for users and groups.
–o	Same as **–l**, except the group name is omitted.
–p	Displays a slash (/) at the end of every directory name.
–q	Lists contents with nonprinting characters represented by a question mark (?).
–r	Lists the contents in reverse order.
–R	Recursively lists subdirectories.
–s	Lists file sizes in blocks, instead of the default bytes.
–t	Lists the contents in order of time saved, beginning with the most recent.
–u	Lists files according to the most recent access time.
–x	Lists files in multicolumn format.

Related Commands

chmod	Changes file-access permissions.
chgrp	Changes group.
chown	Changes file ownership.

find Finds file.
ln Links files.

mkdir — Make Directory

mkdir *options directories*

Purpose

Creates a new directory or directories.

Examples

```
$ mkdir stuff
```

This creates a new directory called **stuff**.

```
$ mkdir -m 444 stuff
```

This creates a new directory called **stuff** and sets up file permissions of 444.

Options

-m *mode* Specifies the *mode* of the new directory.

more — Display File

more *options file(s)*

Purpose

Displays all or parts of a file one screenful at a time. Type **q** to quit; press **space bar** to continue.

Example

```
$ more bigfile
```

This displays a file named **bigfile**.

Options

–c	Clears the screen before displaying the next page of the file. This can be quicker than watching pages scroll by.
–d	Displays a prompt at the bottom of the screen involving brief instructions.
–f	Wraps text to fit the screen width and judges the page length accordingly.
–l	Ignores formfeeds (^L) at the end of a page.
–r	Displays control characters.
–s	Squeezes; ignores multiple blank lines.
–u	Ignores formatting characteristics like underlined text.
–w	Waits for user input before exiting.
–*n*	Sets window size by *n* lines.
+*num*	Starts output at line number *num*.

Options During File Viewing

f	Goes to next full screen.
n	Displays next file.
p	Displays previous file.
q	Quits.

Related Commands

pg	Displays file one page at a time.

mv — Move Files

mv *options sources target*

Purpose

Moves a file or multiple files into another directory or to a new name in the current directory.

Examples

```
$ mv 1999.report /users/home/misc
```

This moves the file **1999.report** to the directory named **/users/home/misc**.

```
$ mv 1998.report 1999.report
```

This renames the file **1997.report** to the new filename **1998.report**.

```
$ mv 1997.report /users/home/misc/1999.report
```

This saves the file **1997.report** under the name **1999.report** in the directory **/users/home/misc**.

```
$ mv -i 1997.report /users/home/misc/1999.report
mv: overwrite 1999.report?
```

This saves the contents of the file **1997.report** to the new name **1999.report** in the directory **/users/home/misc**. The confirmation is required because **1999.report** already exists.

Options

–f Moves file without checking for confirmation in case of an overwrite.

–i Prompts users if action would overwrite an existing file. This is the default with the **bash** shell.

Related Command

cp Copies file.

pack — Compress Files

pack *options file(s)*

Purpose

Compresses a file, decreasing its size by up to 50 percent. The original file is replaced by a new file ending in **.z**. For instance, if you were to pack a file named **text**, the original file **text** is erased and a new file **text.z** appears in the same directory.

Uncompress packed files with the **unpack** command.

Options

–	Displays information about the compression.
–f	Packs the file even if no disk space is saved.

Related Commands

compress	Compresses files.
pcat	Displays contents of packed files.
unpack	Unpacks contents of packed file.

page — Display Files

page *options file(s)*

Purpose

Displays all or parts of a file. Type **q** to quit; press **space bar** to continue.

Example

```
$ page bigfile
```

This displays a file named **bigfile**.

Options

–c	Clears the screen before displaying the next page of the file. This can be quicker than watching pages scroll by.
–d	Displays a prompt at the bottom of the screen involving brief instructions.
–f	Wraps text to fit the screen width and judges the page length accordingly.
–l	Ignores formfeeds (**^L**) at the end of a page.
–r	Displays control characters.
–s	Squeezes; ignores multiple blank lines.
–u	Ignores formatting characteristics like underlined text.

-w	Waits for user input for exiting.
-*n*	Sets window size by *n* lines.
+*num*	Starts output at line number *num*.

Options During File Viewing

f	Goes to next full screen.
n	Displays next file.
p	Displays previous file.
q	Quits.

Related Command

more	Displays file one page at a time.

pcat — Display Packed Files

pcat *file(s)*

Purpose

Displays the contents of a packed file.

Related Commands

pack	Compresses a file.
unpack	Uncompresses a file.

rm — Remove File

rm *options file(s)*

Purpose

Removes files, provided you're either the owner of the file or have write permission to the directory containing the file (though not necessarily to the file itself). If you don't have write permission to the file itself, you'll be prompted as to whether you really want to delete the file. This command can also be used to delete directories (remember, a directory is merely a file containing information about other files).

CAUTION

Use this command with caution. When a file is removed, it's really gone. Unless you have some undelete utilities at your disposal (for instance, there are versions of the Norton Utilities for some UNIX variants), you will want to be very careful with this command. We also use the **–i** option to verify our actions, although this option is not needed with Linux.

Examples

```
$ rm textfile
```

This removes the file named *textfile*.

```
$ rm textfile?
```

This removes all files beginning with **textfile** and having a single extra character, like *textfile1*, *textfile2*, and so on.

```
$ rm -r stuff
```

This removes the directory named **stuff** and all its contents, including files and subdirectories.

Options

–f Removes files without verifying action with user.

–i Removes files after verification from user.

–r Recursively moves through subdirectories.

Related Command

rmdir Removes directory.

rmdir — Remove Directory

rmdir *options directory*

Purpose

Removes a directory. The directory must be empty. To empty a directory that contains other files and directories, use the **rm –r** command.

Options

–p	Removes the directory and any parent directory that is empty as a result of the action.
–s	Ignores error messages.

Related Command

rm Removes file.

sdiff — Compare Files

sdiff *options file1 file2*

Purpose

Compares *file1* with *file2* and reports on the differences as well as on identical lines. Output occurs in four forms:

text text	Lines are identical.
text <	Line exists only in file1.
text >	Line exists only in file2.
text | text	Lines are different.

Options

–l	Reports only on lines that are identical in the left column of file1.
–o *outfile*	Sends identical lines to *outfile*.
–s	Does not return identical lines.
–w*n*	Sets line length to *n* (default is 130).

Related Commands

bdiff	Compares files.
cmp	Compares two files and tells you if the files are different.
diff	Compares files and reports *all* differing lines.
diff3	Compares three files.

split — Split Files

split *option file1 file2*

Purpose

Splits files into smaller files based on line counts. The default is to create 1,000-line files. This command leaves the original file1 intact. If file2 is unnamed, the result files will be named **xaa**, **xab**, **xac**, and so on. If file2 is named, **aa**, **ab**, **ac** (and so on) will be appended to the end of the specified file2 name.

CROSS-REFERENCE

If you're looking for more options when splitting a file—after all, using page lengths is a rather inflexible method of dividing files—use the **csplit** command covered elsewhere in this section.

Example

```
$ split textfile newtext
```

This would split *textfile* into smaller files. If *textfile* was 4,500 lines long, **split** would create five files — **newtextaa**, **newtextab**, **newtextac**, **newtextad**, and **nextextae** — with the first four files containing 1,000 lines and the fifth containing 500 lines.

Option

–n Splits a file into *n*-line segments. (The default is 1,000 lines.)

Related Command

csplit Splits a file.

strings — Look for ASCII Strings

strings *options file(s)*

Purpose

Looks for ASCII strings in binary files. Searches binary or object files for sequences of four or more printable characters, ending with newline or a null character. The **strings** command is useful for identifying binary files, such as object files or word-processor documents made by incompatible software.

Options

–a	Searches an entire file.
–n *n*	Sets minimum string length to *n* (the default is four).

tail — Display End of File

tail *options file*

Purpose

Displays the final 10 lines of a file.

Option

–f	"Follows" growth of file should changes be made while **tail** command is active. Press **Ctrl–D** to stop the process.
–r	Displays lines in reverse order. Not available on all systems.
–n*b*	Displays the last *n* blocks.
+ *n***b**	Displays all blocks after block *n*.
–*n***c**	Displays the last *n* characters.
+ *n***c**	Displays all characters after *n*.
–*n***l**	Displays the last *n* lines.
+ *n***l**	Displays all lines after line *n*.

Related Command

head	Displays first 10 lines of a file.

tar — Tape Archiver

tar *options file(s)*

Purpose

3

Archives files to **tar** files, often on backup tapes. (In UNIX, a tape isn't always a tape — in this instance, it may be a tape, hard disk, or diskette.) Specified files can either replace existing files or be appended to existing files. **Tar** is also used to extract archived files from tape.

The usage for the **tar** command differs slightly from the rest of the UNIX command set. Options have two parts: a function option (each command must contain one of these) followed by other options. In addition, the hyphen (-) is not needed before options.

Examples

```
$ tar cvf /dev/mt0 /usr/users/kevin/memos
```

This creates a new archive of all files in the directory **/usr/users/kevin/memos** on the device **/dev/mt0**; remember, devices in UNIX are treated as files.

```
$ tar xvf /dev/mt0 `memo*`
```

This extracts all files beginning with memo from the tape in **/dev/mt0**.

Function Options

c Creates a new **tar** archive.

r Appends files to the end of the archive.

t Prints out a table of contents.

u Updates archive by appending files if not on the tape or if they have been modified.

x Extracts files from within the **tar** archive.

Options

b*n*	Sets blocking factor to *n* (default is 1; maximum is 64).
f*dev*	Writes archive to *dev*; default is **/dev/mt0** on many systems.
l	Returns error messages about links that cannot be read.
L	Follows symbolic links.
m	Updates file-modification times to the time of extraction.
o	Changes ownership of extracted files to the current user. This is very useful if the archive was made by another user.
v	Verbose mode: prints out status information.
w	Waits for confirmation.

touch — Update File Date

touch *options date file(s)*

Changes a file's access time and modification time to the current date. If you try to change the date for a file that does not exist, **touch** will create a new file.

This value has more worth than meets the eye. For instance, some systems are set up to delete certain types of files that were created before a particular date and time; the **touch** command makes sure that the timestamp can be easily updated to avoid such deletions. In addition, some commands, such as **find** and **make**, occasionally use a file's timestamp.

Touch uses a **MMddhhmmyy** format for date and time:

MM	month (1–12)
dd	day (1–31)
hh	hour (00–23)
mm	minute (00–59)
yy	year (00–99)

Options

–a	Updates only the access time.
–c	Does not create a new file if none exists.
–m	Updates only the modification time.

Related Command

date Displays date and time.

uncompress — Uncompress File

uncompress *option file(s)*

Purpose

Uncompresses a compressed file, which usually has a name ending in **.Z**.

Option

–c Uncompresses without changing original file(s).

Related Command

compress Compresses a file.

unpack — Unpack File

unpack *file(s)*

Purpose

Unpacks a file shrunk with the **pack** command. These files usually end with **.z**.

Related Commands

pack	Compresses a file.
pcat	Views a packed file.

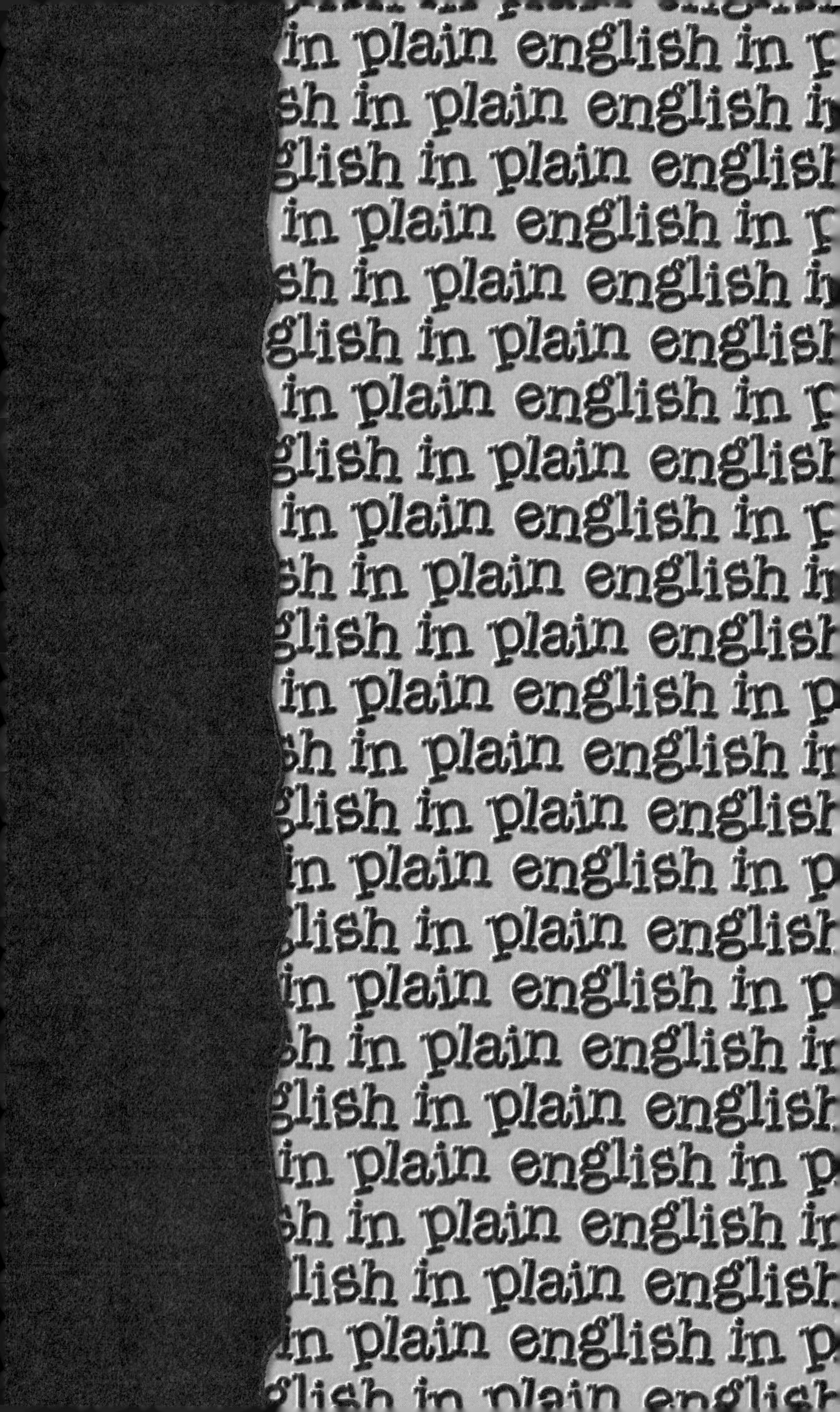
in plain english

4

Text-Processing Commands

These commands cover the various tools needed to edit and format text files, ranging from commands that prepare a file for printing to commands used to compose and edit files.

awk — Text Editing

awk *options 'pattern {action}' files*

Purpose

Actually a rudimentary programming language, **awk** is used mainly with text and database files — any structured file, really. It manipulates these files through editing, sorting, and searching.

Awk is an advanced tool that's far too complicated for this introductory work. There's a whole set of specialized commands that are not even listed here, as you'll see from the short example. See the Bibliography for a list of UNIX tutorials that should cover **awk** in some form.

4

NOTE

Awk has been superseded somewhat by the **nawk** (**new awk**) command, which is also covered in this section. In addition, there's a version in GNU called **gawk** that's common in PC-based UNIX variants like FreeBSD and Linux.

Example

```
$ awk '$1 ~ /Geisha/ {print $0}' workers
```

This command looks in the file workers for the string Geisha in the first column, which is designated by **$1**, and prints the entire record **$0** to the screen.

Option

-F sep	Allows a field separator (specified here as **sep**) other than the default space or tab.

Related Command

nawk	New version of awk.

col — Strip Formatting

col *options*

Purpose

Strips reverse backspaces and other control characters from a file formatted for multiple columns (usually with a text editor such as **tbl** or **nroff**). After these characters are stripped out, you can display the files on older video screens, or print them on printers that do not support reverse linefeeds.

NOTE

Normally you won't find this command used on its own, but rather as part of a longer command line whose eventual destination is a line printer. It's also handy to use with online-manual pages, which are formatted.

Example

```
$ cat kevin.report | col | lp
```

This command sends the file **kevin.report** to **col**, which strips the formatting before printing with the **lp** command.

Options

-b	Ignores backspace commands.
-f	Allows half linefeeds.
-p	Prints unknown escape characters as regular characters. (Don't use this option. It usually makes a mess of the final document.)
-x	Does not convert spaces to tabs.

Related Commands

nroff	Text formatter.
tbl	Table editor.
troff	Text formatter.
vi	Text editor.

cut — Cut Columns

cut *options files*

Purpose

Displays a list of columns (specified with the **-c** option) or fields (specified with the **-f** option) from a file or a set of files. A *column* is exactly what you might expect — a vertical set of characters that occupy the same position on subsequent lines; *fields* are, in effect, positions on a line that are separated by tabs. Numerals identify both the first column and the first field on a particular line, as in the following examples.

Examples

```
$ cut -f1,3 workers > workers_phone
```

This command cuts fields 1 and 3 from the file **workers** and places them in a new file named **workers_phone**.

```
$ cut -c1,3 workers > workers_phone
```

This command cuts columns 1 and 3 from the file **workers** and places them in a new file named **workers_phone**.

Options

-c*list*	Cuts the columns specified by **list** from a given file.
-d*character*	Substitutes **character** for the delimiter when the -f option is used. If a nonalphabetic character is to be used as the delimiter (such as a space), it must be enclosed in single quote marks.
-f*list*	Cuts a field specified by **list** from a given file.
-s	*Suppresses* (does not return) lines that lack a delimiter; used with the **-f** option.

Related Commands

grep	Finds text in files.
join	Joins lines found in multiple files.
paste	Joins two files in vertical columns.

deroff — Strip Formatting

deroff *options files*

Purpose

Removes formatting commands inserted by the **tbl**, **eqn**, **mm**, **nroff**, and **troff** formatting commands.

Examples

```
$ deroff kevin.report
```

This command removes all formatting commands from the file **kevin.report**.

```
$ deroff -mm workers
```

This command removes requests from **mm**-formatted files.

Options

-ml	Deletes lists from **mm**-formatted files.
-mm	Strips formatting from **mm**-formatted files.
-ms	Strips formatting from **ms**-formatted files.

Related Commands

col	Strips control characters.
eqn	Equation editor.
mm	Text formatter.
nroff	Text formatter.
tbl	Table editor.
troff	Text formatter.

ed — Editor

ed *options file*

Purpose

A rudimentary text editor, superseded by more sophisticated tools like **vi** or **ex**. **Ed** works in two modes — input and command — with very little feedback. UNIX still uses this command indirectly (for instance, the **diff** command calls on the **ed** command).

Options

-C	Allows for the editing of encrypted files. (This option can be used only in the United States, due to export regulations.)
-p *string*	Substitutes **string** for the standard command prompt (the **ed** default is *).
-s	Suppresses information about file sizes, diagnostic information, and the ! prompt for shell commands.
-x	Allows for the editing of encrypted files. (This option can be used only in the United States, due to export regulations.)

Related Commands

crypt	Encrypts files.
vi	Text editor.

eqn — Equation Formatter

eqn *options files*

Purpose

Formats equations created by **troff**, for eventual printing by a printer or typesetting machine. UNIX normally places **eqn** commands in a **troff** file, runs the designated file through **eqn**, and pipes the output first to **troff**, and then to a printer.

NOTE

If you are using **nroff** as a text processor, use the **neqn** command.

Macros

Use these within the **troff**-created files, not on an **eqn** command line.

.EQ	Starts typesetting mathematical characters.
.EN	Stops typesetting mathematical characters.

Options

-f*font*	Uses font *font*.
-p*n*	Reduces size of superscripts and subscripts by *n* points.
-s*n*	Reduces size of all text by *n* points.
-T*dev*	Formats for the typesetting *dev*, as defined in the TYPESETTER= environment variable.

Related Commands

mm	Text formatter.
neqn	Equation preprocessor used with **nroff**.
nroff	Text formatter.
tbl	Table editor.
troff	Text formatter.
vi	Text editor.

fmt — Format Text

fmt *options files*

Purpose

Formats text in a limited fashion — usually only to justify text to the right margin. Text editors such as **vi** don't perform this task automatically, so frequently you'll find this command invoked within **vi** (**emacs**, on the other hand, formats text through the **Esc-q** command). In addition, the output of this command is usually piped to a printer command. The **fmt** command is not available on all systems.

Options

-c Does not format the first two lines.

-s Splits long lines, but ignores short lines.

-w*n* Limits the size of lines to *n* columns wide, instead of the default 72.(BSD UNIX does not support this option.)

fold — Format Page Width

fold *options files*

Purpose

Formats text to a specific width, even if the break occurs in the middle of a word.

Options

-*n* Limits the size of lines to *n* columns wide, instead of the default 80, under BSD.

-w *n* Limits the size of lines to *n* columns wide, instead of the default 80. (BSD UNIX does not support this option.)

nawk — New Awk

awk *options 'pattern {action}' files*

Purpose

Actually a rudimentary programming language, **nawk** is used mainly with text and database files — in fact, with any structured file. It manipulates these files in three ways: editing, sorting, and searching.

Nawk is a complicated, advanced tool that has its own entire set of specialized commands that you should learn before you use it. For further study, consult the UNIX tutorials listed in the Bibliography.

NOTE

Nawk has superseded the **awk** command, which is also covered in this section. In addition, there's a version in GNU called **gawk**.

neqn — Format Equations

neqn *options files*

Purpose

Formats equations created by **nroff**, for eventual printing by a printer or typesetting machine. Normally UNIX places **neqn** commands in an **nroff** file, runs the designated file through **neqn**, and pipes the output a printer.

NOTE

If you are using **troff** as a text processor, use the **eqn** command instead of **neqn**.

Macros

Use these within the **nroff**-created files, and not on an **neqn** command line.

.EQ	Starts typesetting mathematical characters.
.EN	Stops typesetting mathematical characters.

Options

-**f***font*	Uses font *font*.
-**p***n*	Reduces size of superscripts and subscripts by *n* points.
-**s***n*	Reduces size of all text by *n* points.
-**T***dev*	Formats for the typesetting *dev*, as defined in the TYPESETTER= environment variable.

Related Commands

eqn	Equation preprocessor used with **troff**.
mm	Text formatter.
nroff	Text formatter.

tbl	Table editor.
troff	Text formatter.
vi	Text editor.

newform — Format Text

newform *options file(s)*

Purpose

Formats text files by adding and removing characters, changing tab settings, and so on. The **newform** command should be viewed as a down-and-dirty text formatter for those who know precisely what they want; there's little interactivity between the user and the command, so it's too easy to make unwanted changes. Output goes to standard output – that is, usually to the screen – and will take standard input if no file is specified.

Options

-a*n*	Appends *n* characters to the end of each line.
-b*n*	Removes *n* characters from the beginning of each line.
-c*char*	Uses *char* instead of the default space with the **-a** and **-p** options. (The **-c** option must appear before **-a** or **-p** on the command line.)
-e*n*	Removes *n* characters from the end of each line.
-i*tabspec*	Sets the tab format defined by *tabspec*. (See the **tabs** command for more information.)
-l*n*	Sets the default line length in *n* characters; the default is 72.
-o*tabspec*	Converts tabs to space, as defined by *tabspec*. (See the **tabs** command for more information.)
-p*n*	Adds *n* characters to the beginning of each line.
-s	Removes characters before the first tab and places them at the end of the line.

nl — Numbering Lines

nl *options file*

Purpose

Inserts line numbers at the beginning of every line of the file and breaks the file into logical page segments, with the first line of each page numbered 1.

Example

```
$ nl -ba -ht -ft textfile
```

This command formats every line in the file *textfile*, including headers and footers.

Options

-b*type*	Numbers lines according to one of four types:
a	All lines.
n	No lines.
p*str*	Lines containing the string *str*.
t	Only lines containing text.
-d*xy*	Changes *xy* as the delimiter for logical page sections.
-f*type*	Numbers the footers; see the **-b** option for types.
-h*type*	Numbers the headers; see the **-b** option for types.
-i*n*	Increases numbers by *n* increments (default is 1).
-l*n*	Compresses *n* blank lines to one line.
-n*format*	Inserts line numbers in one of three formats: **ln** Left-justify, no leading zeroes. **rn** Right-justify, no leading zeroes. **rz** Right-justify.
-p	Does not reset numbering at the beginning of every page.
-s*char*	Inserts the character *char* between line numbers and text (default is tab).
-v*n*	Starts page numbering at *n* (default is 1).
-w*n*	Shows line numbers in *n* columns (default is 6).

nroff — Format Text

nroff *options file(s)*

Purpose

Formats text for printing on a daisywheel or dot-matrix printer. (The related command **troff** prepares files for printing on a laser printer or a typesetter.) The **nroff** command interprets commands already inserted into a text file. For instance, to flush all lines right, you would insert the **.ad r** command within a text file. (This example is called a **dot command** because it begins with a dot.) When you run the **nroff** command, **nroff** will find the **.ad r** command within the text and format the text accordingly.

Most information associated with **nroff** actually focuses on the dot commands that UNIX inserts into files that will be output by **nroff**. For the most part, the same dot commands are used by **troff** and **nroff**, although **troff** also uses its own set of additional files.

NOTE

Many formatting options are available with **troff** and **nroff**—84 formatting requests alone, plus many registers and characters. You might want to check your system documentation for more information about these commands.

Examples

```
$ nroff textfile | lp
```

This command formats the file *textfile* with **nroff** and sends the results to the line printer.

```
$ nroff textfile | more
```

This command formats the file *textfile* and prints the results on the screen, one page at a time.

Related Command

troff Text formatter.

paste — Merge Files

paste *options file(s)*

Purpose

Merges files and places them side by side. For instance, the first line of *file1* can be followed by the first line of *file2* in a second column; a tab separates the two columns.

Options

-	Uses standard input as input (handy when piping output to the command).
D'*char*'	Uses the character *char* as the delimiter between columns, instead of the default tab. *char* can be any character, or one of the following: **n** newline **t** tab \\\\ backslash

Related Commands

cut	Cuts fields.
join	Joins files.

sort — Sort Files

sort *options files*

Purpose

Sorts the lines of named files, usually in alphabetical order. This command is an example of how one UNIX command can affect the functionality of other commands; **comm** and **join** require sorted files in order to work.

Options

-b	Ignores leading spaces and tabs.
-c	Checks if files are already sorted. If they are, **sort** does nothing.
-d	Sorts in dictionary order (ignores punctuation).
-f	Ignores case.
-i	Ignores non-ASCII characters.
-m	Merges files that have already been sorted.
-M	Sorts the files assuming the first three characters are months.
-n	Sorts in numeric order.
-o*file*	Stores output in *file*. The default is to send output to standard output.
-r	Reverses sort.
-t*c*	Separates fields with character *c* (default is tab).
-u	Unique output: If **merge** creates identical lines, uses only the first.
-y*k*	Sets aside *k* kilobytes of memory for the sort. If *k* is not specified, the maximum possible will be allocated.
-z*n*	Provides a maximum of *n* characters per line of input.
+*n* **[-***m***]**	Skips *n* fields before sorting, and then sorts through field *m*.

spell — Check Spelling

spell *options files*

Purpose

Returns incorrectly spelled words in a file. You can also use **spell** to compare spellings against a sorted word file of your own creation. Since it returns only "incorrect" spellings — that is, words not contained in a file of correctly spelled words — **spell** is not as useful as you might think.

NOTE

Operating systems that rely on GNU commands, such as Linux and FreeBSD, feature a spelling command called **ispell**, which has more functionality than the UNIX **spell** command.

Example

```
$ spell textfile
```

This command checks the spellings in the file *textfile*.

```
$ spell +morewords textfile
```

This command checks the spellings in the file *textfile*, against both the main file and the user-created file *morewords*.

Options

-b	Checks for spelling based on British usage.
-l	Checks all included files associated with the target file.
-x	Shows every possible stem of target words.
+ *filename*	Creates a sorted file (*filename*) of correctly spelled words.

tabs — Set Tabs

tabs *tabspec options*

Purpose

Sets the tab settings. The default settings are every eighth column (1, 9, 17, and so on). This command supports several preconfigured tab settings for specific languages (see the Options list), or you can set the tabs manually.

Tabspecs

-8	Sets tabs every eighth column (1, 9, 17, and so on). Default.
-a	IBM S/370 assembler (1, 10, 16, 36, 72).

-a2	IBM S/370 assembler (1, 10, 16, 40, 72).
-c	COBOL (1, 8, 12, 16, 20, 55).
-c2	Compact COBOL (1, 6, 10, 14, 49).
-c3	Expanded COBOL (1, 6, 10, 14, 18, 22, 26, 30, 34, 38, 42, 46, 50, 54, 58, 62, 67).
-f	FORTRAN (1, 7, 11, 15, 19, 23).
-p	PL/1 (1, 5, 9, 13, 17, 21, 25, 29, 33, 37, 41, 45, 49, 53, 57, 61).
-s	SNOBOL (1, 10, 55).
-u	UNIVAC 1100 Assembler (1, 12, 20, 44).

Options

+m*n*	Sets left margin to *n* (default is 10).
-T*type*	Sets terminal *type* (default is TERM).

tbl — Table Formatter

tbl *file*

Purpose

This preprocessor to **nroff** or **troff** formats tables for eventual printing. In this day of WYSIWYG, a tool like **tbl** may seem positively archaic, but it still is useful. With **tbl**, you insert formatting commands into the text file itself. When you run **tbl** on a command line and then pipe the output to **nroff** or **troff**, the formatting commands are interpreted and you end up with a file ready either for printing or viewing on-screen.

CAUTION

These formatting commands are rather complicated for the uninitiated. Beginners, be warned: You may have to put in quite a bit of effort before you get acceptable output from **tbl**.

Examples

```
$ tbl textfile | troff |lp
```

This command formats the file *textfile*, first with **tbl** and then with **troff**, and sends the subsequent formatted file to the line printer.

```
.TS
center, box, tab(%);
cb s s.
Big Ten Standings
_
.T&
l| l | l;
Minnesota%5%1
Michigan%2%3
Wisconsin%1%4
.TE
```

This rather rudimentary and unlikely table would show three columns — headed by Minnesota, Michigan, and Wisconsin — with a bold banner, Big Ten Standings.

Formatting Options

Following is a basic list of major formatting options. Check your documentation or your online-manual pages for more information.

.TS	Table Start. This option must begin the area formatted by tbl.
allbox	Boxes the table and every entry within the table.
box	Boxes the table.
center	Centers the table.
;	End the layout for the table.
c	Center.
l	Flush left.
r	Flush right.
a	Aligns alphabetic entries.
n	Aligns numerical entries.
b	Bold.
i	Italics.
f*fontname*	Font *fontname*.

p*n*	Point size in *n*.
vn	Vertical line spacing, *n* points.
.TE	Table End. This option must end the area formatting by **tbl**.

tr — Translate Characters

tr *options string1 string2*

Purpose

Translates characters as part of a global search-and-replace procedure. **Tr** is a quirky command in its syntax, as you'll see in the following examples.

Examples

```
$ tr '<TAB>' , < textfile
```

This command changes every tab in the file *textfile* to a comma. Note the strange notation for input.

```
$ cat textfile | tr '[A-Z]' '[a-z]' > newtextfile
```

This command takes input from *textfile*, changes every uppercase letter to its lowercase equivalent, and then saves the output to *newtextfile*.

Options

-c	Uses all characters not covered by *string1*.
-d	Deletes the characters covered in *string1*.
-s	Squeezes repeated use of a character into a single use.

troff — Format Text

troff *options file(s)*

Purpose

Formats text for printing on a laser printer or a typesetter. (The related command **nroff** prepares files for printing on a daisy-wheel or dot-matrix printer.) The **troff** command interprets commands already inserted into a text file. For instance, to flush all lines right, you would insert the **.ad r** command within a text file. (This type of command is known as a **dot command** because it begins with a dot.) When you run the **troff** command, **troff** finds the **.ad r** command within the text and formats the text accordingly.

Most information associated with **troff** has to do with the dot commands inserted within files in anticipation of output by **troff**. Although **troff** has its own specialized set of commands, most of the same dot commands are used by **troff** and **nroff**.

NOTE

Many formatting options are available with **troff** and **nroff**—84 formatting requests alone, plus many registers and characters. Check your system documentation for more information about these commands.

Examples

```
$ troff textfile | lp
```

This command formats the file *textfile* with **troff** and sends the results to the line printer, which must be a laser printer or typesetting machine.

```
$ troff textfile | more
```

This command formats the file *textfile* and prints the results on the screen one page at a time.

Related Commands

eqn	Equation formatter.
nroff	Text formatter.
tbl	Table formatter.

uniq — Find Unique Lines

uniq *options file1 file2*

Purpose

Identifies and removes duplicate lines from a sorted file. (Uses the **sort** command to sort the file.)

Examples

```
$ uniq textfile
```

This command removes all duplicate lines in the file *textfile*.

```
$ uniq textfile text.uniq
```

This command removes all duplicate lines in the file *textfile* and saves them to *text.uniq*.

Options

-c	Counts; precedes lines by the number of times they appear.
-d	Prints only the first of duplicated lines and deletes all duplicate lines.
-u	Unique—prints only lines that appear once.
-n	Skips the first *n* fields in a line.
+*n*	Skips the first *n* characters in a field.

Related Command

sort	Sorts a file.

vi — Text Editor

vi *options file(s)*

Purpose

Vi is a full-screen text editor with many useful options. This summary lists the options but not all the editing commands possible when editing a file. For a list of these commands — there are many — either run the **man** command for **vi** or check out a book that contains a reference section on **vi** commands.

The **vi** editor runs mainly in two modes: *command mode* and *insert mode*. In insert mode, you enter text. In command mode, you modify text or issue commands. (We list some of the more useful commands here, but many more are available.) Press Esc to exit input mode and return to command mode.

TIP

For more information on **vi**, we suggest picking up a UNIX tutorial such as **Teach Yourself UNIX** (IDG Books, 1999). Although **vi** isn't exactly the most complex UNIX command, it does require a little background and a little explanation of the underlying concepts.

Examples

```
$ vi
```

This command begins a **vi** text-editing session.

```
$ vi textfile
```

This command starts **vi** with the file *textfile* loaded for editing.

Options

-c *command*	Starts **vi** and runs *command*.
-C	Edits an encrypted file (see the crypt command for more information).
-l	Runs **vi** in LISP mode for editing LISP files.
-L	Lists the files that were saved despite a system failure.
-r*file*	Recovers *file* after a system crash.
-R	Runs in *read-only mode*, which means that files cannot be changed.
-w*n*	Sets window size to *n* lines of text.
-x	Creates an encrypted file (see the **crypt** command for more information).
+	Starts **vi** on the last line of the file.
+ *line*	Starts **vi** with *line* as the top line in the window.

Commands

/pattern	Searches for *pattern*, going forward.
*n***G**	Goes to line number *n*.
h	Same as the left-arrow key. Useful for keyboards lacking arrow keys.
j	Same as the down-arrow key. Useful for keyboards lacking arrow keys.
k	Same as the up-arrow key. Useful for keyboards lacking arrow keys.
l	Same as the right-arrow key. Useful for keyboards lacking arrow keys.
Ctrl-F	Goes forward one screen.
Ctrl-B	Goes backward one screen.
ZZ	Saves file and exits.
:w	Saves file.
:q	Quits without saving file.
:wq	Saves file and quits the command.
:n	Goes to next file on the command line.
:n!	Goes to next file on the command line, even if you haven't saved the current file.
:q!	Quits without saving file.
dw	Deletes word.
dd	Deletes line.
i	Enters insert mode.
a	Enters append mode, inserting after current position.
Esc	Exits inserting or append mode.

Related Commands

crypt	Encrypts files.
mm	Text formatter.
nroff	Text formatter.
tbl	Table editor.
troff	Text formatter.

wc — Word Count

wc *options file(s)*

Purpose

Counts the number of words, characters, and lines in a text file or files. The terse output presents the number of lines, followed by the words and characters.

Options

-c Prints only the number of characters.

-l Prints only the number of lines.

-w Prints only the number of words.

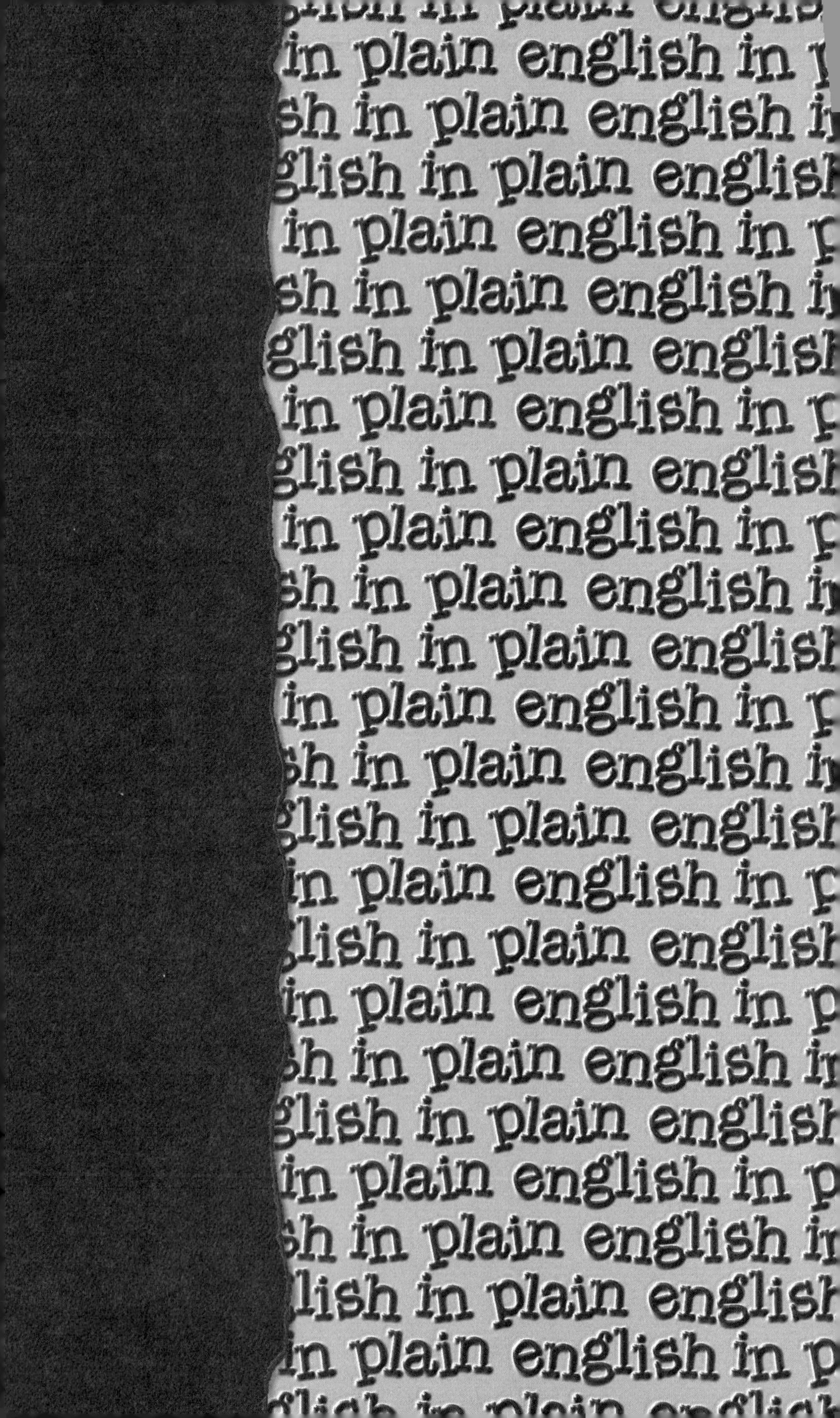
in plain english in
in plain english
in plain english in
in plain english
in plain english in
in plain english
in plain english in
in plain english
in plain english in
in plain english
in plain english in
in plain english
in plain english in
in plain english
in plain english in
in plain english
in plain english in
in plain english
in plain english in
in plain english
in plain english in

5

Printing Commands

This chapter covers not only the actual UNIX printing commands, but also the commands that prepare files for printing, monitor the printer, and schedule jobs in the print queue.

banner — Print Banner

banner *string*

Purpose

Displays up to 10 characters in large letters using asterisks (*) or number signs (#), depending on your system.

Example

```
$ banner kevin
```

This creates the following output:

```
#   #  ######  #    #   #   #    #
#  #   #       #    #   #   ##   #
###    ####    #    #   #   # #  #
# #    #       #    #   #   #  # #
#  #   #        #  #    #   #   ##
#   #  ######    ##     #   #    #
```

cancel — Cancel Printing

cancel *options printer*

Purpose

This cancels pending printer jobs initiated with the **lp** command. You can either specify the job ID or the printer to be canceled. (Privileged users can use the command to cancel jobs created by a specific user.)

Options

job-id	Cancels the specific *job-id*.
-u *user*	Cancels the print requests made by a specific ***user***.

lp — Print

lp *options files*

Purpose

Sends a print request to a printer. This command can be used to print multiple files with one request. On some systems, you may need to use the **lpr** command instead.

NOTE

Not all of the following options are available on every system due to configuration differences. Check with your system administrator to see which options are supported.

Options

-c	Copies the file to a print spooler before sending the request.
-d *printer*	Specifies a *printer* other than the default printer.
-d any	Used with the **-f** and **-s** options to find any printer that supports a form or character set specified by name.
-f *name*	Prints on the form *name*; used in conjunction with the **-d any** option.
-H *action*	Prints according to one of these actions: **hold**: Suspends current or pending print job. **immediate**: Prints immediately after current job is completed. **resume**: Resumes suspended print job.
-m	Sends a mail message to the user when the file is printed.
-n *num*	Prints *num* number of copies (the default is 1).
-o *option*	Sets printer-specific options.
cpi = *n*:	Prints *n* characters per inch; pica, elite, or compressed can be used instead of *n*.
length = *n*	Page length, specified in inches (*n***i**), lines (*n*), or centimeters (*n***c**).

lpi = *n*	Prints *n* lines per inch.
nobanner	Does not print the banner page.
nofilebreak	Does not print form feed between files.
stty = **list:**	Returns a list of options for **stty**.
width = *n*	Page width, specified in inches (*n***i**), lines (*n*), or centimeters (*n***c**).
-P *list*	Prints the page numbers specified by *list*.
-q *level*	Sets a priority *level* for the print job (lowest is 39).
-s	Suppresses messages from **lp**.
-S *name*	Uses the character set or print wheel *name*.
-t *title*	Prints *title* on the banner page.
-T *type*	Prints on a printer that supports type. (See your system administrator about which types are supported.)
-w	Sends a terminal message to the user when the file is printed.
-y *list*	Prints according to locally defined nodes, contained in *list*.

5

Related Commands

cancel	Cancels print requests.
lpsched	Turns on the print spooler.
lpshut	Turns off the print spooler.
lpstat	Shows printer status.

lpsched — Starts Print Spooler

lpsched

Purpose

Turns on a print spooler. A print spooler stores print requests in memory, allocating them to printers. This allows several print requests to be stored in RAM simultaneously, freeing the users who originate the print requests to go on with their work. This command can be run from a prompt but is more effectively used when placed in the **rc** file, where it will be launched when the system starts. Normally, system adminstrators run **lpsched**.

Related Command

lpshut Turns off the print spooler.

lpshut — Stop Print Spooler

lpshut

Purpose

Turns off the print spooler.

Related Command

lpsched Turns on the print spooler.

lpstat — Show Printer Status

lpstat *options*

Purpose

Returns the status of print requests, either individually or systemwide.

Options

-a [*list*]	Tells whether the list of printers or class names is accepting print requests.
-c [*list*]	Displays the names of all class names and printers contained in *list*.
-d	Shows the name of the default destination printer.
-D	Used with **-p** to show a description of the printer.
-f [*list*]	Displays the forms supported by the system in *list*. The **-l** option returns a description of these forms.
-o [*list*]	Returns the status of output requests by printer name, class name, and request ID.

-p [*list*]	Shows the status of all printers in *list*.
-r	Shows whether the print scheduler (or print spooler, as controlled by **lpsched**) is on or off.
-R	Shows the position of a job in the queue.
-s	Summarizes print status.
-S [*list*]	Displays character sets or print wheel supported in *list*.
-t	Shows all status information.
-u [*list*]	Shows the status of requests made by users on *list*. In this instance, *list* refers to:

user	User on the local machine.
all	All users.
host!user	User on machine host.
host!all	All users on host.
all!user	User not on local machine.
all!all	All users.

-v [*list*]	Displays pathnames of devices for all printers (or printers listed in *list*.)

Related Commands

cancel	Cancels print requests.
lp	Prints files.
lpsched	Turns on the print spooler.

pr — Format File

pr *options file(s)*

Purpose

Prepares a file for printing to standard output. If you want to print to the default printer, for instance, you'd pipe the output to **lp**. Each printed page contains a header, which includes a page number, filename, date, and time. Many options are available for formatting the file (for example, multiple columns).

Example

```
$ pr textfile | lp
```

This prepares the file *textfile* for printing and then sends the result to the default line printer.

```
$ pr textfile
```

This prepares the file *textfile* for printing and displays the results on the screen.

Options

-a	Prints multiple columns in rows across the page.
-d	Double-spaces the text.
-e*cn*	Sets tabs (as specified by *c*) to every *n*th position (default is 8).
-f	Separates pages by form feeds, not blank lines.
-F	Folds input lines to avoid truncation.
-h *text*	Prints the header *text* at the beginning of the output instead of default header (if any).
-i*cn*	Replaces white space with *c* (default is tab) every *n*th position (default is 8).
-l*n*	Sets the page length to *n* (default is 66).
-m	Merges input files, placing each in its own column.
-n*cn*	Numbers lines with numbers *n* digits in length (default is 5), separated from the text by *c* (default is a tab).
-o*n*	Offsets each line by *n* spaces.
-p	Pauses between pages; handy when reading off of a screen.
-r	Suppresses messages about files that can't be found.
-s*c*	Separates columns with *c* (default is tab).
-t	Does not print page header.
-w*c*	Sets the page width to *c* (default is 72).
+*num*	Begins printing at page *num*.
-*num*	Prints output with *num* columns.

Related Commands

cat	Concatenates files.
join	Joins files.
paste	Concatenates files horizontally.

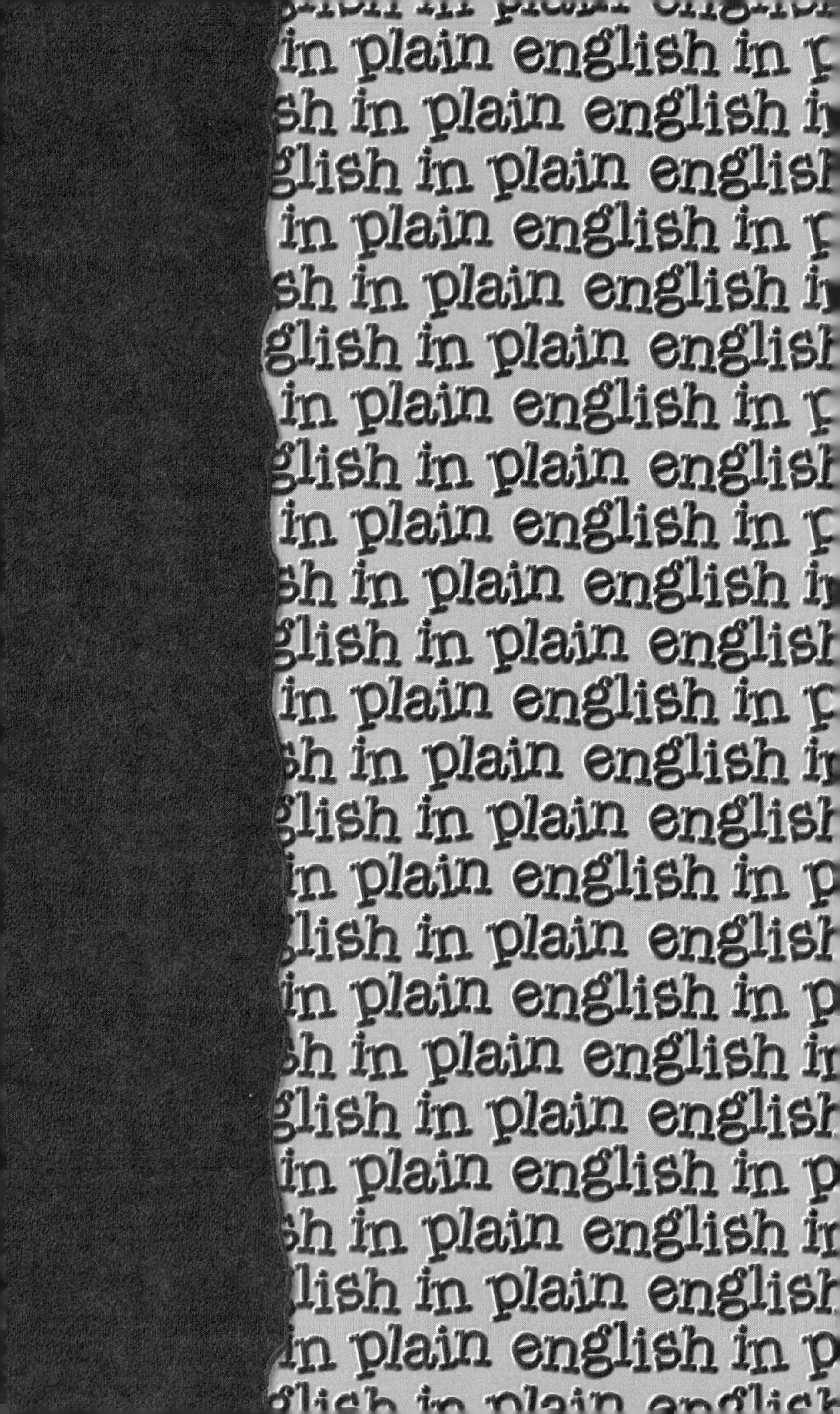
in plain english

6

Networking and Communications Commands

These commands work when you're on the Internet or trying to connect to other UNIX and non-UNIX systems. These commands allow you to do things like transferring files with other systems (with the **ftp** or **rcp** commands). You can also log in to remote systems, using commands like **telnet** or **rlogin**. A further set of commands come from ancient history in UNIX terms and support direct dial-up connections between systems. Usually grouped under the name UUCP (UNIX-to-UNIX Copy Program), this suite of programs supports the ability to transfer files and execute commands on remote systems for which you may only have a telephone connection late at night.

ct — Call Terminal

ct *options -speed* –w –x *system*

Purpose

This command allows you to call another terminal and log on a remote UNIX system via modem or direct line.

Examples

```
$ ct –s9600 5555555
```

This calls the telephone number 555–5555 at 9600 bps.

```
$ ct –s9600 nicollet
```

This calls the remote system **nicollet** at 9600 bps, as long as **nicollet** appears on a list of systems supported by the **uuname** command.

Options

–h	Prevents hang-ups.
–v	Outputs status to standard error output.
–s*speed*	Sets bits-per-second rate.
–w*min*	Waits *min* minutes for remote system to answer.
–x*n*	Debugging mode at *n* level.
system	Phone number or system name.

Related Commands

cu	Calls up another system.
uuname	Listing of UNIX-to-UNIX system names.

cu — Call UNIX

cu *options system*

Purpose

Calls up another UNIX system or terminal, or a non-UNIX bulletin-board service or online service, via modem or direct line. Other computer systems have a separate telecommunications package. In UNIX, telecommunications capabilities are built into the operating system.

Examples

```
$ cu –s9600 5555555
```

This calls the telephone number 555–5555 at 9600 bps.

```
$ cu –s9600 nicollet
```

This calls the remote system **nicollet** at 9600 bps, as long as **nicollet** appears on a list of systems supported by the **uuname** command.

Options

–b*n*	Sets character bit length to 7 or 8.
–c*name*	Searches the UUCP Device file for *name*.
–d	Sets diagnostics mode.
–e	Sets even parity. (Opposite of **–o**.)
–h	Sets half-duplex, which includes a local echo of typed characters.
–l*port*	Specifies *port* (device file such as /dev/tty005) for communications.
–n	Prompts the user for a telephone number.
–o	Sets odd parity. (Opposite of **–e**.)
–s*rate*	Sets bits-per-second *rate* (300, 1200, 2400, 9600, et al.).
–t	Calls an ASCII terminal.

Online Commands

These commands are to be run after a connection to the remote system.

~!*command*	Runs *command* on the local system.
~$*command*	Runs *command* on the local system and then sends the output to the remote system.
~%**cd** *directory*	Changes to directory *directory* on local system.
~%**put** *file*	Copies *file* from the local system to the remote system.
~$**take** file	Copies *file* from the remote system and places it on the local system.
~!	Escapes to a shell on the local system, where you can run commands.
~.	Disconnects the telephone link between the two systems.
~?	Displays a listing of all online commands.

Related Commands

ct	Calls terminal.
uuname	Listing of UNIX-to-UNIX system names.

finger — Find Information on Users

finger *options user(s)*
finger *options user@host ...*

Purpose

Returns the following information about users with accounts on the system: username, full name, terminal, terminal access, time of login, and phone number. In addition, **finger** grabs information from the user's login shell, **.plan** file, and **.project** file. Information is returned in long display or short display.

The **finger** command searches for information based on a specific username or general first and last names. For instance, a search of the name smith on a large system will probably yield quite a few responses. The use of the **finger** command with no username will return a list of all users currently logged on the system.

For remote users, the format of the username is **user@host**.

NOTE

Many systems on the Internet reject **finger**'s requests for information, as this can be considered a security hole.

Example

```
$ finger erc
Login name: erc        In real life: Eric Foster-Johnson
(651) 555-5555
Directory:/home/erc                Shell:/usr/bin/ksh
Last login Wed Nov 10 12:14:45 on term/07
Project: X Window Programming
erc      term/07     Nov 11 19:45
```

Using **finger** to get information on a local user, **erc**.

```
$ finger erc@bigfun.com
[homebase. bigfun.com]
Login name: erc         In real life: Eric Foster-Johnson
Office: Far, far away.
Directory: /usr/home/erc     Shell: /usr/local/bin/bash
On since Jul 22 09:01:22        1 hour 3 minutes Idle Time
   on ttyp0 from yonsen
No Plan.
```

Using **finger** to get information on a remote user.

Options

–b Long display, without information about home directory and shell.

–f Short display, sans header.

–h Long display, without information gleaned from the **.project** file.

–i Shows "idle" status: username, terminal, time of login, and idle lines.

–l Long display.

–m Matches the username exactly, with no searching of first or last names.

–p Long display, without information gleaned from the **.plan** file.

–q Quick display of username, terminal, and time of login (with no searching of first or last names).

–s Short format.

–w Short format, without the user's first name.

Related Commands

who Displays or changes usernames.

rwho Remote who.

ftp — File Transfer Protocol

This command is covered in its own chapter. See Chapter 7, "FTP Commands," for more details.

ifconfig — Query and Configure Network Interfaces

ifconfig *options*

Purpose

The **ifconfig** command serves two purposes: Configuring your network interfaces and telling you the interface status. The command line options for configuring a network interface differ based on the version of UNIX and are simply too advanced for most usage — you don't want to disable your system on the network. Most usage though, uses the **–a** option to see the state of the network interfaces.

Example

```
$ ifconfig –a

tu0: flags=c63<UP,BROADCAST,NOTRAILERS,RUNNING,MULTICAST,SIMPLEX>
     inet 204.220.32.130 netmask ffffff00 broadcast 204.220.32.255 ipmtu 1500
sl0: flags=10<POINTOPOINT>
lo0: flags=c89<UP,LOOPBACK,NOARP,MULTICAST,SIMPLEX>
```

```
    inet 127.0.0.1 netmask ff000000  ipmtu 1536
ppp0: flags=10<POINTOPOINT>
```

Lists information on all configured network interfaces. The loopback test interface is named **lo0** here. On other systems, you might see **lo** or other variations of **loopback**. The other interface names are based on device names and differ per system. A name such as **ppp0**, though, usually tells you this is a PPP (Point-to-Point Protocol) dial-up network link.

Options

–a Lists information on all configured network interfaces.

Related Command

netstat Lists network statistics.

6

logname — Login Name

logname

Purpose

Returns your login name.

Options

None.

Related Command

login Login a system.

mailx — Send Mail

mailx *options users*

Purpose

Used to send mail to other users and to receive mail. This command supersedes the **mail** command found in many older versions of UNIX. Files can be attached to **mailx**-created messages. See the **uuencode** command for more information.

Some system administrators also install other mail front ends in their systems, such as **elm**, **mailtool**, **pine**, or **dtmail**. Check with your system administrator to see if you should be using **mailx** or another mail program.

Examples

```
$ mailx erc
Subject:
```

This sends a mail message to **erc**. After the **mailx** command is given, the system prompts for a subject and a message text. After you're finished editing text, press **Ctrl–D** to end the input.

```
$ mailx erc < memo
```


This sends the contents of the file memo to **erc** in the form of a mail message.

Options

–d	Sets debugging mode.
–e	Checks for mail without printing it.
–f *file*	Stores mail in file named *file* (default is **mbox**).
–F	Stores mail in file named after the first recipient of the message.
–h *n*	Sets number of network hops to *n*.
–i	Ignores interrupts.
–I	Saves newsgroup and article IDs; used in conjunction with **–f**.
–n	Ignores startup **mailx.rc** file.
–N	Doesn't display mail headers.
–r *address*	Specifies a return *address* for your mail.
–s *subject*	Enters subject in the "Subject:" field, avoiding the prompt.
–T *file*	Records message and article IDs in file.
–U	Converts a **uucp** address to an Internet address.
–V	Version number.

Related Commands

uucp UNIX-to-UNIX copy.

uuencode Encodes files for transmission with **mailx**.

mesg — Enable/Disable Messages

mesg *options*

Purpose

Grants or denies permission to other users to send you messages via the **write** or **talk** commands.

Examples

```
$ mesg -y
```

This allows messages.

```
$ mesg -n
```

This forbids messages.

Options

-n Forbids messages.

-y Allows messages.

NOTE

Some versions of UNIX expect **n** and **y** along (with no dash). On other systems, you can use either **-n**, **-y**, **n**, or **y**.

Related Commands

talk Talks with another user via the network.

write Sends a message to a user.

netstat — List Network Statistics

netstat options

Purpose

Lists network statistics. Depending on the version of UNIX, you can gather lots of information about the state of your system on the network. The options listed here are the most commonly supported options. Consult your online manuals for details on your system.

Examples

```
$ netstat
Active Internet connections
Proto Recv-Q Send-Q  Local Address        Foreign Address        (state)
tcp        0      0  unxtest1.3232        ntserv1.domain         TIME_WAIT
tcp        0      0  unxtest1.3214        efoster-johnson.6000   ESTABLISHED
tcp        0      0  unxtest1.3213        efoster-johnson.6000   ESTABLISHED
tcp        0      0  unxtest1.3212        efoster-johnson.6000   ESTABLISHED
tcp        0      0  unxtest1.3211        efoster-johnson.6000   ESTABLISHED
tcp        0      0  unxtest1.3207        efoster-johnson.6000   ESTABLISHED
tcp        0      0  unxtest1.3233        ntserv1.domain         ESTABLISHED
tcp        0      0  unxtest1.199         unxtest1.1334          ESTABLISHED
tcp        0      0  unxtest1.1334        unxtest1.199           ESTABLISHED
tcp        0      0  unxtest1.telnet      modem7.1047            ESTABLISHED
tcp        0      0  unxtest1.199         unxtest1.1332          ESTABLISHED
tcp        0      0  unxtest1.1332        unxtest1.199           ESTABLISHED
tcp        0      0  localhost.1031       *.*                    LISTEN
tcp        0      0  localhost.1030       *.*                    LISTEN
tcp        0      0  localhost.1029       *.*                    LISTEN
tcp        0      0  localhost.1028       *.*                    LISTEN
tcp        0      0  localhost.1027       *.*                    LISTEN
tcp        0      0  unxtest1.1031        *.*                    LISTEN
tcp        0      0  unxtest1.1030        *.*                    LISTEN
udp      187      0  unxtest1.1046        *.*
udp        0      0  localhost.ntp        *.*
udp        0      0  unxtest1.ntp         *.*
udp        0      0  localhost.1043       *.*
udp        0      0  localhost.1042       *.*
udp        0      0  localhost.1041       *.*
```

```
udp        0      0  unxtest1.1043          *.*
udp        0      0  unxtest1.1042          *.*
```

The **netstat** command on a Digital UNIX system.

```
$ netstat

TCP
Local Address        Remote Address       Swind Send-Q Rwind Recv-Q  State
-------------        --------------       ----- ------ ----- ------  -----
sunny.xaudio         204.220.32.101.4545  33580      0  8754      0  CLOSE_WAIT
sunny.xaudio         204.220.32.101.2506  33580      0  8754      0  CLOSE_WAIT
sunny.6000           204.220.32.101.3627  33580      0  8760      0  CLOSE_WAIT
sunny.telnet         204.220.32.118.4892  33580      0  8760      0  ESTABLISHED
sunny.telnet         204.220.32.118.4933  33580      0  8760      0  ESTABLISHED
Active UNIX domain sockets
Address  Type         Vnode     Conn  Local Addr       Remote Addr
ff51d620 stream-ord ff035770       0 /tmp/.X11-unix/X0
ff51d820 stream-ord        0       0
```

The **netstat** command on a Sun Solaris system.

```
$ netstat -i
Name  Mtu   Network     Address              Ipkts Ierrs    Opkts Oerrs  Coll
tu0   1500  <Link>      00:42:82:01:f8:91  27589484     42 25039418    180 3153215
tu0   1500  DLI         none               27589484     42 25039418    180 3153215
tu0   1500  192.63.42   unxtest1           27589484     42 25039418    180 3153215
sl0*  296   <Link>                                0      0        0      0      0
lo0   1536  <Link>                          2183886      0  2183886      0      0
lo0   1536  loop        localhost           2183886      0  2183886      0      0
ppp0* 1500  <Link>                                0      0        0      0      0
```

The **–i** option to **netstat** shows the state of the configured interfaces (such as network adapter cards, etc.).

Options

–a Show state of all socket connections.

–i Shows state of configured network interfaces.

–r Shows state of routing tables.

Related Commands

ifconfig Query and configure network interfaces.

notify — Notify of Mail

notify *options*

Purpose

Notifies a user when new mail arrives. This command is not available on all systems. Some systems have a **checkmail** command instead.

Options

–m *file*	Saves mail messages to *file* when the **–y** option is enabled.
–n	Disables mail notification.
–y	Enables mail notification.

6

Related Command

mailx Sends and receives mail.

nslookup — Lookup Internet Addresses for Hostnames

nslookup *host* [*name_server*]

Purpose

Looks up host names and converts those names to the Internet addresses required for most Internet activity. You can also use this command to help determine whether a host name is valid or not.

The host name should be in the format of a network domain name, such as www.idgbooks.com. To look up names, it helps to know something about the domain name service, or DNS, which is used to convert host names to Internet addresses. At the top level reside domains for each country — using a two-letter country code — as well as special domains such as **com** for commercial organizations:

Top-Level Domain	Usage
com	Commercial organizations
edu	Educational institutions
org	Nonprofit organizations
gov	Government agencies in the United States
mil	US Military MILNET hosts
net	Internet service providers, as well as many commercial organizations

Each country, including the United States, has a top-level domain using a two-letter country code— **fr** for France, **ca** for Canada, **de** for Germany (Deutschland), **uk** for the United Kingdom and **us** for the United States. Very few sites in the United States use the **us** domain, though.

NOTE

The whole domain system is currently undergoing revision and may change.

The **nslookup** command can work in an interactive mode as well, but most calls to this command pass the name of the host to look up on the command line. The interactive mode allows you to look up several hosts, one at a time. The **exit** command exits **nslookup**'s interactive mode and returns you to the shell. To enter interactive mode, supply no options or use a - for the host name.

Examples

```
$ nslookup www.idgbooks.com
Server:  namerserv.bigfun.com
Address:  192.63.42.100

Non-authoritative answer:
Name:    www.idgbooks.com
Address:  206.175.162.15
```

Looks up the Internet address for the site `www.idgbooks.com`, the Web page for the publisher of this book. Note that the name server shown here is not a valid system. The address and name have been changed to protect the innocent.

NOTE

The **nslookup** command is not always in the default path. For example, on Sun Solaris 2.6, you need to look in the **/usr/sbin** directory for the **nslookup** program:

```
$ /usr/sbin/nslookup www.idgbooks.com
Server: namerserv.bigfun.com
Address: 192.43.43.100

Name:     www.idgbooks.com
Address: 206.175.162.15
```

Options

host	name of system to look up.
server	server to use to look up the name.

6

ping — Verify Connection to Remote Host

ping *options hostname*

Purpose

The **ping** command sends an echo request packet to the target hostname. Under normal circumstances, each packet is echoed back to the ping program. If the packets return, then you have verified the network connection is active to the given hostname.

This command normally runs forever, unless you use the **–c** option. In normal operation, use **Ctrl–C** to stop **ping**.

Examples

```
$ ping www.idgbooks.com
PING www.idgbooks.com (206.175.162.15): 56 data bytes
64 bytes from 206.175.162.15: icmp_seq=0 ttl=236 time=156 ms
64 bytes from 206.175.162.15: icmp_seq=1 ttl=238 time=146 ms
64 bytes from 206.175.162.15: icmp_seq=2 ttl=238 time=146 ms
64 bytes from 206.175.162.15: icmp_seq=3 ttl=238 time=146 ms

—www.idgbooks.com PING Statistics—
4 packets transmitted, 4 packets received, 0% packet loss
round-trip (ms)  min/avg/max = 146/149/156 ms
```

Sends a ping request to host www.idgbooks.com and displays the responses. The connection to this machine is alive.

Options

The options for **ping** differ by system. The most common options appear here.

–c *count*	Stop after sending and receiving *count* packets. On some systems, this option is **–n** instead of **–c**.
–f	Floods target hostname with packets to test for dropped packets. This can degrade your network and only the superuser can use this option. Not available on all systems.
–i *delay*	Wait *delay* seconds between each packet. The default is 1 second. This conflicts with the **–f** option. On some systems, this option is **–I** instead of **–i**.
–v	Verbose output. Prints out a lot more data.
hostname	System name or Internet address to connect.

rcp — Remote Copy

rcp *options source target*

Purpose

Copies files to and from remote systems. This command assumes you have permissions in the target directory. Generally, this command is used in conjunction with the **rlogin** command: First you log onto a remote machine with **rlogin** and then transfer files with the **rcp** command. To name remote files, use *hostname:filename*.

NOTE

If you need to use wildcard characters for files on the remote system (the one for which you specify the system name) be sure to escape them with the backslash character, \.

Examples

```
$ rcp nicollet:/u/erc/reports/report.1999 report.copy
```

This copies **/u/erc/reports/report.1999** on remote machine **nicollet** to **report.copy** on the local machine.

```
$ rcp report.1999 attila:/users/kevin
```

This copies local file **report.1999** to the **/users/kevin** directory on remote machine **attila**.

```
$ rcp nicollet:/u/erc/reports\*.txt reports
```

This copies all files ending in **.txt** from the **/u/erc/reports** directory on machine **nicollet** to the **reports** directory on the local system.

6

Options

–p	Preserves the permissions of the source file.
–r	Recursively copies each subdirectory.

Related Commands

ftp	File-transfer protocol.
mailx	Sends and receives mail.
rlogin	Remote login.
uucp	UNIX-to-UNIX copy.

rlogin — Remote Login

rlogin *options hostname*

Purpose

Logs in to a remote system. A list of the available hostnames is stored in the **/etc/hosts/.rhosts** file. If your local hostname is listed in the **.rhosts** file in your home directory on the remote machine, you won't have to enter a password. Your local computing session is suspended while you're logged onto a remote machine. Any UNIX commands you use will be run on the remote machine. When you're finished on the remote system, use an **exit** command or press **Ctrl–D** to end the connection.

CAUTION

If a hostile user can place an **.rhosts** file in your home directory on a remote system, that user can then get into your account on that system (and potentially from there onto other systems). This imposes a security concern.

Options

–8	Uses 8-bit data (default is 7 bits).
–e *c*	Uses *c* as the default escape character (default is ~).
–l *username*	Logs in remotely under the new *username*, instead of the name on your local host.

Related Commands

ftp	File-transfer protocol.
mailx	Sends and receives mail.
rcp	Remote copy.
telnet	Remote login.

rsh — Remote Shell

rsh *options hostname command*

Purpose

Starts a remote shell on a remote machine, executing a command on the remote machine.

NOTE

On some systems, **rsh** refers to the restricted shell. The remote shell is then called **remsh**.

Options

-l *user*	Logs *user* in to the remote machine.
-n	Diverts input to **/dev/null**, which can be useful when the output is not needed or when troubleshooting.

ruptime — List Uptime

ruptime *options*

Purpose

Shows the status of all machines connected to the network. The resulting table shows the name of each host, whether the host is up or down, the amount of time it has been up or down, the number of users on the host, and the average load for that machine.

Options

–a	Includes all users, even those whose machines have been idle for more than an hour.
–l	Sorts by load.
–r	Reverses sort order.
–t	Sorts by uptime.
–u	Sorts by number of users.

Related Commands

uptime	Lists uptime for a single system.

rwho — Remote Who

rwho *option*

Purpose

Shows who is logged on all machines on the network.

Option

–a Includes all users, even those whose machines have been idle for more than an hour.

Related Command

who Shows users logged on the system.

sum — Return Checksum

sum *option filename(s)*

Purpose

Computes and prints a checksum and block count for a specified file. While this command isn't specifically geared toward communications, it's used most often when communicating files back and forth to remote systems, ensuring that the transferred files are the same size on both ends.

The BSD version of this command differs slightly. To match the results of a BSD-generated **sum** command, use the **–r** option.

Option

–r Uses alternative algorithm to compute checksum and size; matches BSD version of command.

Related Command

wc Word count.

talk — Talk to Other User

talk *username*[*@hostname*] *terminal*

Purpose

Carries on a conversation with another user on the network. The command splits your screen into two areas: The top half contains your typing, while the bottom contains messages from the other user. Press **Ctrl–D** to exit.

The **write** command is similar, except that **write** is geared for single messages and not for an ongoing dialog.

Options

user	Other *user*, obviously.
hostname	The *hostname* of the machine the user is logged on, if the user isn't logged on to your local machine.
terminal	Specifies a **tty** should the user be logged on more than one terminal.

Related Commands

mesg	Blocks communications.
write	Writes a message to another terminal.

telnet — Remote Login

telnet *system port*

Purpose

Logs into a remote system using the TELNET protocol. After you login the remote system, your prompt will change to the telnet prompt (**telnet** >), from which you can enter TELNET commands. The **telnet** command also supports an input mode, in which you can enter commands directly on the remote system. Use the escape character (**Ctrl–]** or ^, depending on your system setup) to switch between the two modes.

Options

system	Name of remote *system* or its network address.
port	Optional *port* identification.

Online Commands

close	Ends remote session and exits the program.
display *values*	Displays set and toggle **values**.
mode *mode*	Changes **mode** to character or line.
open *system*	Opens connection to **system**.

quit	Ends remote session and exits the program.	
send *chars*	Sends special characters to the remote system:	
	ao	Abort output.
	ayt	Are you there?
	brk	Break.
	ec	Erase character.
	el	Erase line.
	escape	Escape.
	ga	Go ahead.
	ip	Interrupt process.
	nop	No operation.
	synch	Discards commands that have not been acted upon.
	?	Help for **send** command.
set *value*	Sets one of the following values:	
	echo	Local echo on or off.
	eof	End of file.
	erase	Erase character.
	escape	New **Escape** character.
	flushoutput	Flush output.
	interrupt	Interrupt process.
	kill	Erase line.
	quit	Break.
status	Displays status.	
toggle *values*	Changes one of the following values:	
	autoflush	Send interrupt or quit to remote system.
	autosynch	Synch after interrupt or quit.
	crmod	Convert **CR** to **CR LF**.
	debug	Debugging mode.
	localchars	Convert local commands to remote control.
	netdata	Convert hexadecimal display of network data.
	options	Protocol processing.

6

?	Display settings.
z	Suspends telnet.
?	Displays summary of online commands.

Related Command

rlogin Remote login.

uucp — UNIX-to-UNIX Copy

uucp *options source! destination! file(s)*

Purpose

Copies files to and from remote UNIX system. The file(s) may also be entire directories. Normally the destination is a public, secure directory named **uucppublic**; this prevents unwanted visitors from roaming around a UNIX system where they are not wanted.

Example

```
$ uucp textfile harmar!/usr/users/geisha/uucppublic
```

This copies the file **textfile** to the machine named **harmar** in the directory **/usr/users/geisha/uucpublic**.

Options

–c	Copies the actual file, not a copy from the spool file.
–C	Copies to a spooling file before sending on to the destination machine.
–d	Creates a directory to match the directory sent from the source machine. (This is the default.)
–f	Does not create a directory to match the directory sent from the source machine.
–gp	Sets job priority to **p**.
–j	Prints job number.
–m	Notifies sender via mail when transfer is complete.

–n user	Notifies **user** via mail when transfer is complete.
–r	Queues the file(s), but doesn't send them.
–**s**file	Sends the transfer status to **file** (instead of to user, as specified by **–m**.)
–**x**n	Debugs at level **n**; lowest is 1, highest is 9.

Related Commands

ftp	File-transfer protocol.
mailx	Sends and receive mail.
rlogin	Remote login.
telnet	Remote login.
uulog	Logs **uucp** traffic.
uustat	Returns status of **uucp**.
uux	Executes command on remote system.

6

uudecode — Decode Encoded File

uudecode *file*

Purpose

Reads a file converted by **uuencode** and restores it to original form.

Related Command

uuencode	Encodes file for **mailx**.

uuencode — Encode Binary File

unencode *filename* | **mailx** *username*

Purpose

Converts a binary filename to an encoded form that can be sent with the **mailx** command. This encoded file is in ASCII form.

Related Commands

mailx	Sends mail.
uudecode	Decodes file encoded by **uuencode**.

uulog — UNIX-to-UNIX Log

uulog *options*

Purpose

Prints the log of **uucp** file transfers to and from a specified system.

Options

6

–f*system*	Applies the tail **–f** command to display the most recent file transfers.
–s*system*	Displays all actions on the specified *system*.

Related Commands

tail	Display the tail (end) of a file.
uucp	UNIX-to-UNIX copy.

uuname — UNIX-to-UNIX Names

uuname *options*

Purpose

Lists the UNIX systems that can be accessed with **uucp**.

NOTE

Do not confuse **uuname** with **uname**.

Options

–c	Prints system names that can be accessed with the **cu** command.
–l	Prints the name of the local system.

Related Commands

cu	Calls up another system.
mailx	Sends and receives mail.
uucp	UNIX-to-UNIX copy.

uustat — UNIX-to-UNIX Status

uustat *options*

Purpose

Returns information about the current status of **uucp** commands. It can also be used to cancel **uucp** requests. Not all of the following options are available on all systems. Some options cannot be used together.

Options

–a	Reports on the status for all jobs.
–c	Reports the average time spent in queue.
–d*n*	Used with **-t** to report average for the last *n* minutes (default is last hour).
–j	Reports the total number of jobs.
–k*id*	Kills job *id* (you must own the job).
–m	Shows what systems can be accessed.
–n	Discards normal messages (as for **–k** or **–r**) but continues to display errors (on standard error).
–p	Runs **ps –flp** on current processes.
–q	Reports on the jobs queued for all systems.
–r*n*	Runs touch on its job *n*.
–s*system*	Reports the status of jobs on *system*.
–S*type*	Reports the status of jobs of *type*: **c** completed. **i** interrupted. **q** queued. **r** running.

-t*system*	Reports the average transfer rate on *system*.
-u*user*	Reports on the jobs started with *user*.

Related Commands

cu	Calls up another system.
mailx	Sends and receives mail.
uucp	UNIX-to-UNIX copy.

uux — UNIX-to-UNIX Execute

uux *options system! command*

Purpose

Runs a UNIX command on a remote UNIX system. It also copies files to and from other UNIX systems. A listing of permissible commands can often be found on a remote system in **/etc/uucp/ permissions**.

Options

-a*user*	Notifies *user* when command is completed.
-b	Returns the input if an error interrupts the command.
-c	Copies the actual file, not a copy from the spool file.
-C	Copies to a spooling file before sending on to the destination machine.
-g*p*	Sets job priority to *p*.
-j	Prints **uux** job number.
-n	Does not send mail if the command fails.
-p	Uses standard input for command.
-r	Queues the file(s), but doesn't send them.
-s*file*	Sends the transfer status to *file*. (This option is ignored by Solaris for security reasons.)
-x*n*	Debugs at level *n*; lowest is 1, highest is 9.
-z	Notifies user who initiated command when it is completed.

Related Commands

mailx Sends and receives mail.

rlogin Remote login.

rsh Remote shell.

uucp UNIX-to-UNIX copy.

vacation — Vacation Message

vacation *options*

Purpose

Returns a mail message to the originator indicating that you're on vacation. This lets people know you are not ignoring them. **Vacation** is not available on all systems, and versions vary among systems.

6

CAUTION

If you belong to mailing lists, think twice about using **vacation**. A **mailing list** is list of e-mail addresses, usually of people interested in a particular topic, such as the space shuttle or dinosaurs. Any message sent to the mailing list gets forwarded on to all the recipients of the list. Because **vacation** responds to all the e-mail you receive, your message describing your plans for fun in the sun might get forwarded to thousands of recipients of the mailing list. To make matters worse, since you're a member of the mailing list, you'll get the message, too. And, **vacation** kicks in to answer your e-mail with a polite message that you're gone, sending off another round of messages to the mailing list. If the mailing list maintainer isn't watching carefully, your innocent **vacation** message could set off a storm of messages.

Options

–F *user* Forwards mail to user when *mailfile* is unavailable. This usually just forwards mail and does not return a vacation message to sender.

–l *logfile* Logs names of senders in *logfile* (default is **$HOME/.maillog**).

–m *mailfile* Saves messages in *mailfile* (default is **$HOME/.mailfile**).

–**M** *file* Uses **file** as the message sent to mail originators (default is **/usr/lib/mail/std_vac_msg**).

wall — Write to All

wall

Purpose

Sends a message to all users. After sending the message, you can end input with **Ctrl–D**. This command is most often used by system administrators to warn users about a pending system shutdown.

Example

```
$ wall
WARNING: System will be shut down in 5 minutes.
```

This sends a warning message to all users logged on the system.

who — Who is Logged On

who options file

Purpose

Displays the names and other information about users logged on the system.

Options

am I Displays who you are (your system name).

–a Uses all options listed here.

–b Returns the last time and date the system was booted.

–d Returns expired processes.

–H Inserts column headings.

–l Returns lines available for login.

-n*n*	Displays *n* users per line.
-p	Returns processes started by **init** that are still active.
-q	Quick who; displays only usernames.
-r	Returns run level.
-s	Returns name, line, and time fields (default).
-t	Returns the last time the system clock was updated with clock.
-T	Returns the state of each terminal.
+	Any user can write to the terminal.
–	Only system administrator can write to the terminal.
?	Error with the terminal.
-u	Returns terminal usage in idle time.

6

Related Commands

date	Displays date and time.
login	Login system.
mesg	Sets terminal access.
rwho	Remote who.

write — Write to User

write *user* **tty**

Purpose

Sends a text message to another user. Press **Ctrl–D** to exit. The **tty** is optional and useful for people who are logged in more than once.

Example

```
$ write eric
Hi Eric
Ctrl–D
```

This sends the message "Hi Eric" to user **eric**.

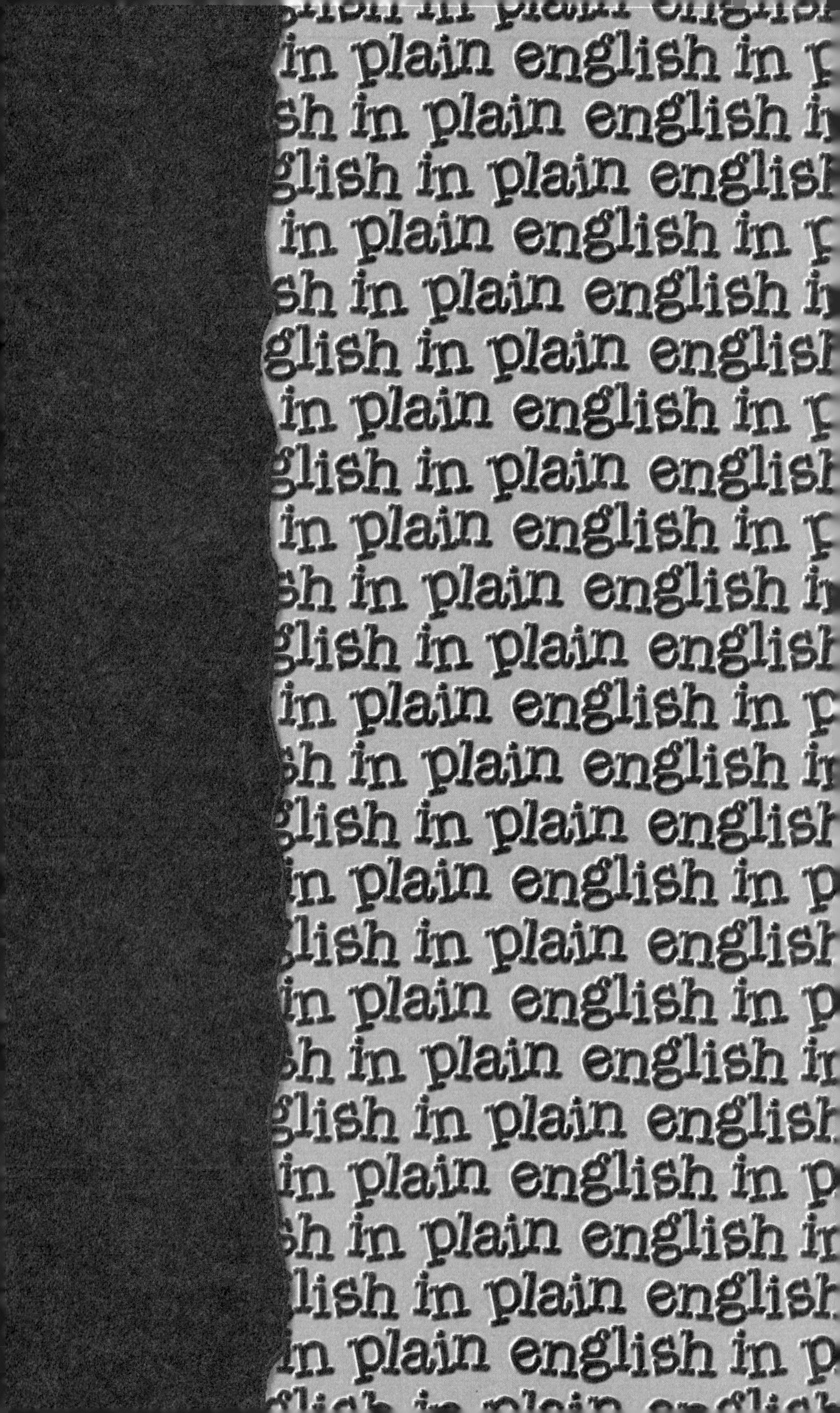
in plain english

7

FTP Commands

One undeniable advantage of being on the Internet is access to widely available free software. Although often we can dial in to remote machines and grab interesting software, this process is not easy for the average computer user. As with almost everything else in the UNIX world, the commands are geared for the expert— they assume that the person using them already knows what he or she is doing.

If you are on the Internet, you can use the **ftp** command to transfer files to and from remote machines. (If you're not sure whether you're on the Internet, check with your system administrator.) **Ftp** stands for **F**ile-**T**ransfer **P**rotocol, and it's rapidly becoming the most popular way to grab files from another networked computer. Although Web browsers like Netscape Navigator are capable of doing anonymous **ftp**, there's still a place for using a simple command line to transfer a file instead of firing up the X Window System and Navigator. The **ftp** command is easy to use. To start it, type

```
$ ftp
ftp>
```

Your shell prompt will be replaced with an **ftp** prompt. At this point, you can enter the commands listed in this chapter.

You can establish a direct connection to a machine in one of two ways: (1) You can specify the machine's name when you begin an **ftp** session, as follows:

```
$ ftp machine_kevin
```

or (2) you can use the **open** command after starting an **ftp** session, with code that looks like this:

```
ftp> open
(to) machine_kevin
Connected to machine_kevin
```

Anonymous FTP

Normal use of the **ftp** command requires the user to have an account set up on the remote machine. Since it's rather impractical to set up an account for every user in a high-traffic situation, the practice of **anonymous ftp** evolved. This allows you to log in to a remote machine as *anonymous*. Your privileges on the machine are extremely limited — you're allowed mainly to upload and download files from a specific directory, and that's about it — but this setup works very well.

To use anonymous **ftp**, you initiate an **ftp** session in the normal way except that you enter **anonymous** as your name, with your e-mail address (referred to as your **ident**) as your password:

```
ftp> open
(to) machine_kevin
Connected to machine_kevin
Name (machine_kevin): anonymous
220 Guest login ok, send ident as password.
Password: reichard@mr.net
230 Guest login ok, access restrictions apply.
```

In our example, we show the password as it was typed to the system. (As a user, you won't see it echoed back to your screen.) After the password is accepted, you can use the regular **ftp** commands.

A Listing of FTP Commands

Table 7.1 lists the **ftp** commands to use once you're online. If you're not sure which command to use, don't be afraid to experiment. You can't do a whole lot of damage; the worst that can happen is that you might get booted off the system.

TIP

Some commands used during an **ftp** session are standard UNIX commands. We've flagged them for you, should you want more information.

Although you're likely to use most of these commands at one point or another, one command is essential if you're transferring anything except text files: the **binary** command, which tells **ftp** that you're transferring a *binary file* (which would include any archive or compressed files, executables, and word-processing files). If you don't use the **binary** command before you try to transfer a binary file, you'll have wasted your time; all you'll get for your efforts is gibberish on your system.

7

Table 7-1 *FTP Commands*

Command	Purpose
! *command*	Runs a shell on your local machine, from where you can run a *command*.
$ *macros arg(s)*	Runs a *macro*, along with an optional argument.
? *command*	Displays help for specified command.
account	Sets up a new account, with a new *password*. This *password* command is frequently unavailable on remote systems.
append *file1 file2*	Appends the local file *file1* to the remote file *file2*.
ascii	Sets transfer mode to ASCII (text) format. This is the default.
bell	Creates a sound (usually a beep) after a file is transferred.
binary	Sets transfer mode to binary format.
bye	Ends **ftp** session and ends the **ftp** command.
cd *directory*	Changes the current remote directory to directory.
	Cd is a standard UNIX command. See Chapter 3 for more information on this command.

Continued

Table 7-1 *Continued*

Command	**Purpose**
cdup	Changes the current directory to one level up on the directory hierarchy. Same as **cd ..**
close	Ends **ftp** session with the remote machine but continues the **ftp** command on the local machine.
debug	Turns debugging on or off. (The default is off.)
delete *filename*	Removes filename from remote directory.
dir *directory filename*	Returns the contents of the specified directory; resulting information is stored in *filename* as specified.
disconnect	Ends **ftp** session and **ftp** command.
get *file1 file2*	Gets *file1* from the remote machine and stores it under the filename *file2*. If *file2* is not specified, the *file1* name will be retained. This command works the same as the **recv** command.
hash	Returns status while transferring numbers by returning feedback for each block transferred usually by displaying the hash (#) symbol.
help *command*	Displays information about specified *command*; displays general help information if no command is specified.
lcd *directory*	Changes the current local directory to the specified directory. If *directory* is not specified, the current local directory changes to the home directory.
ls *directory*	Lists the contents of the directory, provided *directory* is *filename* specified (otherwise the contents of the current directory will be listed). If *filename* is specified, then information about the specified file will be listed. **Ls** is a standard UNIX command. See Chapter 3 for more information on this command.
macdef *macrofile*	Defines a macro, ending with a blank line; the resulting macro is stored in the file *macrofile*.
mdelete *filename(s)*	Deletes *filename(s)* on the remote machine.
mdir *filename(s)*	Returns directory information for multiple, specified *filename(s)*.
mget *filename(s)*	Gets the specified multiple filename(s) from the remote machine.

Command	Purpose
mkdir *directory*	Makes a new directory, named *directory*, on the remote machine. **Mkdir** is a standard UNIX command. See Chapter 3 for more information on this command.
mput *filename(s)*	Puts the specified *filename(s)* on the remote machine.
open *remote_machine*	Opens a connection to the specified *remote_machine*. If no *remote_machine* is specified, the system will prompt you for a machine name.
put *file1 file2*	Puts local file *file1* on the remote machine, under the new filename *file2*. If *file2* is not specified, the file will retain the name *file1*. The command works the same as the **send** command.
pwd	Returns the current directory on the remote machine. (No, this command has nothing to do with a password. This acronym actually stands for **print working directory**, if you find this easier to remember.)
quit	Terminates connection to remote machine and ends the **ftp** command.
recv *file1 file2*	Retrieves *file1* from remote machine and stores it as *file2* on your computer (provided you specify *file2*). This command works the same as the **get** command.
remotehelp *command*	Returns help information about a specific *command* from the remote machine, not from the help files on your computer. This is not always supported.
rename *file1 file2*	Renames *file1* on the remote system as the new *file2*.
rmdir *directory*	Removes directory from the remote machine. **Rmdir** is a standard UNIX command. See Chapter 3 for more information on this command.
send *file1 file2*	Puts local file *file1* on the remote machine, under the new filename *file2*. If *file2* is not specified, the file will be retain the name *file1*. This command works the same as the **put** command.

FTP-Related Commands

rcp Remote copy; found in Chapter 6.

rlogin Remote login; found in Chapter 6.

7

in plain english in p
sh in plain english i
glish in plain englis
in plain english in p
sh in plain english i
glish in plain englis
in plain english in p
glish in plain englis
in plain english in p
sh in plain english i
glish in plain englis
in plain english in p
sh in plain english i
glish in plain englis
in plain english in p
glish in plain englis
in plain english in p
sh in plain english i
glish in plain englis
in plain english in p
sh in plain english i
glish in plain englis
in plain english in p

8

Graphics Commands

Many of these commands, which are used on graphic displays, have an **x** in their names because they come from the X Window System, which provides the base technology for graphics on UNIX. Other commands start with **dt**, which is short for *desktop* and indicates that a command is part of the Common Desktop Environment, or *CDE*, available on many commercial versions of UNIX. An alternative to the CDE interface is called Open Look, available on Sun systems. On Sun Solaris, Open Look is part of Sun's X Window System package called OpenWindows. Solaris also supports the CDE, and most newer Solaris installations provide the CDE applications in place of the older OpenWindows applications.

Many of the CDE, Open Look, and base X Window System commands overlap. To edit a text file, for example, you can choose **dtpad** (on CDE systems), **textedit** (on Open Look systems), or **xedit** (on most X systems, including CDE and Open Look systems). Because of this overlap in function, your system may not have all the individual commands.

All of these commands have something in common: a long list of toolkit options. Depending on the toolkit used to create them, the commands in this section accept either XView or XT options. (You'll notice a lot of overlap between toolkit options.) These options control how the window is displayed; Tables 8–1 and 8–2 describe them.

Table 8–1 *XView Options*

Option	Description
–background *red green blue*	Sets background color to *red green blue* values.
–background *color*	Uses *color* for window background.
–bg *color*	Uses *color* for window background.
–display *host*: *disp_num*	Connects to *disp_num* numbered X server (almost always 0) on a given **host**.
–fg *color*	Uses *color* for window foreground.
–fn *fontname*	Uses given font.
–font *fontname*	Uses given font.
–foreground_color *red green blue*	Sets foreground color to *red green blue* values.
–foreground *color*	Uses *color* for window foreground.
–geometry *Width***x** *Height***+***x***+***y*	Sets window size and position.
–geometry *Width***x** *Height*	Sets window size.
–geometry +*x*+*y*	Sets position of window's upper-left corner.
–height *rows*	Sets height of base window, in *rows*.
–position *x y*	Sets location of upper-left corner of window, in pixels.
–reverse	Reverses foreground and background colors.
–rv	Reverses foreground and background colors.
–size *width height*	Sets base window size, in pixels to *width* x *height*.
–Wb *red green blue*	Sets background color to *red green blue* values.
–Wf *red green blue*	Sets foreground color to *red green blue* values.

Option	Description
–WG *Width***x***Height***+** *x***+***y*	Sets window size and position.
–WG *Width***x***Height*	Sets window size.
–WG +*x***+***y*	Sets position of window's upper-left corner.
–Wh *rows*	Sets height of base window, in *rows*.
–Wi	Starts window as an icon.
–width *columns*	Sets width of base window, in *columns*.
–Wp *x y*	Sets location of upper-left corner of window, in pixels.
–Wr *host:disp_num*	Connects to *disp_num* numbered X server (almost always 0) on given *host*.
–Ws *width height*	Sets base window size, in pixels to *width* x *height*.
–Wt *fontname*	Uses given font.
–Ww *columns*	Sets width of base window, in *columns*.

Table 8–2 *XT Options*

Option	Description
–background *color*	Uses *color* for window background.
–bd *color*	Uses *color* for window border.
–bg *color*	Uses *color* for window background.
–bordercolor *color*	Uses *color* for window border.
–borderwidth *num_pixels*	Sets border to *num_pixels* wide.
–bw *num_pixels*	Sets border to *num_pixels* wide.
–display *host: disp_num*	Connects to *disp_num* numbered X server (almost always 0) on given *host*.
–fg *color*	Uses *color* for window foreground.
–fn *fontname*	Uses given font.
–font *fontname*	Uses given font.
–foreground *color*	Uses *color* for window foreground.

Continued

Table 8–2 *Continued*

Option	Description
–geometry *Width***x** *Height***+***x***+***y*	Sets window size and position.
–geometry *Width***x** *Height*	Sets window size.
–geometry +*x***+***y*	Sets position of window's upper-left corner.
–iconic	Starts window as an icon.
–reverse	Reverses foreground and background colors.
–rv	Reverses foreground and background colors.

bdftopcf — Convert Fonts to X Format

bdftopcf *options font_file.bdf*

Purpose

Converts font from bitmap distribution format (BDF) to portable compiled format (PCF). Use it when you get an X font and want to install it on your system, because most X fonts are distributed in BDF format.

Examples

```
$ bdftopcf times.bdf > times.pcf
```

Converts BDF font file **times.bdf** and redirects output to file **times.pcf**.

```
$ bdftopcf –o times.pcf times.bdf
```

Converts BDF font file **times.bdf**, writing output to PCF file **times.pcf**.

Options

–l	Sets the font bit order to least significant bit first.
–L	Sets the font byte order to least significant byte first.

–m	Sets the font bit order to most significant bit first.
–M	Sets the font byte order to most significant byte first.
–o *filename*	Sends output to *filename*.
–t	Converts to a fixed-width font.

Related Command

mkfontdir	Adds new font.

bitmap — Bitmap Editor

bitmap *options*
bitmap *options filename*
bitmap *options filename basename*

Purpose

Monochrome bitmap editor. The *filename* is the name used to store the bitmap. The *basename* is used for the bitmap name inside the file.

8

NOTE

Most X bitmap files have either no extension or a **.xbm** (short for X bitmap) extension. We've seen some confusing files, though, that use a **.bmp** extension, which is more commonly used for a completely different bitmap format found mostly on Microsoft Windows.

Examples

```
$ bitmap –size 48x32 mybitmap.xbm
```

Creates a new bitmap 48 pixels wide and 32 pixels high to be stored in the file **mybitmap.xbm**.

```
$ bitmap –fr red –hl yellow +dashed
```

Uses solid grid lines, in red and yellow, for selected areas.

Options

–axes	Turns on an X across the bitmap for positioning.
+axes	Turns off an X across the bitmap for positioning.
–background *color*	Uses *color* for window background.
–bd *color*	Uses *color* for window border.
–bg *color*	Uses color for window background.
–bordercolor *color*	Uses *color* for window border.
–borderwidth *num_pixels*	Sets border to *num_pixels* wide.
–bw *num_pixels*	Sets border to *num_pixels* wide.
–dashed	Turns on dashed lines for grid, the default.
+dashed	Turns off dashed lines for grid. Use this if performance is slow.
–display *host*:*disp_num*	Connects to *disp_num* numbered X server (almost always 0) on given *host*.
–fg *color*	Uses color for window foreground.
–fn *fontname*	Uses given font.
–font *fontname*	Uses given font.
–foreground *color*	Uses *color* for window foreground.
–fr *color*	Uses *color* for the frame and grid lines.
–geometry *Width* x*Height*+x+y	Sets window size and position.
–geometry *Width* x*Height*	Sets window size.
–geometry +*x*+*y*	Sets position of window's upper-left corner.
–grid	Turns on grid lines.
+grid	Turns off grid lines.
–hl *color*	Uses *color* for highlighting.
–iconic	Starts window as an icon.

–proportional	Forces all dots to be square.
+proportional	Used with **–sh** and **–sw** to allow for non-square dots.
–reverse	Reverses foreground and background colors.
–rv	Reverses foreground and background colors.
–size *WidthxHeight*	Sets size, in pixels, of bitmap to edit.
–sh *size*	Sets height of each square (for each dot) to *size* pixels.
–sw *size*	Sets width of each square (for each dot) to *size* pixels.

Related Commands

dticon	Desktop icon bitmap editor.
iconedit	Open Look icon bitmap editor.

calctool — Open Look Calculator

calctool *options*

Purpose

Provides a calculator in the Open Look environment.

Options

–2	Uses a two-dimensional look, the default for monochrome systems.
–3	Uses a three-dimensional look, the default for color systems.
–a accuracy_value	Controls number of decimal digits displayed, from 0 to 9. Defaults to 2.
–l	Starts up with a "left-handed" display.
–r	Starts up with a "right-handed" display, the default.
–v	Lists version number of all available options.

–Wn	Starts clock with no title bar.
+Wn	Starts clock with a title bar.

Related Commands

dtcalc	Common Desktop Environment calculator.
xcalc	X calculator.

clock — Open Look Display Current Time

clock *options*

Purpose

Displays current time in a window; Open Look program.

Options

–12	Displays 12-hour time in the digital clock.
–24	Displays 24-hour time in the digital clock.
–analog	Displays a clock with hands.
–digital	Displays a digital clock.
+date	Shows the current date.
–date	Does not show the current date.
–TZ *timezone*	Displays time from *timezone* rather than your normal timezone.
–v	Lists version number of all available options.
–Wn	Starts clock with no title bar.
+Wn	Starts clock with a title bar.

Related Commands

oclock	Displays current time in a round window.
xclock	Displays current time.

cm — Open Look Calendar Manager

cm *options*

Purpose

Appointment calendar in the Open Look environment. Normally started from Open Look window manager.

Options

-background *red green blue*	Sets background color to *red green blue* values.
-background *color*	Uses *color* for window background.
-bg *color*	Uses *color* for window background.
-c *calendar*	Sets name of default *calendar*.
-display *host*: *disp_num*	Connects to *disp_num* numbered X server (almost always 0) on given *host*.
-fg *color*	Uses *color* for window foreground.
-fn *fontname*	Uses given font.
-font *fontname*	Uses given font.
-foreground_color *red green blue*	Sets foreground color to *red green blue* values.
-foreground *color*	Uses *color* for window foreground.
-geometry *Width***x** *Height* + x + y	Sets window size and position.
-geometry *Width***x** *Height*	Sets window size.
-geometry + x + y	Sets position of window's upper-left corner.
-height *rows*	Sets height of base window, in rows.
-i 2	Displays current month when iconified.
-i 3	Displays current date when iconified.
-position *x y*	Sets location of upper-left corner of window, in pixels.

–reverse	Reverses foreground and background colors.
–rv	Reverses foreground and background colors.
–size *width height*	Sets base window size, in pixels to *width* x *height*.
–Wb *red green blue*	Sets background color to *red green blue* values.
–Wf *red green blue*	Sets foreground color to *red green blue* values.
–WG *Width***x** *Height* + x + y	Sets window size and position.
–WG *Width***x***Height*	Sets window size.
–WG + x + y	Sets position of window's upper-left corner.
–Wh *rows*	Sets height of base window, in *rows*.
–Wi	Starts window as an icon.
–width *columns*	Sets width of base window, in *columns*.
–Wp *x y*	Sets location of upper-left corner of window, in pixels.
–Wr *host***:***disp_num*	Connects to *disp_num* numbered X server (almost always 0) on given *host*.
–Ws *width height*	Sets base window size, in pixels to *width* x *height*.
–Wt *fontname*	Uses given font.
–Ww *columns*	Sets width of base window, in *columns*.

Related Command

dtcm Desktop calendar manager.

cmdtool — Open Look Terminal

cmdtool *options*
cmdtool *options* program *args*

Purpose

Provides a shell terminal window, allowing you to enter UNIX commands. You can run multiple **cmdtool** windows on your display and copy and paste between them. Inside the window, **cmdtool** runs your UNIX shell, which is specified in the **SHELL** environment variable. Or, you can specify a program and arguments on the command line.

Options

program args	Runs *program* with *arguments*.
-background *red green blue*	Sets background color to *red green blue* values.
-background *color*	Uses *color* for window background.
-bg *color*	Uses *color* for window background.
-C	Captures system console messages and displays in window.
-display *host:disp_num*	Connects to *disp_num* numbered X server (almost always 0) on given *host*.
-fg *color*	Uses *color* for window foreground.
-fn *fontname*	Uses given font.
-font *fontname*	Uses given font.
-foreground_color *red green blue*	Sets foreground color to *red green blue* values.
-foreground *color*	Uses *color* for window foreground.
-geometry *Width***x** *Height+x+y*	Sets window size and position.
-geometry *Width***x** *Height*	Sets window size.
-geometry *+x+y*	Sets position of window's upper-left corner.
-height *rows*	Sets height of base window, in *rows*.
-I *command*	Passes *command* to the shell.
-position *x y*	Sets location of upper-left corner of window, in pixels.
-reverse	Reverses foreground and background colors.

8

–rv	Reverses foreground and background colors.
–size *width height*	Sets base window size, in pixels to *width* x *height*.
–Wb *red green blue*	Sets background color to *red green blue* values.
–Wf *red green blue*	Sets foreground color to *red green blue* values.
–WG *Width***x***Height* +x+y	Sets window size and position.
–WG *Width***x***Height*	Sets window size.
–WG +x+y	Sets position of window's upper-left corner.
–Wh *rows*	Sets height of base window, in *rows*.
–Wi	Starts window as an icon.
–width *columns*	Sets width of base window, in *columns*.
–Wp *x y*	Sets location of upper-left corner of window, in pixels.
–Wr *host:disp_num*	Connects to *disp_num* numbered X server (almost always 0) on given *host*.
–Ws *width height*	Sets base window size, in pixels to *width* x *height*.
–Wt *fontname*	Uses given font.
–Ww *columns*	Sets width of base window, in *columns*.

Related Commands

shelltool	Open Look terminal.
dtterm	Common Desktop Environment terminal.
xterm	X terminal.

dtcalc — Desktop Calculator

dtcalc *options*

Purpose

Common Desktop Environment calculator utility.

Examples

```
$ dtcalc –b binary –no_menu_bar
```

Starts calculator in binary mode with no menu bar.

```
$ dtcalc –notation engineering –m financial
```

Starts calculator with engineering notation but in financial mode.

Options

–?	Prints a usage message.
–a *accuracy_value*	Controls number of decimal digits displayed, from 0 to 9. Defaults to 2.
–b binary	Starts with binary numeric base.
–b octal	Starts with octal numeric base.
–b decimal	Starts with decimal numeric base, the default.
–b hexadecimal	Starts with hexadecimal numeric base.
–background color	Uses *color* for window background.
–bd color	Uses *color* for window border.
–bg color	Uses *color* for window background.
–bordercolor color	Uses *color* for window border.
–borderwidth num_pixels	Sets border to *num_pixels* wide.
–bw num_pixels	Sets border to *num_pixels* wide.
–display host:disp_num	Connects to *disp_num* numbered X server (almost always 0) on given *host*.
-**fg** color	Uses *color* for window foreground.
–fn fontname	Uses given font for text.
–font fontname	Uses given font.
–foreground color	Uses *color* for window foreground.
–geometry *Width*x*Height* + x + y	Sets window size and position.
–geometry *Width*x*Height*	Sets window size.

–geometry +x+y	Sets position of window's upper-left corner.
–iconic	Starts window as an icon.
–m financial	Starts in financial mode.
–m logical	Starts in logical mode.
–m scientific	Starts in scientific mode, the default.
–no_menu_bar	Displays calculator without a menubar.
–notation engineering	Uses engineering notation.
–notation fixed	Uses fixed notation, the default.
–notation scientific	Uses scientific notation.
–reverse	Reverses foreground and background colors.
–rv	Reverses foreground and background colors.
–trig degrees	Uses degrees for trigonometric data in scientific mode.
–trig gradients	Uses gradients for trigonometric data in scientific mode.
–trig radians	Uses radians for trigonometric data in scientific mode.

8

Related Command

xcalc	Calculator.

dtcm — Desktop Calendar Manager

dtcm *options*

Purpose

Manages a calendar of things to do and remember — part of the Common Desktop Environment.

Example

```
$ dtcm -v day
```

Starts calendar in day view, showing today.

Options

–c calendar	Names the *calendar* to display. Your default calendar is *$USER@$HOST*, for example **erc@eric.com**.
–p printer	Names the *printer* to use. Defaults to system printer.
–v day	Starts with day view.
–v week	Starts with week view.
–v month	Starts with month view.
–v year	Starts with year view.

Related Command

cm	Open Look calendar manager.

8

dtfile — Desktop File Manager

dtfile *options*

Purpose

Manages files in the Common Desktop Environment. The easiest way to launch this program is from the CDE front panel.

Examples

```
$ dtfile -view attributes
```

Views files by name and small icons signifying attributes.

```
$ dtfile -dir /home/erc
```

Starts in directory **/home/erc**.

Options

-dir folder	Displays a window for named *folder* (directory).
-folder folder	Displays a window for named *folder* (directory).
-grid off	Displays file icons where they get placed.
-grid on	Displays file icons in a grid pattern.
-noview	Runs in server mode with no windows until an application requests windows.
-order alphabetical	Displays files in alphabetical order.
-order file_type	Groups files by type.
-order date	Displays files in order of last modified dates.
-order size	Displays files in order of size.
-tree off	Displays files in a single folder.
-tree on	Displays files in tree mode rather than in a single folder.
-view no_icon	Displays files by name.
-view large_icon	Displays files by name and large icon.
-view small_icon	Displays files by name and small icon.
-view attributes	Displays files by name and small attribute icon.

Related Command

filemgr Open Look File Manager.

dthelpview — Desktop Help Viewer

dthelpview *options*

Purpose

Views online help in the Common Desktop Environment. It can also display online manual pages. You start **dthelpview** either with one of the command-line options listed below or by simply clicking on the help icon in the CDE front panel.

Examples

```
$ dthelpview -helpVolume 1
```

Tries to display bogus help volume 1. You can then click on the **Index** button to display an index of all available volumes.

```
$ dthelpview -manPage cal
```

Displays online manual entry for the **cal** command.

```
$ dthelpview -man
```

Prompts you for an online manual page. Does not provide a list of available pages, alas.

```
$ dthelpview -file larry1
```

Displays ASCII file **larry1**.

Options

-file *filename*	Displays given ASCII file.
-helpVolume *volume*	Displays CDE help *volume*.
-manPage *man_page*	Displays named online manual page (entry).
-man	Prompts for an online manual page to display.

Related Commands

man	Prints online manual.
xman	Views online manuals.

dticon — Desktop Icon Bitmap Editor

dticon *options*

Purpose

Common Desktop Environment icon bitmap editor. This icon editor supports XPM (X Pixmap) color and XBM (X Bitmap) monochrome images formats. It can also capture areas of the screen.

NOTE

Most color bitmap files have a **.xpm** extension, short for X pixmap. Most X monochrome bitmap files have either no extension or a **.xbm** (short for X bitmap) extension. We've seen some confusing files, though, that use a **.bmp** extension, which is more commonly used for a completely different bitmap format found mostly on Microsoft Windows.

Examples

```
$ dticon -x 32x48
```

Creates a new bitmap for editing, 32 pixels wide and 48 pixels high.

```
$ dticon -f recycle.xbm
```

Edits existing bitmap file **recycle.xbm**.

Options

8

–f *filename*	Edits given *filename*.
–x *Width***x***Height*	Specifies size of icon to create, in pixels.

Related Command

bitmap Bitmap editor.

dtksh — Desktop Korn Shell

dtksh *options*

Purpose

Provides an extended Korn shell, **ksh**, with windowing commands. Your scripts can create windows and access the CDE help system. For most usage, though, **dtksh** acts like ksh, the Korn shell, one of UNIX's many command-line interfaces. See Chapter 11, "Shell Commands and Variables," for more information on the Korn shell.

dtlp — Desktop Printer Manager

dtlp *options*
dtlp *options filename*

Purpose

Presents a print dialog window in which you can specify all the printing options, then it prints a file. As the name suggests, **dtlp** acts as a front-end to **lp**, described earlier in this book. The command is located in **/usr/dt/bin/dtlp**.

Examples

```
$ dtlp –b "This is MY file so there"
```

Displays the print dialog with the printing title banner set to "This is MY file so there."

```
$ dtlp -n 5 –d bigprinter –s secret_report
```

Silently prints 5 copies of the file **secret_report** on the printer named **bigprinter**. Does not display a print dialog box.

Options

–a	Formats file with the **man** command.
–b banner	Sets text of the banner page to *banner*.
–d printer_name	Names the printer.
–e	Erases file after printing it.
–h	Prints out a help message.
–m print_command	Replaces the printer command, **lp**, with *print_command*.
–n copy_count	Sets number of copies to *copy_count*.
–o *other_options*	*Sets extra options to pass to the print -* command, which defaults to **lp**.
–r	Format file with the **pr –f** command before printing it.
–s	Prints the file silently, without displaying the print dialog box.

–u user_*filename*	Sets name of file to appear in the print dialog box.
–v	Prints out verbose messages as **dtlp** works.
–w	Sends raw file data to printer, without special handling for tabs, backspaces, formfeeds and other binary characters.

Related Commands

lp	Prints files.
man	Shows online manual.

dtmail — Send and Receive E-mail Messages

dtmail *options*

Purpose

This Common Desktop Environment e-mail program allows you to send and receive messages. Located in **/usr/dt/bin/dtmail**.

Examples

```
$ dtmail –f ~/Mail/my_mailbox
```

Starts **dtmail** and uses the file ~ **/Mail/my_mailbox** as the mailbox file.

```
$ dtmail –c
```

Starts **dtmail** with just the compose message window.

```
$ dtmail
```

Starts **dtmail** with the normal message window.

Options

–a *filename*	Brings up compose window with **filename** included as an attachment.

–a *filename1 ... filenameN*	Brings up compose window with all listed files included as attachments.
–background color	Uses **color** for window background.
–bd color	Uses **color** for window border.
–bg color	Uses **color** for window background.
–bordercolor color	Uses **color** for window border.
–borderwidth num_pixels	Sets border to **num_pixels** wide.
–bw num_pixels	Sets border to **num_pixels** wide.
–c	Starts **dtmail** with an empty compose message window.
–display host: disp_num	Connects to **disp_num** numbered X server (almost always 0) on given **host**.
–f mailfile	Uses **mailfile** instead of your default mailbox file (named by the **MAIL** environment variable).
–fg color	Uses **color** for window foreground.
–fn fontname	Uses given font.
–font fontname	Uses given font.
–foreground color	Uses **color** for window foreground.
–geometry *Width***x***Height* + x + y	Sets window size and position.
–geometry *Width***x***Height*	Sets window size.
–geometry + x + y	Sets position of window's upper-left corner.
–h	Prints summary of command-line options.
–iconic	Starts window as an icon.
–reverse	Reverses foreground and background colors.
–rv	Reverses foreground and background colors.

8

Related Commands

mail	Sends and receives e-mail.
mailx	Sends and receives e-mail.
mailtool	Open Look program that sends and receives e-mail.

dtpad — Desktop Text Editor

dtpad *options*
dtpad *options filename*

Purpose

GUI text editor for the Common Desktop Environment.

Examples

```
$ dtpad filename.txt
```

Starts **dtpad** editing file **filename.txt**.

```
$ dtpad –saveOnClose –statusLine filename.txt
```

Starts **dtpad** editing file **filename.txt**; saves files when closed and shows a status line.

Options

–background color	Uses **color** for window background.
–bd color	Uses **color** for window border.
–bg color	Uses **color** for window background.
–bordercolor color	Uses **color** for window border.
–borderwidth num_pixels	Sets border to **num_pixels** wide.
–bw num_pixels	Sets border to **num_pixels** wide.
–display host:disp_num	Connects to **disp_num** numbered X server (almost always 0) on given **host**.
–exitOnLastClose	Quits when last file is closed.

-fg color	Uses **color** for window foreground.
-fn fontname	Uses given font.
-font fontname	Uses given font.
-foreground color	Uses **color** for window foreground.
-geometry *Width***x** *Height* + x + y	Sets window size and position.
-geometry *Width***x** *Height*	Sets window size.
-geometry + x + y	Sets position of window's upper-left corner.
-iconic	Starts window as an icon.
-missingFile Warning	Alerts you when a filename cannot be found.
-noReadOnly Warning	Doesn't alert you when a file is read only.
-noNameChange	Doesn't change default filename when you use Save As on the File menu. The default option is to change the name.
-reverse	Reverses foreground and background colors.
-rv	Reverses foreground and background colors.
-saveOnClose	Automatically saves files when closed.
-statusLine	Displays status line at bottom of window.
-viewOnly	Doesn't allow you to change files.
-workspaceList workspace_list	Displays window in given workspace (or workspaces).
-wrapToFit	Wraps text to fit. Default is not to wrap.

Related Commands

textedit	Open Look text editor.
vi	Text editor.
xedit	X Window Text editor.

8

dtstyle — Control Desktop Colors and Fonts

dtstyle

Purpose

Calls up Common Desktop Environment style manager, from which you can select fonts and colors for all Common Desktop Environment applications.

Options

None.

dtterm — Desktop Terminal Window

dtterm *options*
dtterm –e *program options*

Purpose

Opens a shell terminal window, allowing you to enter UNIX commands. You can run multiple **dtterm** windows on your display and copy and paste between them. Inside the window, **dtterm** runs your UNIX shell, which is specified in the **SHELL** environment variable.

Examples

```
$ dtterm &
```

Runs **dtterm** in the background.

```
$ dtterm –e rlogin eric
```

Launches **dtterm** and executes **rlogin** to remotely login to machine **eric** rather than launching your shell.

Options

–background color	Uses **color** for window background.
–bd color	Uses **color** for window border.
–bg color	Uses **color** for window background.
–bordercolor color	Uses **color** for window border.
–borderwidth num_pixels	Sets border to **num_pixels** wide.
–bw num_pixels	Sets border to **num_pixels** wide.
–C	Captures output sent to **/dev/console** and displays in this window.
–display host:disp_num	Connects to **disp_num** numbered X server (almost always 0) on given **host**.
–e program *options*	Executes **program** and passes all following **options** to program.
–fg color	Uses **color** for window foreground.
–fn fontname	Uses given font.
–font fontname	Uses given font.
–foreground color	Uses **color** for window foreground.
–geometry *Width***x** *Height* + x + y	Sets window size and position.
–geometry *Width***x** *Height*	Sets window size.
–geometry + x + y	Sets position of window's upper-left corner.
–iconic	Starts window as an icon.
–ls	Starts a login shell (reads **.profile** or **.login**.)
–map	Maps (deiconifies) window if it is iconified and new output arrives.
–name progname	Uses **progname** as program's name; default for icon name.
–reverse	Reverses foreground and background colors.
–rv	Reverses foreground and background colors.
–title titlestring	Sets window title.
–usage	Displays a usage message explaining the options.

Related Commands

xterm	Terminal window.
cmdtool	Open Look terminal window.
shelltool	Open Look terminal window.

dtwm — Desktop Window Manager

dtwm *options*

Purpose

Controls placement and size of windows on the screen.

NOTE

You normally won't start **dtwm** yourself. Instead, **dtwm** is normally started automatically when you log into Common Desktop Environment systems.

Example

8

```
$ dtwm -display eric:0
```

Starts **dtwm** as the window manager for display **eric:0**, that is, the first X server on machine **eric**.

Options

-display host:disp_num	Connects to **disp_num** numbered X server (almost always 0) on given **host**.
-name name	Uses **name** for finding resources, rather than the default resource name of **Dtwm**.

Related Commands

twm	Tab window manager.
mwm	Motif window manager.
olwm	Open Look window manager.

filemgr — Open Look File Manager

filemgr *options*

Purpose

The Open Look file manager program allows you to view, copy, move, rename, and delete files. It is normally started from the Open Look window manager, **olwm**.

Options

-a	Checks both file and directory modification times, limiting performance.
-background red green blue	Sets background color to **red green blue** values.
-background color	Uses **color** for window background.
-bg color	Uses **color** for window background.
-C	Doesn't use system for typing files. With **-C**, **filemgr** only understands generic documents, folders, and programs.
-c	Displays in columns, not rows.
-d directory	Starts in given **directory**.
-display host: disp_num	Connects to **disp_num** numbered X server (almost always 0) on given **host**.
-fg color	Uses **color** for window foreground.
-fn fontname	Uses given font.
-font fontname	Uses given font.
-foreground_color red green blue	Sets foreground color to **red green blue** values.
-foreground color	Uses **color** for window foreground.
-geometry *Width***x** *Height* +x+y	Sets window size and position.
-geometry *Width***x** *Height*	Sets window size.
-geometry +x+y	Sets position of window's upper-left corner.

–height rows	Sets height of base window, in **rows**.
–i secs	Checks directories (and files with **–a**) for modification every **secs** seconds.
–position x y	Sets location of upper-left corner of window, in pixels.
–r	Displays in rows, not columns; the default.
–reverse	Reverses foreground and background colors.
–rv	Reverses foreground and background colors.
–size width height	Sets base window size, in pixels to **width** x **height**.
–Wb red green blue	Sets background color to **red green blue** values.
–Wf red green blue	Sets foreground color to **red green blue** values.
–WG *Width***x** *Height* + x + y	Sets window size and position.
–WG *Width***x***Height*	Sets window size.
–WG + x + y	Sets position of window's upper-left corner.
–Wh rows	Sets height of base window, in **rows**.
–Wi	Starts window as an icon.
–width columns	Sets width of base window, in **columns**.
–Wp x y	Sets location of upper-left corner of window, in pixels.
–Wr host:disp_num	Connects to disp_num numbered X server (almost always 0) on given **host**.
–Ws width height	Sets base window size, in pixels to **width** x **height**.
–Wt fontname	Uses given font.
–Ww columns	Sets width of base window, in **columns**.

Related Command

dtfile Desktop File Manager.

8

fsinfo

Get Information on Font Server

fsinfo *options*

Purpose

Prints out information about font servers, which provide scaled fonts.

Options

–server host:port	Returns information on the font server located on the given **host**, using the given network **port** number, instead of the font server named in the **FONTSERVER** environment variable.

Related Commands

fslsfonts	Lists fonts provided by a font server.
xfs	Font server.

fslsfonts

List Fonts Provided by Font Server

fslsfonts *options*

Purpose

Lists the available fonts that a font server provides and can scale.

Options

–1	(One) Prints output using only one column.
–C	Prints output in multiple columns.
–fn pattern	Lists fonts that match the pattern. * and ? wildcards are allowed.
–l	(Ell) Lists some attributes of font as well as names.

–ll	(Ell ell) Lists font properties in addition to output from **–l** option.
–m	Prints minimum and maximum bounds of each font.
–n columns	Sets number of columns to columns.
–server host:port	Lists fonts on the given font server, located on the given **host**, using the given network port number, instead of the font server named in the **FONTSERVER** environment **variable**.
–u	Doesn't sort output.
–w width	Sets total width of output to **width** characters.

Related Commands

fsinfo	Prints information on font server.
xfs	Font server.

8

fstobdf — Extract Font Server Fonts

fstobdf –server server **–fn** fontname
fstobdf –fn fontname

Purpose

Converts a font from the font server into the bitmap distribution format, or BDF. You can have the font server scale a font and then convert that font to BDF format for installing on another system.

Options

–fn fontname	Names font to extract to BDF format.
–server host:port	Extracts fonts from the given font server, located on the given **host**, using the given network **port** number, instead of the font server named in the **FONTSERVER** environment variable.

Related Commands

fsinfo	Prints information on font server.
fslsfonts	Lists fonts provided by a font server.
xfs	Font server.

ghostview

View PostScript Documents

ghostview *options filename*

Purpose

Displays PostScript documents in a window.

NOTE

This command is not available on all systems.

Examples

```
$ ghostview budget.ps
```

Displays PostScript document **budget.ps**.

Options

-10x14	Sets standard page size to 10 x 14 inches.
-a3	Uses A3 paper size.
-a4	Uses A4 paper size.
-a5	Uses A5 paper size.
-b4	Uses B4 paper size.
-b5	Uses B5 paper size.
-center	Centers page within viewport.
-color	Uses a color palette.
-date	Shows PostScript **%%Date** comment.
-dpi dpi	Sets resolution to **dpi** dots per inch.
-executive	Sets standard page size to 7.5 x 10 inches.
-folio	Sets standard page size to 10 x 14 inches.

–grayscale	Uses a grayscale palette.
–landscape	Sets default orientation to Landscape.
–ledger	Sets standard page size to 17 x 11 inches.
–legal	Sets standard page size to 8.5 x 14 inches.
–letter	Sets standard page size to 8.5 x 11 inches.
–locator	Displays locator.
–magstep	Sets default magnification step. Defaults to 0.
–monochrome	Displays only in monochrome.
–ncdwm	Workaround if window appears extremely small.
–nocenter	Doesn't center page within viewport.
–nodate	Doesn't show PostScript %%**Date** comment.
–nolocator	Doesn't display locator.
–noncdwm	Turns off workaround for extremely small windows.
–noopenwindows	Turns off workaround for Sun OpenWindows systems.
–noquiet	Prints informational messages.
–notitle	Doesn't show PostScript %%**Title** comment.
–openwindows	Workaround for errors on Sun OpenWindows systems.
–portrait	Sets default orientation to Portrait.
–quiet	Doesn't print informational messages.
–resolution dpi	Sets resolution to **dpi** dots per inch.
–seascape	Rotates orientation 90 degrees counterclockwise.
–statement	Sets standard page size to 5.5 x 8.5 inches.
–tabloid	Sets standard page size to 11 x 17 inches.
–title	Shows PostScript %%**Title** comment.
–upsidedown	Sets orientation to upside down.
–xdpi dpi	Sets horizontal resolution of window to **dpi** dots per inch.
–ydpi dpi	Sets vertical resolution of window to **dpi** dots per inch.

Related Command

xdvi Previews DVI Documents.

iconedit — Open Look Icon Editor

iconedit *filename options*
iconedit *options*

Purpose

Open Look program that edits icons and cursors.

Example

```
$ iconedit myicon.icon
```

Starts **iconedit** with icon file **myicon.icon**. If the file exists, you'll see that icon in the window. Otherwise, it will create a new icon named **myicon.icon**.

Options

-background red green blue	Sets background color to **red green blue** values.
-background color	Uses **color** for window background.
-bg color	Uses **color** for window background.
-display host:disp_num	Connects to **disp_num** numbered X server (almost always 0) on given **host**.
-fg color	Uses **color** for window foreground.
-fn fontname	Uses given font.
-font fontname	Uses given font.
-foreground_color red green blue	Sets foreground color to **red green blue** values.
-foreground color	Uses **color** for window foreground.
-geometry *Width***x** *Height* + x + y	Sets window size and position.

–geometry *Width***x** *Height*	Sets window size.
–geometry +x+y	Sets position of window's upper-left corner.
–height rows	Sets height of base window, in **rows**.
–position x y	Sets location of upper-left corner of window, in pixels.
–reverse	Reverses foreground and background colors.
–rv	Reverses foreground and background colors.
–size width height	Sets base window size, in pixels to **width** x **height**.
–Wb red green blue	Sets background color to **red green blue** values.
–Wf red green blue	Sets foreground color to **red green blue** values.
–WG *Width***x** *Height*+x+y	Sets window size and position.
–WG *Width***x***Height*	Sets window size.
–WG +x+y	Sets position of window's upper-left corner.
–Wh rows	Sets height of base window, in **rows**.
–Wi	Starts window as an icon.
–width columns	Sets width of base window, in **columns**.
–Wp x y	Sets location of upper-left corner of window, in pixels.
–Wr host:disp_num	Connects to **disp_num** numbered X server (almost always 0) on given **host**.
–Ws width height	Sets base window size, in pixels to **width** x **height**.
–Wt fontname	Uses given font.
-**Ww** columns	Sets width of base window, in **columns**.

Related Commands

bitmap	Bitmap editor.
dticon	Desktop icon bitmap editor.

8

mailtool

Send and Receive E-mail Messages

mailtool *options*

Purpose

This Open Look e-mail program allows you to send and receive messages. This command is located in **/usr/openwin/bin/mailtool**.

Options

-background red green blue	Sets background color to **red green blue** values.
-background color	Uses **color** for window background.
-bg color	Uses **color** for window background.
-display host:disp_num	Connects to **disp_num** numbered X server (almost always 0) on given **host**.
-fg color	Uses **color** for window foreground.
-fn fontname	Uses given font.
-font fontname	Uses given font.
-foreground_color red green blue	Sets foreground color to **red green blue** values.
-foreground color	Uses **color** for window foreground.
-geometry *Width***x** *Height* + x + y	Sets window size and position.
-geometry *Width***x** *Height*	Sets window size.
-geometry + x + y	Sets position of window's upper-left corner.
-height rows	Sets height of base window, in **rows**.
-Mx	Works in expert mode. Won't ask you to confirm deleting messages.
-Mi interval	Checks for new mail every **interval** seconds.

8

–Mf mailfile	Uses **mailfile** instead of the default in-box, in /**var**/**mail**/username.
–position x y	Sets location of upper-left corner of window, in pixels.
–reverse	Reverses foreground and background colors.
–rv	Reverses foreground and background colors.
–size width height	Sets base window size, in pixels to **width** x **height**.
–v	Prints **mailtool** version number.
–Wb red green blue	Sets background color to **red green blue** values.
–Wf red green blue	Sets foreground color to **red green blue** values.
–WG *Width*x*Height* +x+y	Sets window size and position.
–WG *Width*x*Height*	Sets window size.
–WG +x+y	Sets position of window's upper-left corner.
–Wh rows	Sets height of base window, in **rows**.
–Wi	Starts window as an icon.
–width columns	Sets width of base window, in **columns**.
–Wp x y	Sets location of upper-left corner of window, in pixels.
–Wr host:disp_num	Connects to **disp_num** numbered X server (almost always 0) on given **host**.
–Ws width height	Sets base window size, in pixels to **width** x **height**.
–Wt fontname	Uses given font.
-**Ww** columns	Sets width of base window, in **columns**.

8

Related Command

dtmail	Common Desktop Environment e-mail program.
mail	Sends and receives e-mail.
mailx	Sends and receives e-mail.

mkfontdir — Add New Font

mkfontdir
mkfontdir directory

Purpose

Scans all the font files in a directory and creates the **fonts.dir** file with a listing of these fonts. Once this is done, the X server should be able to use the new font. You must run **mkfontdir** after you have copied a new font file into a font directory, usually under **/usr/lib/X11/fonts**. You normally have to be the root user to run **mkfontdir**, because the font directories usually have restrictive permissions.

Options

The only option is a directory name. If one is omitted, **mkfontdir** works in the current directory.

Related Command

xlsfonts	Lists installed fonts.

mwm — Motif Window Manager

mwm *options*

Purpose

Controls the placement and size of windows on the screen. Usually, a window manager gets started when you begin an X session. **Mwm** displays window titlebars with a Motif look and feel.

OPTION

-display host: disp_num	Connects to **disp_num** numbered X server (almost always 0) on given **host**.

Related Commands

dtwm	Common Desktop Environment window manager.
olwm	Open Look window manager.
twm	Tab window manager.

oclock — Round Clock

oclock *options*

Purpose

Displays the time in a round window.

Examples

```
$ oclock -hour red -jewel gold
```

Starts a round clock with a red hour hand and a gold jewel.

```
$ oclock –transparent
```

Starts a round clock with a transparent background.

Options

–bd color	Uses **color** for window border.
–bg color	Uses **color** for window background.
–bw num_pixels	Sets border to **num_pixels** wide.
–display host: disp_num	Connects to **disp_num** numbered X server (almost always 0) on given **host**.
–fg color	Uses **color** for window foreground.
–geometry *Width***x** *Height* + x + y	Sets window size and position.
–geometry *Width***x** *Height*	Sets window size.
–geometry + x + y	Sets position of window's upper-left corner.
–hour color	Uses **color** for hour hand.
–jewel color	Uses **color** for clock jewel.

–minute color	Uses **color** for minute hand.
–noshape	Creates a rectangular clock.
–shape	Creates a rounded clock.
-transparent	Creates a clock with a transparent background.

Related Commands

clock	Open Look clock.
xclock	X clock.

olwm — Open Look Window Manager

olwm *options*

Purpose

Controls the placement and size of all windows on the display and provides window title bars with an Open Look appearance.

Examples

```
$ olwm -follow -3d
```

Starts **olwm** with keyboard focus following the mouse — rather than having to click to type — and with a three-dimensional look.

```
$ olwm -2d -fg maroon
```

Starts **olwm** with a foreground color of maroon and with a two-dimensional look.

Options

–2d	Uses a two-dimensional look, the default for monochrome systems.
–3d	Uses a three-dimensional look, the default for color systems.

–background color	Uses **color** for window background.
–bd color	Uses **color** for window border.
–bg color	Uses **color** for window background.
–bordercolor color	Uses **color** for window border.
–c	You must click a mouse button in a window to make it active.
–click	You must click a mouse button in a window to make it active.
–display host: disp_num	Connects to **disp_num** numbered X server (almost always 0) on given **host**.
–f	As you move the mouse, windows underneath the mouse become active.
–follow	As you move the mouse, windows underneath the mouse become active.
–fn font_name	Sets titlebar font to **font_name**.
–font fontname	Uses given font.
–fg color	Sets titlebar foreground color to **color**.
–foreground color	Uses **color** for window foreground.
-name name	Uses **name** for finding resources, rather than the default **olwm**.

8

Related Commands

dtwm	Desktop window manager.
mwm	Motif window manager.
twm	Tab window manager.

openwin — Starts OpenWindows

openwin *options*

Purpose

Starts the X server in an OpenWindows environment, usually called from your **.login** or **.profile** file. The **openwin** file is a shell script designed to make starting X easier.

Options

-auth protocol	Uses **protocol** instead of the default **MIT-MAGIC-COOKIE** protocol for access security.
-noauth	Turns off default **MIT-MAGIC-COOKIE** user-based access security.
-server server	Tells **openwin** which program to start as the X server. Defaults to **$OPENWINHOME/bin/Xsun**.
-**wm** window _mgr	Starts **window_mgr** as an alternate window manager instead of the default **olwm**. If you have a **.xinitrc** file in your home directory, this option is likely to be ignored.

Related Commands

olwm	Open Look window manager.
startx	Starts X server.
xauth	Creates and modifies X authorization file.

shelltool — Open Look Terminal

shelltool *options*
shelltool *options* program *args*

Purpose

Provides a shell terminal window, much like **cmdtool**, allowing you to enter UNIX commands. You can run multiple **shelltool** windows on your display and copy and paste between them. Inside the window, **shelltool** runs your UNIX shell, which is specified in the **SHELL** environment variable. Or, you can specify a program and arguments on the command line.

Options

program *args*	Runs **program** with arguments *args* instead of your default shell.
-background red green blue	Sets background color to **red green blue** values.

–background color	Uses **color** for window background.
–bg color	Uses **color** for window background.
–C	Captures system console messages and displays in window.
–display host: disp_num	Connects to **disp_num** numbered X server (almost always 0) on given **host**.
–fg color	Uses **color** for window foreground.
–fn fontname	Uses given font.
–font fontname	Uses given font.
–foreground_color red green blue	Sets foreground color to **red green blue** values.
–foreground color	Uses **color** for window foreground.
–geometry *Width***x** *Height* + x + y	Sets window size and position.
–geometry *Width***x** *Height*	Sets window size.
–geometry + x + y	Sets position of window's upper-left corner.
–height rows	Sets height of base window, in **rows**.
–I command	Passes **command** to the shell.
–position x y	Sets location of upper-left corner of window, in pixels.
–reverse	Reverses foreground and background colors.
–rv	Reverses foreground and background colors.
–size width height	Sets base window size, in pixels to **width** x **height**.
–Wb red green blue	Sets background color to **red green blue** values.
–Wf red green blue	Sets foreground color to **red green blue** values.
–WG *Width***x** *Height* + x + y	Sets window size and position.
–WG *Width***x***Height*	Sets window size.
–WG + x + y	Sets position of window's upper-left corner.
–Wh rows	Sets height of base window, in **rows**.
–Wi	Starts window as an icon.

–width columns	Sets width of base window, in **columns**.
–Wp x y	Sets location of upper-left corner of window, in pixels.
–Wr host:disp_num	Connects to **disp_num** numbered X server (almost always 0) on given **host**.
–Ws width height	Sets base window size, in pixels to **width** x **height**.
–Wt fontname	Uses given font.
-**Ww** columns	Sets width of base window, in **columns**.

Related Commands

cmdtool	Open Look terminal.
dtterm	Common Desktop Environment terminal.
xterm	X terminal.

startx — Start X Server

8

startx client_*options* -- server_*options*

Purpose

Shell script that starts the X server. **Startx** is useful for environments where you do not have a graphical login (a feature that is usually provided by **xdm**).

Options

The client options may be either a program to launch in place of the commands in the **.xinitrc** file or options to the default **xterm** program (if no **.xinitrc** file exists in your home directory).

The server options may either be a program to use in place of **X** — the X server — along with options for that program, or options to **X**. See the entry on **X** for the server options.

Related Commands

openwin	Starts X server in OpenWindows.
xdm	X display manager.
xinit	Starts X server.

tapetool

Open Look Tape Backup Manager

tapetool *options*

Purpose

Presents a friendly interface over the **tar** command to allow you to make backups and restore data from tape.

Options

–background red green blue	Sets background color to **red green blue** values.
–background color	Uses **color** for window background.
–bg color	Uses **color** for window background.
–display host: disp_num	Connects to **disp_num** numbered X server (almost always 0) on given **host**.
–fg color	Uses **color** for window foreground.
–fn fontname	Uses given font.
–font fontname	Uses given font.
–foreground_color red green blue	Sets foreground color to **red green blue** values.
–foreground color	Uses **color** for window foreground.
–geometry *Width***x** *Height* + x + y	Sets window size and position.
–geometry *Width***x** *Height*	Sets window size.
–geometry + x + y	Sets position of window's upper-left corner.
–height rows	Sets height of base window, in **rows**.
–position x y	Sets location of upper-left corner of window, in pixels.
–reverse	Reverses foreground and background colors.
–rv	Reverses foreground and background colors.
–size width height	Sets base window size, in pixels to **width** x **height**.

8

–Wb red green blue	Sets background color to **red green blue** values.
–Wf red green blue	Sets foreground color to **red green blue** values.
–WG *Width*x*Height* +x+y	Sets window size and position.
–WG *Width*x*Height*	Sets window size.
–WG +x+y	Sets position of window's upper-left corner.
–Wh rows	Sets height of base window, in **rows**.
–Wi	Starts window as an icon.
–width columns	Sets width of base window, in **columns**.
–Wp x y	Sets location of upper-left corner of window, in pixels.
–Wr host:disp_num	Connects to **disp_num** numbered X server (almost always 0) on given **host**.
–Ws width height	Sets base window size, in pixels to **width** x **height**.
–Wt fontname	Uses given font.
-**Ww** columns	Sets width of base window, in **columns**.

8

Related Command

tar Tape archiver.

textedit — Open Look Text Editor

textedit *options filename*

Purpose

Open Look text editor with mouse support.

Options

–auto_indent	Indents new lines to match line above.
–background red green blue	Sets background color to **red green blue** values.
–background color	Uses **color** for window background.

–bg color	Uses **color** for window background.
–display host: disp_num	Connects to **disp_num** numbered X server (almost always 0) on given **host**.
–Ei on	Indents new lines to match line above.
–Ei off	Does not indent new lines to match line above.
–En lines	Sets number of lines in window to **lines**.
–Eo on	Allows you to overwrite an existing file.
–Eo off	Presents an error if you try to overwrite an existing file.
–Er on	Prevents you from changing a file; the default is off.
–Er off	Allows you to change files; the default.
–fg color	Uses **color** for window foreground.
–fn fontname	Uses given font.
–font fontname	Uses given font.
–foreground_color red green blue	Sets foreground color to **red green blue** values.
–foreground color	Uses color for window foreground.
–geometry *Width***x** *Height* + x + y	Sets window size and position.
–geometry *Width***x** *Height*	Sets window size.
–geometry + x + y	Sets position of window's upper-left corner.
–height rows	Sets height of base window, in rows.
–number_of_lines lines	Sets number of lines in window to **lines**.
–okay_to_ overwrite	Allows you to overwrite an existing file.
–position x y	Sets location of upper-left corner of window, in pixels.
–read_only	Prevents you from changing a file.
–reverse	Reverses foreground and background colors.
–rv	Reverses foreground and background colors.
–size width height	Sets base window size, in pixels to **width** x **height**.

8

-Wb red green blue	Sets background color to **red green blue** values.
–**Wf** red green blue	Sets foreground color to **red green blue** values.
–**WG** *Width*x*Height* +x+y	Sets window size and position.
–**WG** *Width*x*Height*	Sets window size.
–**WG** +x+y	Sets position of window's upper-left corner.
–**Wh** rows	Sets height of base window, in **rows**.
–**Wi**	Starts window as an icon.
–**width** columns	Sets width of base window, in **columns**.
–**Wp** x y	Sets location of upper-left corner of window, in pixels.
–**Wr** host:disp_num	Connects to **disp_num** numbered X server (almost always 0) on given **host**.
–**Ws** width height	Sets base window size, in pixels to **width** x **height**.
–**Wt** fontname	Uses given font.
-**Ww** columns	Sets width of base window, in **columns**.

8

Related Commands

dtpad Common Desktop Environment text editor.

xedit Text editor.

toolwait — Wait For X Program to Start

toolwait *options* application *args*

Purpose

Starts an X application, then waits for the application to start up and create windows. The application and any necessary arguments for the application appear at the end of the **toolwait** command.

Examples

```
$ toolwait xclock -digital
```

Starts the **xclock** and passes the **-digital** option to **xclock**.

```
$ toolwait -timeout 5 xclock -digital
```

Starts the **xclock** and passes the **-digital** option to **xclock**, waiting a maximum of 5 seconds for **xclock** to start up.

OPTION

–display host: disp_num	Connects to **disp_num** numbered X server (almost always 0) on given **host**.
application *args*	Runs **application** and passes arguments *args* to the program.

twm — Tab Window Manager

twm *options*

8

Purpose

Provides a window manager that controls the size and location of all windows on the screen. Window managers also create the titlebars, many of which are very distinctive.

Options

–display host: disp_num	Connects to **disp_num** numbered X server (almost always 0) on given **host**.
–f initfile	Uses **initfile** instead of **.twmrc** in your home directory to configure **twm**.
–s	Manage only windows on the default screen. (Few systems have more than one screen, anyway.)
-v	Prints verbose error messages.

Related Commands

dtwm	Common Desktop Environment window manager.

mwm	Motif window manager.
olwm	Open Look window manager.

X — X Server

X *options*

Purpose

X is the actual X server program, normally started by **openwin**, **startx**, **xdm**, or **xinit**. X controls the monitor screen, keyboard, and mouse. Sometimes the X program has an extended name, such as **Xsun** on Sun Solaris systems.

Options

Some special X servers accept extra options. The options listed here are used by all X servers.

–a acceleration	Sets mouse **acceleration** ratio; defaults to 2.
–audit level	Sets audit trail **level**; defaults to 1. Level 2 logs more information about client applications that connect to the X server. Level 0 disables auditing.
–bs	Disables backing store.
–c	Turns off key click sounds.
c volume	Sets key click volume to a value from 0 to 100.
–co *filename*	Uses **filename** for the database of color names.
–core	Server dumps a core file on errors.
–dpi resolution	Sets screen **resolution** in dots per inch. Used when the X server cannot figure this out on its own.
–f volume	Sets bell volume to a value from 0 to 100.
–fc cursor_font	Uses **cursor_font** as font for cursor shapes, defaults to **cursor**.

–fn font	Uses **font** for the default font.
–fp path1,path2,...	Sets list of directories searched for fonts to a comma-delimited list of directories.
–help	Prints a summary of the command-line options.
–I	Ignores everything after the **–I**.
–logo	Uses X logo in screen saver.
–nologo	Doesn't use X logo in screen saver.
–p minutes	Sets screen saver pattern cycle time to given number of **minutes**.
–pn	Tells server to continue running if a number of socket connections fail, but it gets at least one successfully set up.
–r	Turns off keyboard auto-repeat.
r	Turns on keyboard auto-repeat.
–s minutes	Sets screen saver timeout to given number of **minutes**.
–su	Disables save under support for all windows.
–t number	Sets mouse acceleration threshold in pixels.
–terminate	Terminates server instead of resetting.
–to seconds	Sets connection timeout to **seconds**, defaults to 60.
–tst	Disables all testing extensions including **XTEST**, **XTestExtension1**, and **XTrap**.
–v	Tells screen saver to leave video on.
v	Tells screen saver to turn video off.

Related Commands

openwin	Starts X server in OpenWindows.
startx	Starts X server.
xdm	X display manager.
xinit	Starts X server.
xset	Sets X server values.

xauth — Create Authorization File

xauth *options* command arguments
xauth command arguments

Purpose

Creates and modifies a file that controls who can access an X server. **Xauth** has a finer grain of control than **xhost**, which allows any user on a given host to access your display. Table 8-3 provides descriptions of **xauth** commands.

Table 8-3 *Xauth Commands*

Command	Meaning
add *display protocol hexkey*	Adds an entry for the given **display**; a period (.) is shorthand for a protocol of **MIT-MAGIC-COOKIE-1**.
extract *filename* display	Extracts entries for **display** and writes to **filename**; - means **stdout**.
nextract *filename display*	Extracts entries for **display** and writes to **filename** using numeric format; - means **stdout**.
list *display*	Lists all entries for a given **display**.
nlist *display*	Lists all entries for a given **display** using numeric output.
merge *filename*	Merges entries from **filename**; - means **stdin**.
nmerge *filename*	Merges entries from **filename** using numeric format; - means **stdin**.
remove display	Removes all entries for **display**.
source *filename*	Treats **filename** as a script of **xauth** commands.
info	Prints info on authority file.
exit	Exits and saves authority file.

Continued

Table 8-3 *Continued*

Command	Meaning
quit	Exits and doesn't save authority file.
help	Lists all **xauth** commands.
help string	Lists all **xauth** commands starting with **string**.
?	Prints short help message.

Examples

```
$ xauth add `hostname`/unix:0 . 6666
```

Adds an X authority entry for **unix:0**, a common default display name, using the **hostname** command to get the current hostname. The period tells **xauth** to use the **MIT-MAGIC-COOKIE-1** protocol, the default protocol. The number 6666 is a random number made up for the occasion.

```
$ xauth add eric:0 . 6666
```

8

Adds an X authority entry for the display name of **eric:0**, the first X server on machine **eric**. Again, the default protocol and the random number 6666 are used.

```
$ xauth list

DISPLAY NAME PROTOCOL NAME          DISPLAY KEY
============ =============          ===========
unix:0       MIT-MAGIC-COOKIE-1     6666
eric:0       MIT-MAGIC-COOKIE-1     6666
```

Prints a list of all the displays in the **.Xauthority** file.

```
$ xauth extract - $DISPLAY | \
   rsh eric xauth merge -
```

Extracts all X authority entries for the current display and passes them on over the network to another program, merging these entries in with the authority file on the target machine, **eric**. This is a very common use of **xauth**, passing the information needed to log on from one display to another.

Options

–b	Breaks any file locks on the authorization file.
–f authfile	Tells **xauth** to use **authfile** as the authorization file. The default is the file named in the **XAUTHORITY** environment variable or a file named **.Xauthority** in your home directory.
–i	Ignores file locks on the authorization file.
–q	Runs in quiet mode and doesn't print out messages.
-v	Runs in verbose mode and prints out lots of messages to explain what is going on.

Related Commands

rsh	Remote shell.
xdm	X Display Manager.
xhost	Controls access to X server.

xbiff — Announce New E-mail

8

xbiff *options*

Purpose

Announces new e-mail messages.

Options

–bd color	Uses **color** for window border.
–bg color	Uses **color** for window background.
–bw num_pixels	Sets border to **num_pixels** wide.
-display host: disp_num	Connects to **disp_num** numbered X server (almost always 0) on given **host**.
–file *filename*	Uses **filename** instead of default mailbox file, **/usr/spool/mail/**username.
–fg color	Uses **color** for window foreground.

–geometry *Width***x** *Height* + x + y	Sets window size and position.
–geometry *Width***x** *Height*	Sets window size.
–geometry + x + y	Sets position of window's upper-left corner.
–help	Prints a summary of the command-line options.
–rv	Reverses foreground and background colors.
–shape	Uses a nonrectangular window.
–update secs	Checks for incoming e-mail every **secs** seconds.
-**volume** percentage	Sets volume of bell from 0 to 100.

Related Commands

dtmail	Common Desktop Environment e-mail program.
mailtool	Open Look e-mail program.

8

xcalc — Calculator

xcalc *options*

Purpose

Performs calculations.

Options

–background color	Uses **color** for window background.
–bd color	Uses **color** for window border.
–bg color	Uses **color** for window background.
–bordercolor color	Uses **color** for window border.
–borderwidth num _pixels	Sets border to **num_pixels** wide.
–bw num_pixels	Sets border to **num_pixels** wide.
–display host: disp_num	Connects to **disp_num** numbered X server (almost always 0) on given **host**.

–**fg** color	Uses **color** for window foreground.
–**fn** fontname	Uses given font.
–**font** fontname	Uses given font.
–**foreground** color	Uses **color** for window foreground.
–**geometry** *Width***x** *Height* + x + y	Sets window size and position.
–**geometry** *Width***x** *Height*	Sets window size.
–**geometry** + x + y	Sets position of window's upper-left corner.
–**iconic**	Starts window as an icon.
–**reverse**	Reverses foreground and background colors.
–**rpn**	Uses Reverse Polish Notation.
–**rv**	Reverses foreground and background colors.
-**stipple**	Draws background using a stipple of the foreground and background colors, which makes **xcalc** look better on monochrome systems.

Related Command

dtcalc Common Desktop Environment calculator utility.

8

xclipboard — Show Clipboard

xclipboard *options*

Purpose

Displays the contents of the clipboard and allows you to select that text for pasting into applications.

Options

–**background** color	Uses **color** for window background.
–**bd** color	Uses **color** for window border.
–**bg** color	Uses **color** for window background.
–**bordercolor** color	Uses **color** for window border.

–borderwidth num _pixels	Sets border to **num_pixels** wide.
–bw num_pixels	Sets border to **num_pixels** wide.
–display host: disp_num	Connects to **disp_num** numbered X server (almost always 0) on given **host**.
–fg color	Uses **color** for window foreground.
–fn fontname	Uses given font.
–font fontname	Uses given font.
–foreground color	Uses **color** for window foreground.
–geometry *Width***x** *Height* + x + y	Sets window size and position.
–geometry *Width***x** *Height*	Sets window size.
–geometry + x + y	Sets position of window's upper-left corner.
–iconic	Starts window as an icon.
–nw	Doesn't wrap long lines of text; this is the default.
–reverse	Reverses foreground and background colors.
–rv	Reverses foreground and background colors.
-w	Wraps long lines of text.

8

Related Commands

dtpad	Common Desktop Environment text editor.
textedit	Open Look text editor.
xedit	X text editor.

xclock — Display Current Time

xclock *options*

Purpose

Displays the time in a window.

Examples

```
$ xclock -digital
```

Displays a digital clock.

```
$ xclock -analog -padding 50 -update 1
```

Displays an analog clock face with 50 pixels of empty space around the clock in all directions, updating every second with a second hand.

Options

–analog	Displays an analog clock (with hands).
–background color	Uses **color** for window background.
–bd color	Uses **color** for window border.
–bg color	Uses **color** for window background.
–bordercolor color	Uses **color** for window border.
–borderwidth num_pixels	Sets border to **num_pixels** wide.
–bw num_pixels	Sets border to **num_pixels** wide.
–chime	Chimes once on the half hour and twice on the hour.
–d	Displays a 24-hour digital clock.
–digital	Displays a 24-hour digital clock.
–display host:disp_num	Connects to **disp_num** numbered X server (almost always 0) on given **host**.
–fg color	Uses **color** for window foreground.
–fn fontname	Uses given font.
–font fontname	Uses given font.
–foreground color	Uses **color** for window foreground.
–geometry *Width***x** *Height* + x + y	Sets window size and position.
–geometry *Width***x** *Height*	Sets window size.
–geometry + x + y	Sets position of window's upper-left corner.

8

–hands color	Sets the hands to display using the given **color**.
–h color	Sets the hands to display using the given **color**.
–highlight color	Sets the **color** for the edges of the clock hands.
–help	Prints a summary of the command-line options.
–hl color	Sets the **color** for the edges of the clock hands.
–iconic	Starts window as an icon.
–padding pixels	Sets number of **pixels** of blank space between the border and the clock.
–reverse	Reverses foreground and background colors.
–rv	Reverses foreground and background colors.
-**update** seconds	Controls update interval. If less than 30 seconds, **xclock** will display a second hand. In that case, it is best to update each second.

Related Commands

clock	Open Look clock.
oclock	Rounded clock.

xcmap — Display Colormap

xcmap *options*

Purpose

Displays the contents of the default colormap. This is useful for helping with color problems.

Options

–display host:disp_num	Connects to **disp_num** numbered X server (almost always 0) on given **host**.

–geometry *Width***x** *Height* + x + y	Sets window size and position.
–geometry *Width***x** *Height*	Sets window size.
-geometry + x + y	Sets position of window's upper-left corner.

xconsole — Display System Messages

xconsole *options*

Purpose

Displays system console messages in a window.

Options

–background color	Uses **color** for window background.
–bd color	Uses **color** for window border.
–bg color	Uses **color** for window background.
–bordercolor color	Uses **color** for window border.
–borderwidth num_pixels	Sets border to **num_pixels** wide.
–bw num_pixels	Sets border to **num_pixels** wide.
–daemon	Runs in the background.
–display host:disp_num	Connects to **disp_num** numbered X server (almost always 0) on given **host**.
–exitOnFail	Tells **xconsole** to exit if it cannot redirect the console output.
–fn fontname	Uses given font.
–font fontname	Uses given font.
–foreground color	Uses **color** for window foreground.
–geometry *Width***x** *Height* + x + y	Sets window size and position.
–geometry *Width***x** *Height*	Sets window size.
–geometry + x + y	Sets position of window's upper-left corner.
–iconic	Starts window as an icon.

8

–notify	If iconified, adds a "*" to the icon name to let you know a system message has arrived; the default.
–nonotify	Doesn't change icon name to notify of new messages.
–reverse	Reverses foreground and background colors.
–rv	Reverses foreground and background colors.
-verbose	Displays an informative message in the text buffer.

Related Command

xterm	Shell window.

xditview — Display Ditroff Output

xditview *options*

Purpose

8

Displays **ditroff** output files from the device-independent suite of formatting programs called **ditroff**.

Options

–backingStore backing_store	Set to **Always** or **WhenMapped** to improve performance when redisplaying pages; leave at **NotUseful** if performance is OK.
–background color	Uses **color** for window background.
–bd color	Uses **color** for window border.
–bg color	Uses **color** for window background.
–bordercolor color	Uses **color** for window border.
–borderwidth num _pixels	Sets border to **num_pixels** wide.
–bw num_pixels	Sets border to **num_pixels** wide.
–display host:disp_ num	Connects to **disp_num** numbered X server (almost always 0) on given **host**.
–fg color	Uses **color** for window foreground.

–fn fontname	Uses given font.
–font fontname	Uses given font.
–foreground_color red green blue	Sets foreground color to **red green blue** values.
–foreground color	Uses **color** for window foreground.
–geometry *Width*x *Height* + x + y	Sets window size and position.
–geometry *Width*x *Height*	Sets window size.
–geometry + x + y	Sets position of window's upper-left corner.
–iconic	Starts window as an icon.
–noPolyText	If text is displayed improperly, this may correct the situation.
–page page_number	Starts with given page.
–resolution screen _resolution	Sets screen resolution used when choosing fonts.
–reverse	Reverses foreground and background colors.
-rv	Reverses foreground and background colors.

8

xdm — X Display Manager

xdm *options*

Purpose

Manages X displays. **Xdm** presents a graphical login screen and starts your X session. If you don't have a graphical login screen, then chances are you use **openwin**, **startx**, or **xinit** to start your X session instead of **xdm**.

Normally, **xdm** starts at machine boot time from an entry in /etc/**inittab**, so you will rarely start it from a command line.

Options

–config config_file	Uses **config_file** as the configuration file rather than the default, which is typically **/var/X11/xdm/xdm–config** or **/usr/lib/X11/xdm/xdm–config**.

–debug debug_level	Any value above 0 causes **xdm** to run synchronously and print lots of debugging information.
–error log_file	Errors get logged to the given **log_file**.
–nodaemon	Stops **xdm** from running in the background as a daemon process.
–resources res_file	Names a resource file that customizes the login widget.
–server server_entry	Lists the X servers that **xdm** should manage. An entry for the local machine appears like the following: **:0 local /usr/X11/bin/X :0**
–session session_program	Names the program to run as a session when the user logs in.
-udpPort port_number	Sets the UDP network port for **xdm** to monitor.

Related Commands

openwin	Starts OpenWindows X server.
startx	Starts X server.
X	X server.
xinit	Initializes X server.

xdpr — Dump Window and Print

xdpr *options*
xdpr *filename options*

Purpose

Acts as a front end to **xwd**, **xpr** and **lp** or **lpr**. **Xwd** captures a screen image, **xpr** prepares the image to print and **lp** or **lpr** prints the image. **Xdpr** combines all this into one handy command. If you pass an **xwd**-captured filename to **xdpr**, it prints that file rather than capturing a screen image.

Example

```
$ xdpr -device ps -Pmyhp
```

Captures a screen image, formats the image for a PostScript printer, and sends the results to the printer named **myhp**.

Options

–device devtype	Names the output device type: **la100** (Digital LA100), **ljet** (HP LaserJet), **ln03** (Digital LN03), **pjet** (HP PaintJet in color), **pjetxl** (HP PaintJet XL color), **pp** (IBM PP3812), or **ps** (generic PostScript).
–display host: disp_num	Connects to **disp_num** numbered X server (almost always 0) on given **host**.
–help	Prints a summary of the command-line options.
-**P**printer	Names the **printer** to use for printing. Note there is no space after the -**P**.

Any other options get passed on to **xwd**, **xpr**, **lp** or **lpr**, as appropriate.

8

Related Commands

lp	Prints files.
lpr	Prints files.
xpr	Prints X screen image.
xwd	Captures X screen image.

xdpyinfo — X Display Information

xdpyinfo option

Purpose

Prints information about your graphics display, much of which is confusing.

Examples

```
$ xdpyinfo
```

This prints information on your default X server, normally the screen in front of you.

```
$ xdpyinfo | more
```

This prints information on your default X server, and sends the reams of output to the **more** command to display it one page at a time.

```
$ xdpyinfo -display yonsen:0
```

This prints information on X server **yonsen:0**, the first—often only—X server running on a machine named **yonsen**.

OPTION

-display host: disp_num	Connects to **disp_num** numbered X server (almost always 0) on given **host**.

Related Commands

more	Display file.
X	X server.
xrdb	Loads X resource files.
xwininfo	Prints information on windows.

xdvi — Preview DVI Documents

xdvi *options filename*

Purpose

Previews DVI files, which are created by TeX.

Options

+	Displays last page.
+page_number	Displays page numbered **page_number**.

–expert	Works in expert mode; doesn't display interface buttons.
–hush	Avoids displaying warning messages.
–hushchars	Avoids displaying warnings about characters not in the current font.
–thorough	Ensures that overstrike characters get properly displayed on color screens.
-version	Prints version number and exits.

Related Command

ghostview Views PostScript Documents.

xedit — Text Editor

xedit *options filename*

Purpose

Edits text files in a window.

Example

```
$ xedit sigs.txt
```

Edits file **sigs.txt**.

Options

–background color	Uses **color** for window background.
–bd color	Uses **color** for window border.
–bg color	Uses **color** for window background.
–bordercolor color	Uses **color** for window border.
–borderwidth num _pixels	Sets border to **num_pixels** wide.
–bw num_pixels	Sets border to **num_pixels** wide.
–display host: disp_num	Connects to **disp_num** numbered X server (almost always 0) on given **host**.
–fg color	Uses **color** for window foreground.

8

–fn fontname	Uses given font.
–font fontname	Uses given font.
–foreground color	Uses **color** for window foreground.
–geometry *Width*x *Height* + x + y	Sets window size and position.
–geometry *Width*x *Height*	Sets window size.
–geometry + x + y	Sets position of window's upper-left corner.
–iconic	Starts window as an icon.
–reverse	Reverses foreground and background colors.
-rv	Reverses foreground and background colors.

Related Commands

dtpad	Desktop Text Editor.
textedit	Open Look Text Editor.

8

xfd — Display Font

xfd *options fn fontname*

Purpose

Displays the characters in a font. **Xfd** is better for showing all of a font, while **xfontsel** is better for choosing a font.

Example

```
$ xfd -fn "-*-courier-medium-r-normal-*-240-*-*-m-*-*"
```

Displays a Courier font.

Options

–bc color	Uses **color** for boxes with the **–box** option.
–background color	Uses **color** for window background.
–bd color	Uses **color** for window border.

–bg color	Uses **color** for window background.
–bordercolor color	Uses **color** for window border.
–borderwidth num _pixels	Sets border to **num_pixels** wide.
–box	Shows a box around the actual extents of each character in the font.
–bw num_pixels	Sets border to **num_pixels** wide.
–center	Centers each character in its grid.
–columns numcols	Sets the number of columns in the grid display.
–display host: disp_num	Connects to **disp_num** numbered X server (almost always 0) on given **host**.
–fg color	Uses **color** for window foreground.
–fn fontname	Uses given font.
–font fontname	Uses given font.
-**foreground_color** red green blue	Sets foreground color to **red green blue** values.
–foreground color	Uses color for window foreground.
–geometry *Width***x** *Height* + x + y	Sets window size and position.
–geometry *Width***x** *Height*	Sets window size.
–geometry + x + y	Sets position of window's upper-left corner.
–iconic	Starts window as an icon.
–reverse	Reverses foreground and background colors.
–rows numrows	Sets the number of rows in the grid display.
–rv	Reverses foreground and background colors.
-**start** number	Starts with the character at the given position in the font. Defaults to 0.

Related Command

xfontsel	Selects fonts.
xlsfonts	List fonts.

xfontsel — Select Fonts

xfontsel *options*

Purpose

Displays fonts that match a pattern. You can use this to select a desired font style and size.

Examples

```
$ xfontsel -sample "Help me choose a font"
```

Starts **xfontsel** and uses given text to show current font.

```
$ xfontsel -pattern "*adobe*"
```

Selects only **adobe** fonts.

NOTE

Since this pattern has asterisks, you need to enclose the pattern in double quotes or it will be interpreted by your shell and not by the **xfontsel** program.

8

Options

–background color	Uses **color** for window background.
–bd color	Uses **color** for window border.
–bg color	Uses **color** for window background.
–bordercolor color	Uses **color** for window border.
–borderwidth num_pixels	Sets border to **num_pixels** wide.
–bw num_pixels	Sets border to **num_pixels** wide.
–display host:disp_num	Connects to **disp_num** numbered X server (almost always 0) on given **host**.
–fg color	Uses **color** for window foreground.
–fn fontname	Uses given font.
–font fontname	Uses given font.
–foreground color	Uses **color** for window foreground.

–geometry *Width***x** *Height* + x + y	Sets window size and position.
–geometry *Width***x** *Height*	Sets window size.
–geometry + x + y	Sets position of window's upper-left corner.
–iconic	Starts window as an icon.
–noscaled	Doesn't display scaled fonts.
–pattern partial_ fontname	Displays only fonts whose names match **partial_fontname**. Enclose this pattern in double quotes.
–print	Prints selected font name to screen at exit.
–reverse	Reverses foreground and background colors.
–rv	Reverses foreground and background colors.
-sample sample_text	Uses **sample_text** rather than alphabet.

Related Commands

xfd	Displays font.
xlsfonts	Lists fonts.

8

xfs — Font Server

xfs *options*

Purpose

Launches the X font server (previously known as **fs** — without the **x**), which can provide fonts to the X server. It normally adds the ability to scale fonts to a requested size.

Options

–config configuration _file	Sets the configuration file.
-port tcp_port	Sets the TCP port number on which the font server will listen for connections.

Related Commands

fsinfo	Gets information on font server.
fslsfonts	Lists fonts provided by a font server.

xhost — Allow Others Access

xhost *options*

Purpose

Controls which machines — hosts — can access your X server. Once it is enabled, any user on that machine can connect to your X server. This creates a potential security risk, as a user could track all the keystrokes you enter (including passwords).

Example

```
$ xhost +eric
```

Allows any user on machine **eric** to connect to your X server.

8

Options

+hostname	Allows any user on host **hostname** to connect to your display.
–hostname	Disallows any user on host **hostname** to connect to your display.
+	Allows any user on any machine to connect to your display.
-	Disallow any extra machines access beyond the list that **X** starts up with (usually just your machine).

Related Command

xauth	Creates authorization file.

xinit — Initialize X Server

xinit client_*options* -- server_*options*

Purpose

Initializes X server. Normally, **xinit** is run from a script such as **startx**. By default, the **client_options** are stored in a file named **.xinitrc** in your home directory and the server options in a file named **.xserverrc**. In most cases, you don't need any **server_options**.

Examples

```
$ xinit
```

Starts X server program X and uses **.xinitrc** in your home directory to name the applications to start. If there is no **.xinitrc** file, it starts **xterm**.

```
$ xinit -- /usr/bin/X11/X -bpp 16
```

Starts X server with 16 bits-per-plane rather than the default 8 bits of color.

```
$ xinit -- /usr/bin/X11/X -auth $HOME/.Xauthority
```

Starts X server using the authorization file **$HOME/.Xauthority** in your home directory. Usually, **xauth** would create this file for use by **X**.

Options

The client options may be either a program to launch in place of the commands in the **.xinitrc** file or options to the default **xterm** program (if no **.xinitrc** file exists in your home directory).

The server options may be either a program to use in place of **X** — the X server — along with options for that program, or options to **X**.

CROSS-REFERENCE

See entry in this chapter on X for the server options.

Related Commands

startx	Starts X server.
X	X server.
xauth	Creates authorization file to control access to X server.
xdm	X display manager.

xkill — Kill Errant Programs

xkill *options*

Purpose

Kills a window and usually the program that created the window. This is useful for stopping runaway programs.

Options

-all	Kills all top-level windows.
-button number	Determines which mouse button (normally 1 to 3) is used to select the window. Useful for killing popup windows. Defaults to leftmost mouse button, 1.
-display host: disp_num	Connects to **disp_num** numbered X server (almost always 0) on given **host**.
-frame	Kills framing window rather than window inside a window-manager frame.
-id ID	Names the window **ID** to kill. If you omit this, **xkill** asks you to select a window with the mouse.

Related Command

xwininfo	Prints information on windows.

xload — View System Load

xload *options*

Purpose

Displays system load average.

Examples

```
$ xload -highlight maroon -jumpscroll 1
```

Starts **xload** with maroon-colored scale lines and smooth scrolling.

```
$ xload -fg red -bg lightgrey
```

Starts **xload** with a graph line color of red and a background color of light grey.

Options

–background color	Uses **color** for window background.
–bd color	Uses **color** for window border.
–bg color	Uses **color** for window background.
–bordercolor color	Uses **color** for window border.
–borderwidth num _pixels	Sets border to **num_pixels** wide.
–bw num_pixels	Sets border to **num_pixels** wide.
–display host: disp_num	Connects to **disp_num** numbered X server (almost always 0) on given **host**.
–fg color	Uses **color** for window foreground.
–fn fontname	Uses given font.
–font fontname	Uses given font.
–foreground color	Uses **color** for window foreground.
–geometry *Width***x** *Height* + x + y	Sets window size and position.
–geometry *Width***x** *Height*	Sets window size.

8

-geometry +x+y	Sets position of window's upper-left corner.
-hl color	Uses **color** for scale lines.
-highlight color	Uses **color** for scale lines.
-iconic	Starts window as an icon.
-jumpscroll pixels	Specifies number of **pixels** to shift graph to left when it reaches the end of the window.
-jumpscroll	Uses smooth scrolling.
-label string	**String** appears above graph as a label. Default label is system host name.
-lights	Uses keyboard LEDs instead of a window to display load.
-nolabel	Doesn't display a label.
-reverse	Reverses foreground and background colors.
-rv	Reverses foreground and background colors.
-scale number	Sets minimum number of tick-marks in graph to **number**.
-update seconds	Sets interval in **seconds** between updates to be displayed. Defaults to 10.

8

xlock — Lock Screen

xlock *options*

Purpose

Locks display until you enter your password. The screen is blanked with a display based on the mode selected.

Examples

```
$ xlock -mode bouboule
```

Locks screen with moving dots display.

```
$ xlock -mode world
```

Locks screen and displays spinning globes.

Options

–**batchcount** num	Controls number of things based on the mode. For example, in **ant** mode, **num** controls the number of ants.
–**bg** color	Uses **color** for window background.
–**cycles** num	Sets number of cycles until a timeout.
–**delay** usecs	Sets speed for mode drawing in microseconds.
–**display** host: disp_num	Connects to **disp_num** numbered X server (almost always 0) on given **host**.
–**fg** color	Uses **color** for window foreground.
–**font** fontname	Uses given font.
–**lockdelay** seconds	Sets number of seconds before you need to enter a password. Good for stopping **xlock** before it kicks in.
-**mode** mode	Selects mode to blank screen: **ant**, **bat**, **blank**, **blot**, **bouboule**, **bounce**, **braid**, **bug**, **clock**, **demon**, **eyes**, **flag**, **flame**, **forest**, **galaxy**, **geometry**, **grav**, **helix**, **hop**, **hyper**, **image**, **kaleid**, **laser**, **life**, **life1d**, **life3d**, **lissie**, **marquee**, **maze**, **mountain**, **nose**, **petal**, **puzzle**, **pyro**, **qix**, **random**, **rock**, **rotor**, **shape**, **slip**, **sphere**, **spiral**, **spline**, **swarm**, **swirl**, **triangle**, **wator**, **world**, or **worm**.

xlogo — Display X Window Logo

xlogo *options*

Purpose

Displays X Window System logo in a window.

Options

–**background** color	Uses **color** for window background.
–**bd** color	Uses **color** for window border.

–bg color	Uses **color** for window background.
–bordercolor color	Uses **color** for window border.
–borderwidth num _pixels	Sets border to **num_pixels** wide.
–bw num_pixels	Sets border to **num_pixels** wide.
–display host: disp_num	Connects to **disp_num** numbered X server (almost always 0) on given **host**.
–fg color	Uses **color** for window foreground.
–fn fontname	Uses given font.
–font fontname	Uses given font.
–foreground color	Uses **color** for window foreground.
–geometry *Width***x** *Height* + x + y	Sets window size and position.
–geometry *Width***x** *Height*	Sets window size.
–geometry + x + y	Sets position of window's upper-left corner.
–iconic	Starts window as an icon.
–reverse	Reverses foreground and background colors.
–rv	Reverses foreground and background colors.
-shape	Creates a window that is shaped (i.e., X-shaped) rather than rectangular.

xlsfonts — List Fonts

xlsfonts *options*

Purpose

Lists fonts available to the X server.

Examples

```
$ xlsfonts | grep courier
```

Lists all fonts and pipes output to **grep**, which searches for the text string **courier**.

```
$ xlsfonts -lll | more
```

Lists all fonts, producing copious output including character metrics, and pipes results to **more**.

Options

–1	(One) Prints output using only one column; this is the same as **–n 1**.
–C	Prints output in multiple columns; this is the same as **–n 0**.
–display host: disp_num'	Connects to **disp_num** numbered X server (almost always 0) on given **host**.
–fn pattern	Lists fonts that match the **pattern**. * and ? wildcards are allowed. Omitting the pattern is the same as *.
–l	(Ell) Lists some attributes of fonts as well as names.
–ll	(Ell ell) Lists font properties in addition to output from **–l** option.
–lll	(Ell ell ell) Prints all of **–ll** output as well as character metrics.
–m	Prints minimum and maximum bounds of each font.
–n columns	Sets number of columns to **columns**.
–o	Gets information on fonts by an alternate means; this is useful if normal listing fails.
–u	Doesn't sort output.
-w width	Sets total width of output to width characters.

Related Commands

fslsfonts	List fonts provided by font server.
more	Display file.
xfontsel	Selects fonts.
xlsfonts	List fonts.

xmag — Magnify Part of Screen

xmag *options*

Purpose

Captures a small screen image and enlarges the data so you can see individual pixels.

Options

–background color	Uses **color** for window background.
–bd color	Uses **color** for window border.
–bg color	Uses **color** for window background.
–bordercolor color	Uses **color** for window border.
–borderwidth num _pixels	Sets border to **num_pixels** wide.
–bw num_pixels	Sets border to **num_pixels** wide.
–display host: disp_num	Connects to **disp_num** numbered X server (almost always 0) on given **host**.
–fg color	Uses **color** for window foreground.
–fn fontname	Uses given font.
–font fontname	Uses given font.
–foreground color	Uses **color** for window foreground.
–geometry *Width***x** *Height* + x + y	Sets window size and position.
–geometry *Width***x** *Height*	Sets window size.
–geometry + x + y	Sets position of window's upper-left corner.
–iconic	Starts window as an icon.
–mag factor	Magnifies by the given **factor**, which defaults to 5.
–reverse	Reverses foreground and background colors.
–rv	Reverses foreground and background colors.
–source *Width***x** *Height* + x + y	Sets source area size and position.

8

–source *Width***x** *Height*	Sets source area size.
-source +x+y	Sets source area upper-left corner. If you don't use a **-source** option, **xmag** asks you to select an area to magnify using the mouse.

xman — View Online Manuals

xman *options*

Purpose

Displays online manuals.

Examples

```
$ xman &
```

Starts **xman** in background.

```
$ xman -bothshown
```

Show both manual entries and the list of available entries.

```
$ xman -notopbox
```

Skips small control window and displays manual entry right away.

Options

–background red green blue	Sets background color to **red green blue** values.
–background color	Uses **color** for window background.
–bd color	Uses **color** for window border.
–bg color	Uses **color** for window background.
–bordercolor color	Uses **color** for window border.
–borderwidth num_pixels	Sets border to **num_pixels** wide.
–bothshown	Shows both manual entries and list of available entries.

-bw num_pixels	Sets border to **num_pixels** wide.
-display host: disp_num	Connects to **disp_num** numbered X server (almost always 0) on given host.
-fg color	Uses **color** for window foreground.
-fn fontname	Uses given font.
-font fontname	Uses given font.
-foreground color	Uses **color** for window foreground.
-geometry *Width***x** *Height* + x + y	Sets window size and position.
-geometry *Width***x** *Height*	Sets window size.
-geometry + x + y	Sets position of window's upper-left corner.
-iconic	Starts window as an icon.
-notopbox	Doesn't display small control panel window.
-pagesize *Width*x *Height* + x + y	Displays manual pages in window at given size and location.
-reverse	Reverses foreground and background colors.
-rv	Reverses foreground and background colors.

8

Related Command

man	Prints online manual.

xpr — Print Window Dump

xpr *options*
xpr *options filename*

Purpose

Formats an image captured by **xwd** and prepares the image for printing. If you pass a filename, **xpr** formats that file. Otherwise, **xpr** expects data from standard input. The output is sent to standard output unless you specify the **-output** option.

Example

```
$ xpr -device ps capture1.xwd | lp
```

Formats a previously captured image in file **capture1.xwd** for a PostScript printer and pipes the results to the **lp** command.

Options

–append *filename*	Appends output to **filename**.
–compact	Compresses windows with lots of white pixels using run-length encoding.
–cutoff level	Sets cutoff **level** where colors get mapped to black or white to level percentage of full brightness.
–density dpi	Sets dot-per-inch density for HP printers.
–device devtype	Names the output device type: **la100** (Digital LA100), **ljet** (HP LaserJet), **ln03** (Digital LN03), **pjet** (HP PaintJet in color), **pjetxl** (HP PaintJet XL color), **pp** (IBM PP3812), or **ps** (generic PostScript).
–gamma correction	Changes intensity of colors for PaintJet XL printers to a **correction** value between 0.00 and 3.00, set according to the printer's manual.
–gray 2	Uses a 2x2 grayscale conversion.
–gray 3	Uses a 3x3 grayscale conversion.
-**gray 4**	Uses a 4x4 grayscale conversion.
–header text	Uses **text** as a header printed above the image.
–height inches	Sets maximum height of output.
–landscape	Sets landscape output.
–left inches	Sets left margin.
–output *filename*	Sends output to **filename** rather than to standard output.
–noff	With **–append**, appends image to same page as previous image.
–noposition	Bypasses header, trailer, and positioning for HP LaserJet, PaintJet, and PaintJet XL printers.
–plane number	Uses only the given bitplane of the color image.

–portrait	Sets portrait output.
–psfig	Doesn't translate PostScript output to center of page.
–render algorithm	Renders image using named **algorithm** from HP PaintJet XL manual.
–rv	Reverses foreground and background colors in output.
–scale scale	Sets scaling factor for output.
–slide	Allows HP PaintJet and PaintJet XL printers to create overhead transparencies.
–split num_pages	Splits image into a number of pages.
–top inches	Sets top margin.
–trailer text	Uses **text** as a footer printed below the image.
-width inches	Sets maximum width of output.

Related Commands

lp	Prints files.
lpr	Prints files.
xdpr	Captures and prints X screen image.
xwd	Captures X screen image.

xprop — Print Window Properties

xprop *options*

Purpose

Returns window property information for a given window. You can either specify the window as a command-line option or select the window with the mouse.

X uses window properties to store data about windows, such as requests to the window manager, data exchange, and other information. The root window has interesting properties.

Options

-display host: disp_num	Connects to **disp_num** numbered X server (almost always 0) on given **host**.
-font font	Prints properties of given **font**, rather than of a window.
-frame	Selects window-manager frame, rather than window inside frame.
-grammar	Prints detailed information on command-line options.
-help	Prints a summary of the command-line options.
-id ID	Prints information for given window **ID**.
-len length	Prints at most **length** bytes of any property.
-name name	Prints information for window with given **name**.
-notype	Doesn't print the types of properties.
-remove prop_ name	Removes named property from window.
-root	Prints information for root window (screen background).
-spy	Keeps checking for property change events and prints them out as they occur.

8

Related Commands

xwininfo	Prints window information.
xrdb	Loads resource files.

xrdb — Loads Resource Files

xrdb *options*
xrdb *options filename*

Purpose

Maintains a database of X resource values. With X, you can either use resource files or load the files with **xrdb** into a resource database. Many newer systems, like the Common Desktop Enviroment, make extensive use of **xrdb** and resource databases. If you change a resource in a file such as **.Xdefaults** and it seems to have no effect, you probably need to look into **xrdb**.

For most usage, **xrdb** loads or saves data in a property on the root window called RESOURCE_MANAGER. (If this property exists, resource settings in the **.Xdefaults** file will be ignored by most X applications.) If you pass a filename on the command line, **xrdb** will load that file.

Examples

```
$ xrdb -query > res1.txt
```

Reads value of resources in **RESOURCE_MANAGER** property and writes out data to file **res1.txt**.

```
$ xrdb -edit .Xdefaults
```

Reads value of resources in **RESOURCE_MANAGER** property and writes out data to file **.Xdefaults**, but preserves anything else already in file **.Xdefaults**.

```
$ xrdb -load .Xdefaults
```

Loads in resources from file **.Xdefaults** into **RESOURCE_MANAGER** property on the root window.

8

Options

-all	Sets resources into both **RESOURCE_MANAGER** and **SCREEN_RESOURCES** on every screen.
-backup suffix	Appends **suffix** to filename used with **-edit** to create a backup file of the original contents.
-cpp *filename*	Uses **filename** in place of **cpp**, the C preprocessor.
-display host: disp_num	Connects to **disp_num** numbered X server (almost always 0) on given **host**.
-edit *filename*	Places all resources in the property into the given file, but preserving the rest of the file. This allows you to keep your comments in the file.

–global	Works with **RESOURCE_MANAGER** property (the default).
–help	Prints a summary of the command-line options.
–load	Loads data from standard input into property, replacing all old values.
–merge	Loads input into property and merges differences.
–n	Prints changes to standard output, but doesn't actually make the changes.
–nocpp	Doesn't preprocess files with cpp.
–query	Reads resource values from property.
–quiet	Doesn't print warning messages.
–remove	Removes properties from X server.
–screen	Works with **SCREEN_RESOURCES** property on the default screen.
–screens	Works with **SCREEN_RESOURCES** property on all screens.
-symbols	Prints symbols defined by **cpp**.

Related Commands

cpp	C preprocessor.
xprop	Prints window properties.

xrefresh — Refresh Screen

xrefresh *options*

Purpose

Repaints all or part of the screen, with a surprisingly large number of options.

Examples

```
$ xrefresh
```

Repaints the screen.

```
$ xrefresh -solid orange
```

Briefly paints the screen orange, then repaints everything.

Options

-black	Turns off all electron guns so screen goes black, then repaints.
-display host: disp_num	Connects to **disp_num** numbered X server (almost always 0) on given **host**.
-geometry *Width***x** *Height* + x + y	Sets window size and position.
-geometry *Width***x** *Height*	Sets window size.
-geometry + x + y	Sets position of window's upper-left corner.
-none	Repaints all windows with no funny options; the default.
-root	Fills in screen with root window's background color, then repaints.
-solid color	Fills in screen with given **color**, then repaints.
-white	Fills in screen with a white background, then repaints.

8

xset — Change X Server Settings

xset *options*

Purpose

Controls and queries settings in the X server for things like the screen saver blanking timeouts and keyboard repeat rates.

Examples

```
$ xset fp rehash
```

Reloads list of available fonts. Normally done after adding a new font.

```
$ xset led on
```

Turns on all the keyboard LED lights.

```
$ xset s off
```

Turns off screen saver.

Options

b on	Turns on bell.
b off	Turns off bell.
b -	Turns off bell.
b percent	Sets bell volume to **percent** of maximum.
b percent pitch duration	Sets bell volume to **percent** of maximum, at **pitch** hertz and for **duration** milliseconds. Not all hardware allows this control.
c percent	Sets key click volume, if supported, to **percent** of maximum.
c on	Restores defaults for key click volume.
c off	Turns off key click sounds, if supported by hardware.
c -	Turns off key click sounds, if supported by hardware.
-display host: disp_num	Connects to **disp_num** numbered X server (almost always 0) on given **host**.
fp= path,path,...	Sets font search path to comma-delimited list of directories.
fp default	Restores default set of font search directories.
fp rehash	Tells X server to reload list of available fonts.
-fp path,path,...	Removes comma-delimited list of directories from font search path.
fp- path,path,...	Removes comma-delimited list of directories from font search path.
+fp path,path,...	Adds comma-delimited list of directories to font search path.

8

fp+ path,path,...	Adds comma-delimited list of directories to font search path.
led –	Turns off all keyboard LED lights.
led on	Turns on all keyboard LED lights.
led off	Turns off all keyboard LED lights.
led number	Turns on keyboard LED light **number**, e.g., 3 for the third light.
–led number	Turns off keyboard LED light **number**.
m accelt_mult threshold	Sets mouse acceleration. The **accelt_mult** setting controls how much faster the mouse should move when accelerating, e.g., two times faster, while **threshold** controls the distance the mouse must move, in pixels, in a short period of time to start accelerating.
p pixel color	Sets colormap ID number **pixel** to given **color**.
r	Turns on key autorepeat (when you hold down a key).
–r	Turns off key autorepeat.
s off	Turns off screen saver.
s on	Turns on screen saver.
s noblank	Uses a pattern rather than a blank screen for screen saver.
s timeout pattern	Sets screen saver to turn on with **timeout** seconds of inactivity and change its pattern (if there is any) every **pattern** seconds.

xsetroot — Change Screen Background

xsetroot *options*

Purpose

Changes the root window—the screen background—from the default X cross-hatch pattern to a bitmap pattern or solid color.

If you use the Common Desktop Environment, you must set the screen background to "No Background" in the Style Manager (**dtstyle**) before calling **xsetroot** to change the screen background, or you will see no effect.

Examples

```
$ xsetroot -cursor_name gumby
```

Sets default cursor to the Gumby shape.

```
$ xsetroot -cursor_name gumby -bg green
```

Sets default cursor to the Gumby shape with a green background color.

```
$ xsetroot -solid bisque2
```

Sets screen background color to **bisque2**, which is easy on the eyes.

Options

-bg color	Uses **color** for window background.
-bitmap filename	Tiles bitmap in given file for screen background, using current screen foreground and background colors.
-cursor cursorfile maskfile	Sets default cursor to given image and mask. Both files can be created by the **bitmap** program.
-cursor_name cursorname	Sets default cursor to given named cursor, e.g., **gumby**.
-def	Resets all unspecified values to defaults. The screen background gets a black and white cross-hatch mesh and the cursor becomes an X.
-display host: disp_num	Connects to **disp_num** numbered X server (almost always 0) on given **host**.
-fg color	Uses given foreground **color**; only works with **-bitmap**, **-cursor**, **-cursor_name**, or **-mod**.
-gray	Sets entire background gray.

8

–grey	Sets entire background gray.
–help	Prints summary of the command-line options.
–mod x y	Creates a plaid using numbers **x** and **y** from 1 to 16.
–name name	Sets name of root window to **name**.
–rv	Reverses foreground and background colors.
-solid color	Fills screen background with given **color**.

Related Commands

bitmap	Creates bitmap files.
dtstyle	Sets Common Desktop Environment settings.

xterm — X Terminal Window

xterm *options*

8

Purpose

Provides a shell terminal window that acts much like a VT102 terminal, allowing you to enter UNIX commands. You can run multiple **xterm** windows on your display and copy and paste between them. Inside the window, **xterm** runs your UNIX shell, which is specified in the **SHELL** environment variable. You can control the fonts used and whether or not to display a scrollbar. **Xterm** remains the most-used X application because it allows you to directly enter UNIX commands.

Examples

```
$ xterm -sb &
```

Starts **xterm** with a scrollbar in the background — very useful.

```
$ xterm -fn "-*-courier-medium-r-normal-18-*-*-*-m-*-*"
&
```

Starts **xterm** using the given courier font. See **xlsfonts** for a list of fonts.

Options

-132	Allows **xterm** to honor the DECCOLM escape sequence that switches between 80 and 132 column mode.
-ah	Always highlights text cursor.
+ah	Only highlights the text cursor when the window has the keyboard focus; the default.
-background color	Uses **color** for window background.
-bd color	Uses **color** for window border.
-bg color	Uses **color** for window background.
-bordercolor color	Uses **color** for window border.
-borderwidth num _pixels	Sets border to **num_pixels** wide.
-bw num_pixels	Sets border to **num_pixels** wide.
-C	Captures console output. Makes **xterm** similar to **xconsole**.
-cn	Doesn't cut newlines when selecting to the end of a line.
+cn	Cuts newlines when selecting to the end of a line.
-cr color	Sets text cursor **color**.
-display host: disp_num	Connects to **disp_num** numbered X server (almost always 0) on given **host**.
-e program *args*	Executes **program** with its arguments *args* instead of the default shell.
-fb fontname	Uses **fontname** for bold items.
-fg color	Uses **color** for window foreground.
-fn fontname	Uses given font.
-foreground color	Uses **color** for window foreground.
-geometry *Width***x** *Height* + x + y	Sets window size and position.
-geometry *Width***x** *Height*	Sets window size.
-geometry + x + y	Sets position of window's upper-left corner.

8

–help	Prints a summary of the command-line options.
–iconic	Starts window as an icon.
–j	Turns on jump scrolling.
+j	Turns off jump scrolling.
–ls	Starts **xterm** as a login shell. Use this if **xterm** doesn't properly read your startup files, like **.login** for the C shell or **.profile** for the Korn shell.
–mb	Rings a bell when you type near the end of the line. Very annoying.
–reverse	Reverses foreground and background colors.
–rv	Reverses foreground and background colors.
–rw	Allows reverse wraparound. This means the cursor can back up from the start of one row to the end of the previous row.
–s	Allows asynchronous scrolling, which is useful for slow networks.
–sb	Displays a scrollbar to allow you to recall data that scrolls by.
+sb	Doesn't display a scrollbar.
–si	Scrolls window to bottom when new output appears.
+si	Turns off **–si** mode.
–sk	Scrolls window to bottom when you type in text.
+sk	Turns off **–sk** mode.
–sl number	Sets the **number** of lines in the scrolling buffer, defaults to 64.
–t	Starts in Tektronix mode, not VT102 mode.
+t	Starts in VT102 mode, the default.
-title string	Sets window title.

Related Commands

cmdtool	Open Tool shell window.
dtterm	Common Desktop Environment shell window.

shelltool Open Tool shell window.

xconsole Displays console messages.

xlsfonts Lists available fonts.

xv — Display Graphic Images

xv *options filenames*

Purpose

This wonderful graphics display and screen capture program supports most image file formats. You can display single images or use the "visual schnauzer" to view directories. The right mouse button displays the **xv** controls window, from which most functions are available.

NOTE

This command is not available on all systems. This is actually shareware from John Bradley; if this command is on your system and you find it useful, you should send a contribution to Bradley in support of his programming efforts.

Examples

```
$ xv &
```

Starts image browser in background.

```
$ xv lion.gif
```

Displays image file **lion.gif**.

```
$ xv -quit -root -max lion.gif
```

Displays image file **lion.gif** on the background of the screen — the root window — and expands as necessary to fit the screen. Quits the application once the image is loaded.

Options

–cemap	Starts with color editor window, too.
+cemap	Starts without color editor window.
–cmap	Starts with control window, too.
+cmap	Starts without control window.
–display host: disp_num	Connects to **disp_num** numbered X server (almost always 0) on given **host**.
–dir directory	Starts visual schnauzer in given **directory**.
–help	Prints a summary of the command-line options.
–iconic	Starts window as an icon.
–imap	Starts with image information window, too.
+imap	Starts without image information window.
–quit	Quits after performing actions requested on command line.
–wait seconds	Waits for given time.
–root	Displays images on root window rather than in **xv**'s window.
–vsmap	Starts with visual schnauzer window, too.
+vsmap	Starts without visual schnauzer window.

8

Related Commands

xwd	Captures screen image.
xwud	Displays captured screen image.

xwd — Dump X Window

xwd *options*

Purpose

Captures an image of a window and saves it to a file. Unfortunately, the **xwd** image format tends to be rather obscure and works mostly with tools like **xwud** and **xpr**. The **xv** program can convert this format to other more common image formats, such as GIF or JPEG.

Xwd will prompt you to select a window if you have not selected a window by its ID, name, or the root window.

Example

```
$ xwd -name xterm -add 45 -out image1.xwd
```

Captures the window named **xterm**, adds 45 to every color pixel value to darken the image, and writes the output to the file **image1.xwd**.

Options

–add value	Adds **value** to every pixel. Can be used to lighten or darken an image. Negative numbers generally lighten; positive numbers darken.
–display host: disp_num	Connects to **disp_num** numbered X server (almost always 0) on given **host**.
–frame	Captures window manager frame along with window; used only in interactive mode.
–help	Prints a summary of the command-line options.
–icmap	Uses the first installed colormap of the screen for colors rather than the colormap for the window.
–id window_id	Captures the window with the given ID.
–name name	Captures the window with the given **name**.
–nobdrs	Doesn't include the window border when capturing image.
–out *filename*	Stores output in **filename** rather than sending output to the terminal.
–root	Captures the root window.

8

–screen	Captures any areas that overlap the window, too.
-xy	Uses XY format for dumping color images, rather than the default Z format.

Related Commands

xv	Image viewer.
xwud	Undumps an X window.

xwininfo — Print Window Information

xwininfo *options*

Purpose

Prints information about a given window. In interactive mode, you can select the window with the mouse or use a window ID.

Examples


```
$ xwininfo -root -children -all
```

Displays all possible information about the root window, as well as information about all of its children, that is, all windows.

```
$ xwininfo -all
```

Asks you to select a window, then displays all available information.

Options

–all	Displays all possible information.
–bits	Prints out the bit flags for the selected window, including the backing-store and save-under hints.
–children	Prints information about the selected window as well as the names and IDs of all children and the parent of the selected window.

–display host: disp_num	Connects to **disp_num** numbered X server (almost always 0) on given **host**.
–english	Displays data in inches as well as pixels.
–events	Prints out the event masks for the selected window.
–frame	Selects the frame rather than the inner window.
–help	Prints a summary of the command-line options.
–id window_id	Prints information about the given window.
–int	Prints window IDs as decimal rather than hexadecimal values.
–metric	Displays data in millimeters as well as pixels.
–name window _name	Prints information about the window with the given name.
–root	Prints information about the root window (screen background).
–shape	Prints the window's border and shape extents (if not rectangular).
–size	Prints the requested sizes (including maximum and minimum) of the selected window.
–stats	Prints information about the location and color map for the selected window.
–tree	Prints full information about the selected window, its parent, and all of its children. Very useful with the **–root** option.
-wm	Prints the window manager hints for the selected window.

xwud — Undump X Window

xwud *options*

Purpose

Displays an image captured by **xwd**. **Xwud** quits when you click a mouse button in the window or when you type **q**, **Q**, or **Ctrl-C**.

Examples

```
$ xwud -in image3.xwd
```

Loads up image stored in file **image3.xwd**.

```
$ xwd -root | xwud
```

Captures the root window and then displays the image captured.

Options

-bg color	Uses **color** for window background.
-display host: disp_num	Connects to **disp_num** numbered X server (almost always 0) on given **host**.
-fg color	Uses **color** for window foreground.
-geometry *Width***x** *Height* + x + y	Sets window size and position.
-geometry *Width***x** *Height*	Sets window size.
-geometry + x + y	Sets position of window's upper-left corner.
-help	Prints a summary of the command-line options.
-in *filename*	Displays image stored in **filename** rather than the default, which assumes the image is passed as standard input.
-new	Creates a new colormap to display the image.
-noclick	Disables mouse clicks from quitting **xwud**.
-plane *number*	Displays a single bit plane of an image. This can be used with **xpr** for printing a single bit plane.
-raw	Uses the raw color IDs in the default colormap.
-rv	Reverses the foreground and background colors for monochrome images.

8

Related Commands

xdpr	Dumps an X window and prints it.
xpr	Prints an X window dump.
xwd	Dumps an X window.

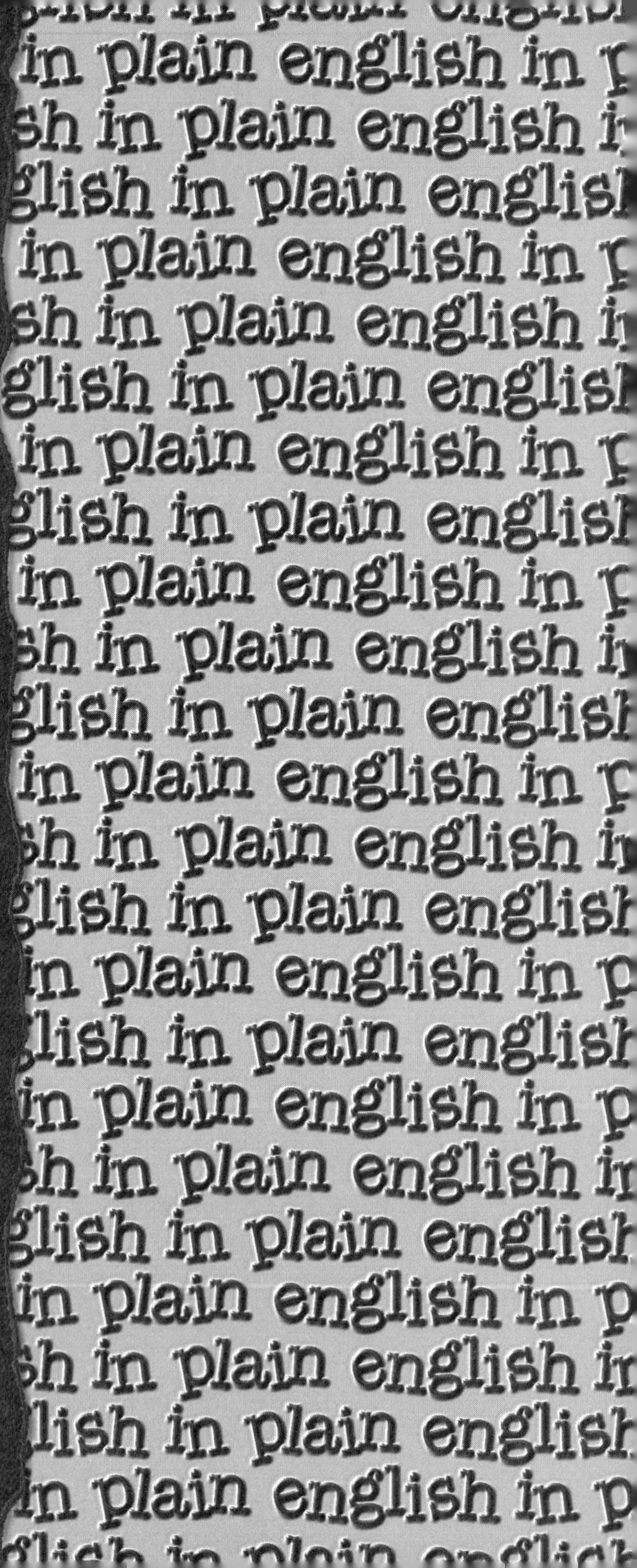
in plain english

9

Programming Commands

UNIX is a great programming environment. In this short section, we've listed some of the most commonly used programming commands. These commands won't make you into a programmer, but they should give you an idea of the UNIX conventions regarding programming. If you are a programmer, these commands will help you to figure out how to program on UNIX systems.

ar — Create Software Libraries

ar key archive_name files

PURPOSE

Maintains an archive — called a **library** — of compiled software modules. These library routines are then used when creating UNIX programs. The archive name usually ends in **.a**. Most of the files you'd place in an archive end in **.o**, and are compiled object modules.

EXAMPLE

```
$ ar rv libFOO.a module1.o module2.o
```

Adds — or replaces if necessary — the modules **module1.o** and **module2.o** in the library file **libFOO.a**.

OPTIONS

- **r** Replaces files in archive with new files.
- **s** Updates symbol table.
- **t** Prints table of contents (list of files in archive).
- **v** Works in verbose mode; combined with another option, prints messages.

You must supply one of the **r**, **s**, or **t** options.

RELATED COMMANDS

- **cc** C compiler.
- **CC** C+ + compiler.

cc — C Compiler

cc options files

PURPOSE

This command compiles C language programs (source files, assembler source files, or preprocessed C source files).

In general, C source code files have a **.c** extension (See Table 9-1).

Table 9-1 *Common C Programming Filename Extensions*

Extension	Common Usage
.a	Compiled library of functions (binary).
.c	C source code file (text).
.h	C header file, called an "include" file (text).
.o	Compiled source code file, called an "object module" (binary).

NOTE

There are literally dozens of options available for this command. Check your system documentation or online manual page for a full set.

EXAMPLES

```
$ cc -o hello hello.o
```

This creates an executable file named **hello** from an object module named **hello.o**.

```
$ cc -o hello hello.c
```

This creates an executable file named **hello** from a C source code file named **hello.c**. The command will first compile the **hello.c** file.

9

OPTIONS

-c filename	Specifies the name of the file to compile to generate an **.o** file.
-g	Generates debugging information.
-l library	Link in the given **library**, e.g., **-lX11**, for the library file named **libX11.a**.
-o filename	Specifies the name of the executable file to generate.
-On	Optimizes while compiling; some UNIX versions also allow you to set an optimization level with a numeral.

RELATED COMMAND

ar	Creates software libraries.
CC	C++ compiler.
make	Builds programs efficiently.

CC — C++ Compiler

CC options files

PURPOSE

Compiles C++ files and creates executable programs. Note that **CC**, which compiles C++ code, differs from **cc** (all lowercase), which compiles C code.

Typically, C++ source code files have a **.C**, **.cpp**, **.cxx**, or **.cc** extension (see Table 9-2).

Table 9-2 *Common C++ Programming Filename Extensions*

Extension	Common Usage
.a	Compiled library of functions or classes (binary).
.C	C++ source code file (text).
.cc	C++ source code file (text).
.cpp	C++ source code file (text).
.cxx	C++ source code file (text).
.h	C++ header file, called an "include" file (text).
.hxx	C++ header file, called an "include" file (text).
.o	Compiled source code file, called an "object module" (binary).

NOTE

There are literally dozens of options available for this command. Check your system documentation or online manual page for a full set.

9

EXAMPLE

```
$ CC -o myprog myprog.cxx
```

Compiles the C++ code file **myprog.cxx** and creates an executable program named **myprog**.

OPTIONS

-**c** filename	Specifies the name of the file to compile to generate an .**o** file.
-**g**	Generates debugging information.
-**l** library	Link in the given **library**, e.g., -**lm** for **libm.a** (the math library).
-**o** filename	Specifies the name of the executable file to generate.
-**O**	Optimizes while compiling.

RELATED COMMANDS

ar	Creates software libraries.
cc	C compiler.
make	Builds programs efficiently.

ci — Check In Files to RCS

ci options file
ci options file1 file2 ...

PURPOSE

Checks a file or files into the Revision Control System, or RCS. You must have a directory named **RCS** for this command to work.

NOTE

There's a lot more to the Revision Control System, or RCS. See the online manual information on **rcsintro** for a good overview of RCS.

EXAMPLE

```
$ ci -l fred.cxx
```

Checks in file **fred.cxx** and then checks out again, locking the file.

OPTIONS

-l	Checks in file and then checks out again using **co -l**.
-rrev	Assigns revision number **rev** to checked-in file.
-u	Checks in file and then checks out again — unlocked. This gives you a read-only version of the file you just checked in.

RELATED COMMANDS

co	Checks out files from RCS.
rcs	Manipulates files in RCS.

co — Check Out Files from RCS

co options file
co options file1 file2 ...

PURPOSE

Checks a file or files out of the Revision Control System, or RCS. You must have a directory named **RCS** for this command to work.

NOTE

There's a lot more to the Revision Control System, or RCS. See the online manual information on **rcsintro** for a good overview of RCS.

EXAMPLES

```
$ co -l fred.cxx
```

Checks out file **fred.cxx**, locking the file so you can modify it.

```
$ co -u fred.cxx
```

Checks out file **fred.cxx**, but does not lock the file.

OPTIONS

-l	Checks out file and locks it.
-rrev	Checks out revision **rev**, or the latest version earlier than **rev**.
-u	Checks out file, unlocked.

RELATED COMMANDS

ci	Checks in files to RCS.
rcs	Manipulates files in RCS.

dbx — UNIX Debugger

dbx program
dbx program core

PURPOSE

One of many UNIX debuggers. The most common are **dbx**, **gdb**, and **xdb**. It is likely your system will have only one of these three debuggers. A debugger helps you find bugs in a running program by allowing you to examine the parts of the code as they get executed. To make this happen, you must compile your code with the **-g** option to **cc** or **CC** to provide information crucial to the debugger. Debuggers can usually work in one of two modes: with a running program or in postmortem mode by examining the **core** file created when the program crashed.

The **dbx** debugger is common on Sun and Silicon Graphics systems.

EXAMPLES

```
$ dbx myprog
```

Starts debugger working with program **myprog**.

```
$ dbx myprog core
```

Starts debugger working with program **myprog** and using core dump file named **core**.

RELATED COMMAND

xdb Hewlett-Packard UNIX debugger.

make — Build Programs Efficiently

make options

PURPOSE

Builds programs the most efficient way, based on file modification dates. If a code file has changed, **make** will rebuild the code file but won't rebuild everything else. To use make, you need to create a **Makefile (or makefile)**, much like the following:

```
OBJS=	str.o mytest.o
mytest:		$(OBJS)
	CC -o mytest $(OBJS)
INC=	-I.
str.o:	   str.cxx
	CC -c $(INC) str.cxx
mytest.o:	mytest.cxx
	CC -c $(INC) mytest.cxx
```

The rules in the file above describe how to recompile the executable program **mytest** if either of the code files, **str.cxx** or **mytest.cxx**, has changed. The lines starting with CC must be indented with tabs, not spaces.

EXAMPLES

```
$ make -f MyMakefile
```

Uses the file **MyMakefile** instead of the default **Makefile**.

```
$ make str.o
```

Builds **str.o** rather than the default target — the first target in the **Makefile**.

OPTIONS

-**f** Makefile	Names an alternative **Makefile**.
-n	Works in no-execute mode; **make** just prints out the commands it would execute.
target	Builds given target.

RELATED COMMANDS

ar	Creates software libraries.
cc	C compiler.
CC	C++ compiler.

rcs — Manipulate Files in RCS

rcs options file
rcs options file1 file2...

PURPOSE

Changes attributes of files stored within the Revision Control System, or RCS.

NOTE

There's a lot more to the Revision Control System, or RCS. See the online manual information on **rcsintro** for a good overview of RCS.

OPTIONS

-i Creates and initializes a new file without any file contents.

-l Locks file without modifying it. Useful if you've made changes but didn't first check out the file.

-u Abandons changes to file, unlocking it.

RELATED COMMANDS

ci Checks in files to RCS.

co Checks out files from RCS.

xdb — UNIX Debugger

xdb program
xdb program core

PURPOSE

One of many UNIX debuggers. The most common are **dbx**, **gdb**, and **xdb**. It is likely your system will have only one of these three debuggers. A debugger helps you find bugs in a running program by allowing you to examine the parts of the code as they get executed. To make this happen, you must compile your code with the **-g** option to **cc** or **CC** to provide information crucial to the debugger. Debuggers can usually work in one of two modes: with a running program or in postmortem mode by examining the **core** file created when the program crashed.

The **xdb** debugger is typically found under HP-UX on Hewlett-Packard systems. It works best from an **hpterm** window rather than an **xterm** window.

EXAMPLE

```
$ xdb myprog core
```

Starts debugger working with program **myprog** and using core dump file named **core**.

RELATED COMMAND

dbx UNIX debugger.

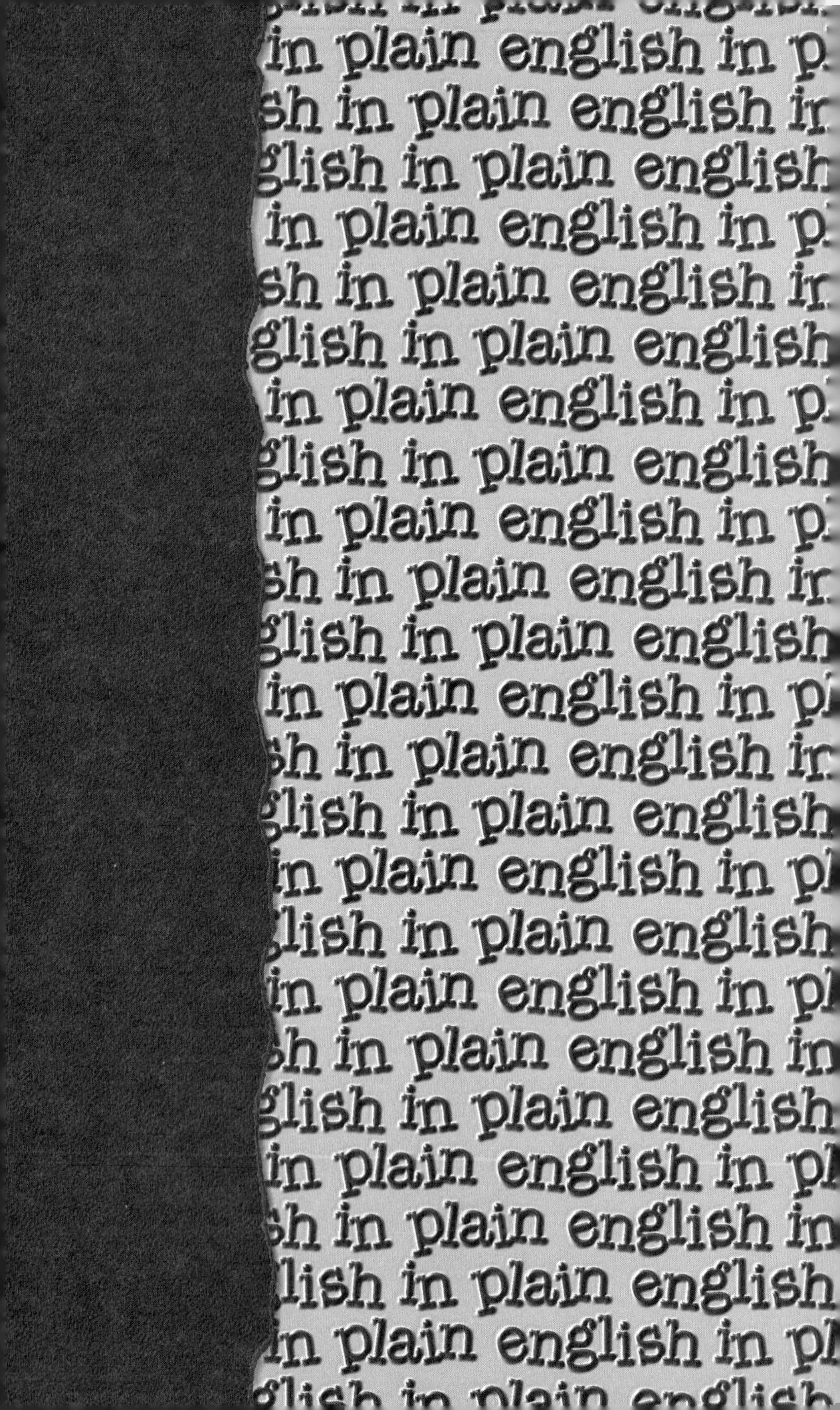
in plain english

10

System-Administration Commands

These system-administration commands are geared primarily to the needs of system administrators; some of them are available only for privileged users. Other commands — particularly **at** and related commands — can come in handy for the majority of UNIX system users. If you think you could use any of these commands but are currently barred from doing so, check with your system administrator.

at — Perform Task At

at *option1 time* [*date*] *increment*
at *option2* [*job-id*]

Purpose

The **at** command performs specified commands at given times and dates, as long as the commands require no additional input from you. For instance, you may want to print a series of long documents at midnight so you won't tie up the laser printer for hours when other people may need it. You don't need to interact with the laser printer at midnight (although you should make sure its paper tray is filled before leaving work!), so you can use the **at** command to print at that time.

Two sets of options are available with the **at** commands. One set, which we'll call **option1**, relates to setting the targeted time and date. The second set of options, which we'll represent with **option2**, allows changes to jobs already scheduled. After you enter the **at** command, you type in the commands to execute at that time. You type in these commands at the keyboard. When you're finished, press **Ctrl-D**. At the given time, **at** runs your commands. Any output from the commands is sent to you via electronic mail.

NOTE

Even though the **at** command is used primarily by system administrators, it can also be used by regular users, but this usage must be set by the system administrator. If you are not authorized to use **at**, you'll see an error message like the following:

```
at: you are not authorized to run at. Sorry.
```

If you want to use the **at** command, talk with your system administrator.

Examples

```
$ at 11am
ls
Ctrl-D
```

The **at** command reads the command to run from standard input. On the line following the command line, you enter commands and end with **Ctrl-D**.

```
$ at 11am nov 1
$ at 11am nov 1, 1997
$ at 11am sun
$ at now + 2 weeks
$ at [option2] [job-id]
```

NOTE

Job-IDs are issued by the system when a job is scheduled.

Scheduling Options

-f *filename*	Executes the commands listed in *filename*. Not available on all systems.
-m	Notifies user when job is completed.

Time Options

time	Obviously, the time when the commands should run. Unless you specify otherwise (with am or pm as a suffix), the system assumes military time.
midnight **noon** **now**	These options are used in lieu of a specific time. If you use now as an option, you must specify an increment (see "Increment Option").

Date Options

date	Format is usually specified as **month day, year**, with **year** optional.
day	The specific day when the command should run, with the name either spelled out (**Sunday**) or referred to by the first three letters (**Sun**).
today	This option can be used in lieu of a specific date.
tomorrow	This option can be used in lieu of a specific date.

Already-Scheduled-Jobs Options

-l	Lists current job.
-r	Removes specified job.

Increment Option

increment	A numerical value relative to the current time and date. The increment must contain a reference to **minute**, **hour**, **day**, **week**, **month**, or **year**. In the example at the beginning of this command's listing (**at now + 2 weeks**), the job would be performed two weeks from now.

Related Commands

atq	Immediately lists jobs scheduled with the **at** command.
atrm	Removes jobs scheduled by **at**.
batch	Runs a series of commands in order in the background.

atq — List At Jobs

atq *option user*

Purpose

10

Lists jobs already scheduled with the **at** command. There's not a lot of control available with the command: You can list all the jobs, list all the jobs generated by a specific user, or list the jobs in the order they were generated through the **at** command.

NOTE

Even though the **atq** command is used primarily by system administrators, it can also be used by regular users, but this usage must be set by the system administrator. If you want to use the **atq** command, talk with your system administrator.

Examples

```
$ atq ericfj
ericfj.899996400.a      Thu Jul  9 10:00:00 1998
ericfj.900000000.a      Thu Jul  9 11:00:00 1998
```

Displays the jobs for the **at** command for user **ericfj** in time order.

```
$ atq -c ericfj
ericfj.900000000.a      Thu Jul  9 11:00:00 1998
ericfj.899996400.a      Thu Jul  9 10:00:00 1998
```

Displays the jobs for the **at** command for user **ericfj** in order of when the **at** commands were set up.

```
$ atq -n ericfj
2 files in the queue
```

Lists the number of **at** commands for user **ericfj**.

Options

-c Sorts the queue in the order jobs were generated through the **at** command.

-n Returns the number of jobs in the queue but does not list them.

Related Commands

at Schedules jobs to be performed at a specific time.

atrm Removes jobs scheduled by **at**.

atrm — Remove At Job

atrm *option user job-id*

Purpose

Removes jobs already scheduled with the **at** command. Privileged users can remove all jobs or the jobs of a specific user, while other users can remove only those jobs generated by themselves.

Options

-a Removes all jobs generated by the current user only.

-i Removes the job only after the approval of the user (**y** or **n**).

Related Commands

at Schedules jobs to be performed at a specific time.

atq Immediately lists jobs scheduled with the **at** command.

batch — Run Commands

batch

Purpose

Runs a series of commands one command at a time in the background, avoiding the performance issue of running several commands simultaneously in the background.

Example

```
batch
pr -a kevinstuff
lp kevinstuff
Ctrl-D
```

Use **Ctrl-D** to end the list of commands.

Options

None.

chgrp — Change Group

chgrp *options groupname filename(s)*

Purpose

This changes the ownership of a file or files to a new or existing group, specified by either name (stored in **/etc/group**) or ID number. You can use groups to allow all users in the engineering department (group), for example, to access a file or directory, and prevent all other users, such as those in accounting, from accessing the engineering data.

File owners can use the command to change the ownership of only their own files, while privileged users can use the command to change ownership of any file. This command can also be used to change the IDs for an entire directory and the files within.

Example

```
$ chgrp restricted kevin.report
```

This changes the group for **kevin.report** to **restricted**.

```
$ chgrp -R restricted /usr/users/kevin/reports
```

This changes the group for all the files and subdirectories within **/usr/users/kevin/reports** to **restricted**.

Options

-h	Changes a symbolic link, not the file referenced by a symbolic link. Not available on all systems.
-R	Recursively changes through subdirectories and files.
group	Either a group name (stored in **/etc/group**) or ID number.

Related Commands

chown	Changes file ownership.
chmod	Changes file-access permissions.
newgrp	Changes to a new working group.

10

cpio — Create Archives

cpio *-i options*
cpio *-o options*
cpio *-p options*

Purpose

Copies archived files to and from backup storage devices like tape drives. This rather involved command is meant for true system administrators, not for those of us who putz around with system-administration commands as the need arises. Because of this, we suggest that you check your system documentation before using this command. Besides, the **tar** command is much easier to work with.

crontab — Schedule Tasks

crontab *filename*

Purpose

The **crontab** command sets up a file containing a list of tasks to be performed regularly, such as data backups and regular correspondence. The **crontab** command creates the file (if none exists) from keyboard entry, or processes a text file generated by a text editor. The **cron** program then runs those commands.

The syntax of this file is very rigid. There are six fields to a file, each separated by a space. The first five fields specify exactly when the command is to be run; the sixth field is the command itself. The first five fields are:

Field	Meaning
1	Minutes after the hour (0-59)
2	Hour, in 24-hour format (0-23)
3	Day of the month (1-31)
4	Month (1-12)
5	Day of the week (0-6; the 0 refers to Sunday)

Asterisks (*) specify when commands are to be run in every instance of the value of the field. For instance, an asterisk in the Month field would mean that the command should be run every month. In addition, multiple events can be scheduled within a field; merely separate all instances with commas — with no space between.

Examples

To run a command every morning at 9:30 a.m., the line in the **crontab**-generated file would look like this:

```
30 9 * * * command
```

To run a command at 1 p.m. only on the 1st and 15th of the month, the line in the **crontab**-generated file would look like this:

```
0 13 1,15 * * command
```

To install the events file in your system, making it operational, use the **crontab** command:

```
$ crontab events_file
```

NOTE

Although **crontab** is a command primarily meant for system administrators, it's useful for any user. BSD or pre-System V users, however, are out of luck, as those systems allow use of **crontab** only for system administrators. If you're using a newer version of UNIX and want to use this command, check with your system administrator.

Options

-e Edits the current **crontab** file or creates a new one. Not available on all systems.

-l Lists the contents of the **crontab** file.

-r Removes the **crontab** file.

Related Command

at Runs a command at a specified time.

iostat — Report Input/Output Statistics

iostat [*drive(s)*] [*interval*] [*number_reports*]

Purpose

Reports on Input/Output (I/O) activity.

NOTE

Although this command differs on a number of versions of UNIX, it always reports on I/O activity. Check your system's online manuals to verify thc output.

Examples

```
$ iostat
      tty      rz0       dk1       dk2       dk3      cpu
 tin tout bps tps  bps tps  bps tps  bps tps  us ni sy id
   0   10   5   1    0   0    0   0    0   0   3  0  2 95
```

Reports on terminal (**tty**), disk (**rz0**, **dk1**, **dk2**, **dk3**), and CPU (**cpu**) activity since the last boot.

For terminals, **tin** is the number of characters read in, and **tout** the number of characters output.

For disks, **iostat** shows the number of kilobytes transferred per second (**bps**), transfers per second (**tps**). Some disks also provide average seek times in milleseonds (not shown here).

For the CPU, **iostat** outputs the percentage of time the system spent in user mode (**us**), in user mode but running low-priority — *nice* — tasks (**ni**), in system mode (**sy**), and idling (**id**).

```
$ iostat 1 6
      tty      rz0       dk1       dk2       dk3      cpu
 tin tout bps tps  bps tps  bps tps  bps tps  us ni sy id
   0   10   5   1    0   0    0   0    0   0   3  0  2 95
   0    0   0   0    0   0    0   0    0   0  98  0  2  0
   0    0   0   0    0   0    0   0    0   0  97  0  2  0
   0    0   0   0    0   0    0   0    0   0  92  0  5  4
   0    0   0   0    0   0    0   0    0   0  49  0 24 26
   0    0   0   0    0   0    0   0    0   0  13  0 18 69
```

Reports on terminal (**tty**), disk (**rz0**, **dk1**, **dk2**, **dk3**), and CPU (**cpu**) activity since the last boot, and then reports five more times, at one-second intervals, for a total of six reports.

10

```
$ iostat
      tty          fd0            sd3            nfs1         cpu
 tin tout kps tps serv  kps tps serv  kps tps serv  us sy wt id
   0    0   0   0    0    3   0  129    0   0    0   4 19  0 77
```

Output on Sun's Solaris version of UNIX.

```
$ iostat
  device    bps     sps    msps
  c0t6d0      0     0.0     1.0
  c0t1d0      0     0.0     1.0
```

Output on Hewlett-Packard's HP-UX.

Options

drive(s)	Displays information on specific *drives*. By default, **iostat** reports information on the first four drives.
interval	Reports every *interval* seconds.
number_reports	Provides *number_reports* of output.

Related Command

vmstat	Reports virtual memory usage statistics.

login — Login System

login *options*

Purpose

This command logs you in to the UNIX system. Without this command, there isn't much computing work you can finish.

If you do not supply a username with the **login** command, you'll be prompted for one. In addition, **login** may ask you for a password, if your system is so configured.

Options

username	Supplies a *username* when you log in.
var=value	Changes the *value* of an environment variable.

Related Command

logname	Login name.

newgrp — New Group

newgrp *option group*

Purpose

Logs you in to a new group during a current session. If you do not have permission to join a group, the request will be denied.

Option

- \- Changes to the new group, with new environment associated with the new group.

Related Commands

chgrp Changes group associated with files.

env Sets environment.

stty — Set Terminal Modes

stty *options modes*

Purpose

Displays your terminal configuration and options. If you use **stty** with no options or modes, your current configuration will be returned in basic format; use **stty -a** for a more complete — and cryptic — listing of your current configuration.

As UNIX hardware evolves, the use of the **stty** command becomes less and less common. Unless you're really into hardware and want to start mucking around with modes and settings, we advise you to shy away from the **stty** command, except in one situation: When you dial into a UNIX host and find that the **Backspace** key does not work. Try the following:

```
$ stty erase backspace
```

Don't type the word *backspace*; instead, press the actual **Backspace** key on your terminal (and then the **Enter** key to end the command). This should fix the problem.

Options

-a Displays current options and their settings.

-g Displays current settings in a cryptic format that can be used as input to **stty**.

tput — Query Terminal

tput *options capname*

Purpose

Displays information about your terminal's capabilities, as contained in the **terminfo** database (usually stored in the **/usr/lib/terminfo** directory). While you can use the **tput** command to directly manipulate your terminal — for instance, the command **tput clear** will clear the screen — this capability is used mostly by programmers and certainly not by beginning UNIX users.

Options

-**T***type*	Returns the capabilities of terminal *type*. If no *type* is specified, **tput** uses the current terminal as the default.
init	Returns initialization strings and expands tabs.
longname	Returns the long name of your terminal.

Related Command

stty	Sets terminal modes.

tty — Get Terminal Name

tty *options*

Purpose

Returns the operational settings for your terminal. This command is often used in shell scripts to see if the script is being run from a terminal.

Options

-a	Displays all settings. Not available on all systems.
-s	Displays only codes: 0 (terminal), 1 (not a terminal), or 2 (invalid option).

Related Command

stty Changes terminal settings.

uptime — Reports Up Time

uptime *options*

Purpose

Returns the time your system has been running since the last reboot, as well as the CPU load average.

Examples

```
$ uptime
09:34 up 33 days, 19:52, 13 users, load average: 0.00, 0.26, 0.40
```

This example shows that this system has been up for 33 days. The load average shows the number of processes in the run queue for the last 5 seconds, last 30 seconds, and last 60 seconds.

Related Command

ruptime Reports uptime for systems on the network.

vmstat — Report Virtual Memory Statistics

10

vmstat *options*
vmstat *interval* [*number_reports*]

Purpose

Reports on virtual memory and CPU activity.

Examples

```
$ vmstat
 procs    memory            page              disk          faults      cpu
 r b w   swap  free  re  mf pi po fr de sr f0 s3 - -   in   sy   cs us sy id
 0 0 0   4048  1264   0 214  0  0  0  0  0  0  0  0  0    5  472   67  4 19 77
```

Reports on processes (**procs**), virtual memory usage (**memory** and **page**), interrupts (**faults**), and CPU activity (**cpu**) since last boot on a Sun Solaris system. The brief column headings have the following meanings:

r number of runnable processes.

b number of blocked processes that are not interruptible.

w number of processes swapped out.

swap amount of virtual memory used, in kilobytes.

free amount of free memory, in kilobytes.

re number of page reclaims.

mf number of minor faults.

pi number of kilobytes paged in.

po number of kilobytes paged out.

fr number of kilobytes freed.

de anticipated shortfall in free memory in kilobytes.

sr pages scanned by clock algorithm.

f0 disk actrivity for floppy drive 0.

s3 disk activity for SCSI drive 3.

in number of interrupts per second, not including the clock.

cs number of context switches per second.

us percent of total CPU time spent in user mode.

sy percent of total CPU time spent in system mode.

id percent of total CPU time idle.

10

NOTE

The **vmstat** command differs on a number of flavors of UNIX. Check your online manual entry to verify the actual output. You will see output similar to this, but the actual values may differ. All versions of **vmstat** output virtual memory statistics, just the output format differs. To help get a better idea of the output to expect, we show the data on a number of versions of UNIX.

```
$ vmstat
Virtual Memory Statistics: (pagesize = 8192)
  procs    memory           pages                                 intr        cpu
  r  w  u  act  free wire fault cow zero react pin pout  in  sy  cs  us  sy  id
  3 79 17   14K  13K 3031  15M   1M   8M 1774   2M  706  23  30 258   3   2  95
```

Reports on processes (**procs**), virtual memory usage (**memory** and **pages**), interrupts (**intr**), and CPU activity (**cpu**) since last boot on a Digital UNIX system. The output appears as follows:

r number of running or runnable threads.

w number of waiting threads that can be interrupted.

u number of waiting threads that cannot be interrupted.

act number of virtual memory pages on the active and inactive but allocated lists.

free number of free virtual memory pages.

wire number of pages currently in use that cannot be used for paging.

fault number of addessing faults (which cause a page of virtual memory to get loaded into real memory).

cow number of copy-on-write page faults.

zero number of zero-filled page faults (new pages which have never been referenced yet and must be filled with zeroes).

react number of pages faulted while on the list of inactive pages.

pin number of pages paged in from disk.

pout number of pages that have been paged out to disk.

in number of interrupts—excluding clock interrupts—per second.

sy number of system calls per second.

cs number of context switches between threads or tasks per second

us percentage of total CPU time in user mode.

sy percentage of total CPU time in system mode.

id percentage of total CPU time idling.

```
$ vmstat
 procs                  memory     swap        io    system         cpu
 r b w  swpd  free  buff cache  si  so   bi   bo   in   cs  us  sy  id
 0 0 0     0   452  1776  4684   0   0    1    0  100    4   0   0 100
```

Output on a Linux system, showing different data than the previous example:

r	number of runnable processes.
b	number of blocked processes that are not interruptable
w	number of processes swapped out.
swpd	amount of virtual memory used, in kilobytes.
free	amount of free memory, in kilobytes.
buff	amount of buffer memory, in kilobytes.
si	amount of memory swapped in from disk, in kilobytes per second.
so	amount of memory swapped out to disk, in kilobytes per second.
bi	blocks sent to a block device, in number of blocks per second.
bo	blocks read in from a block device, in number of blocks per second.
in	number of interrupts per second, including the clock.
cs	number of context switches per second.
us	percent of total CPU time spent in user mode.
sy	percent of total CPU time spent in system mode.
id	percent of total CPU time idle.

```
$ vmstat
procs          memory                   page                          faults     cpu
r  b  w   avm   free  re  at   pi  po   fr  de   sr    in   sy    cs  us sy id
0 22  0  1611    405   1   2    1   0    0   0    3   116   76    32   1  0 99
```

Output on Hewlett-Packard's HP-UX.

```
$ vmstat
kthr      memory               page                 faults         cpu
------ ---------- ------------------------ ------------ -----------
 r  b   avm   fre  re  pi  po  fr   sr  cy  in   sy  cs us sy id wa
 0  0  4694   383   0   0   0   0    0   0 107    7  25  0  0 99  0
```

10

Output on IBM'S AIX.

```
$ vmstat 1 6
Virtual Memory Statistics: (pagesize = 8192)
  procs    memory          pages                                intr         cpu
  r  w  u  act  free wire fault cow zero react pin pout  in  sy  cs  us  sy  id
  3 79 17   14K  13K 3031  15M   1M   8M 1774   2M  706  23  30 258   3   2  95
  2 79 18   14K  13K 3031  116    7   95    0    9    0 365 344 839  29  25  46
  4 78 17   14K  13K 3031   63    0   63    0    0    0 227 254 613  50  21  30
  3 78 18   14K  13K 3031   90    0   89    0    1    0 467 459  1K  21  29  50
  2 79 18   14K  13K 3031   71    0   71    0    0    0 369 370 850  36  25  39
  5 77 17   14K  13K 3031   86    0   86    0    0    0 162 198 423  26  58  17
```

Reports on system usage since the last time the system booted, and provides five more reports (once per second) for a total of six reports.

```
$ vmstat -s
Virtual Memory Statistics: (pagesize = 8192)
        340   active pages
       3517   inactive pages
      13755   free pages
       3025   wired pages
   15239937   virtual memory page faults
    1023079   copy-on-write page faults
    8619404   zero fill page faults
       1774   reattaches from reclaim list
    2162468   pages paged in
        706   pages paged out
  647806853   task and thread context switches
   57945833   device interrupts
   76032600   system calls
```

Reports the accumulated information on a Digital UNIX system.

```
$ vmstat -s
33898 swap ins
33898 swap outs
14504 pages swapped in
6568 pages swapped out
10077187 total address trans. faults taken
5069158 page ins
371338 page outs
1577552 pages paged in
917097 pages paged out
4393436 reclaims from free list
4403277 total page reclaims
2552 intransit blocking page faults
6441115 zero fill pages created
```

```
3566751 zero fill page faults
5014643 executable fill pages created
785811 executable fill page faults
0 swap text pages found in free list
2475032 inode text pages found in free list
17114 revolutions of the clock hand
3747760 pages scanned for page out
780020 pages freed by the clock daemon
39365945 cpu context switches
379574957 device interrupts
1036728 traps
92090912 system calls
```

Reports on accumulated information on Hewlett-Packard's HP-UX.

Options

-s	Displays accumulated statistics.
interval	Reports every *interval* seconds.
number_reports	Prints *number_reports* (at given *interval*) and then stops.

NOTE

Different versions of UNIX may support more options. The options listed here are the most common.

Related Command

iostat Reports I/O statistics.

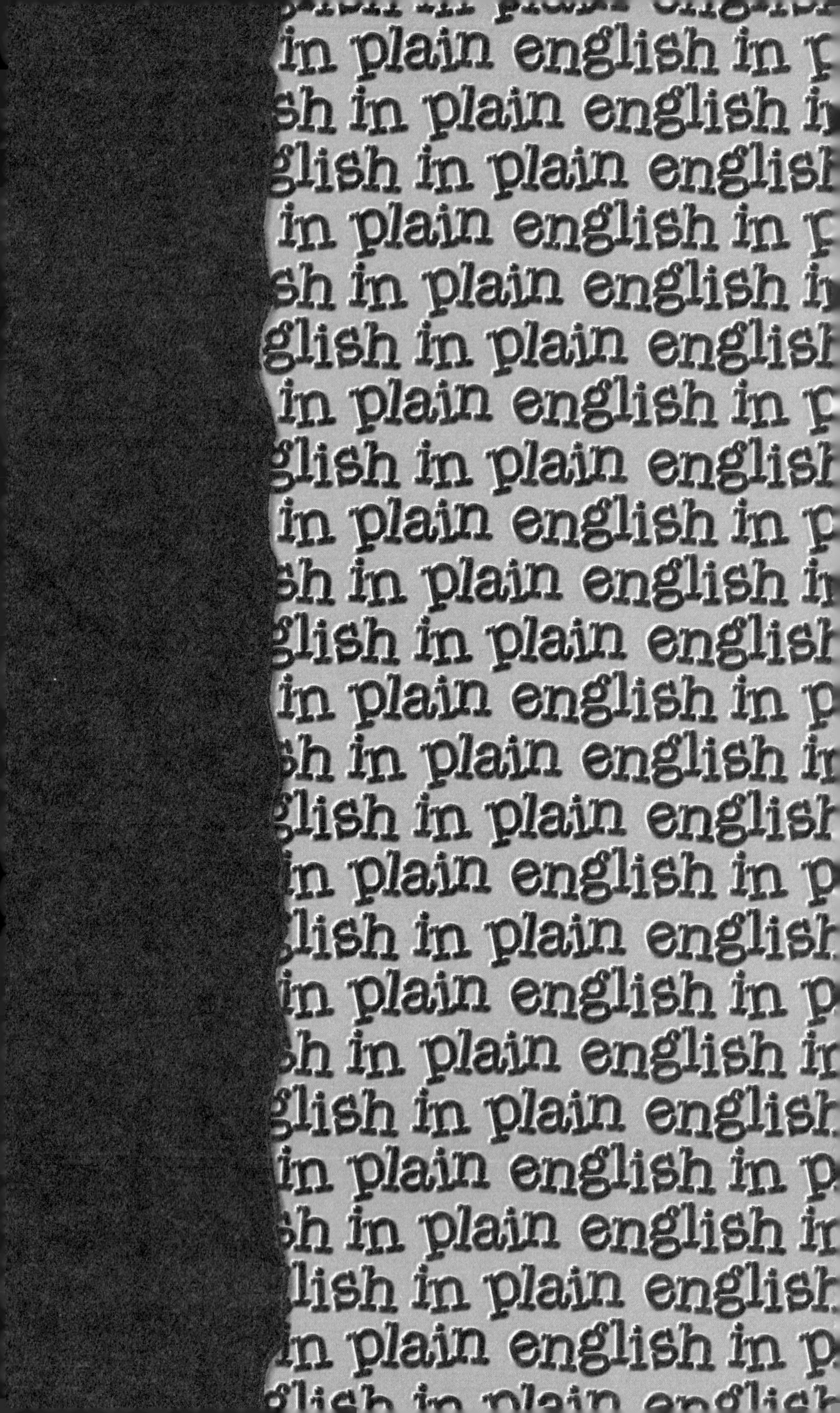

11

Shell Commands and Variables

A shell is a command, no less than every other UNIX command. If you've already browsed through the commands listed in Chapter 2, you'll see that the C shell, the Bourne shell, and the Korn shell were all listed as commands. All three shells do the same thing: They act as interpreters, translating your commands into a form the operating system can understand. When you log in to a UNIX system, you automatically launch a shell program; without it, you wouldn't be able to do much with UNIX.

As noted in Chapter 1, a shell uses a special symbol to show that it's ready and waiting for a command from you, called a *prompt*. The Bourne and Korn shells typically use the **$** symbol, while the C shell uses the % symbol. (If you're logged on the system as a *privileged user* — also known as the *superuser* or the *root user* — you'll have a hash mark (#) as your prompt.)

Most users configure their systems with the shell when they log in to the system (this is known as setting your *environment variables*, which are contained in a file referenced in your **.profile** file) or perform some special tasks with **shell scripts**. The analog to DOS batch files, shell scripts are exactly what the name implies: They are a script of commands performed by the system on command.

This chapter covers the most important shell variables, followed by some choice shell commands; it isn't necessary (or useful) to cover every shell variable and every shell command here. By the time you're using variables and shell commands, you're well into an intermediate to advanced topic; see the Bibliography for a listing of books that can help you on your way toward advanced shell usage.

Bourne and Korn Shell Variables

The *Bourne shell* has the distinction of being the original shell in UNIX. The newer *Korn shell* was designed as an improvement of the Bourne shell, incorporating several useful traits from the C shell (such as command history) while retaining the familiar structure of the Bourne shell.

Unless noted, the variables in the list that follows are valid for both the Korn and Bourne shells. The following is not an exhaustive list of shell variables, but rather the most useful and popular ones. Check your documentation or a book listed in the Bibliography for more information on shell variables.

VARIABLE	MEANING
CDPATH	Tells the shell where to look for a relative pathname, which allows you to enter shorter command lines. For instance, if you used the following line: **CDPATH=/usr/users/kevin/data in your .profile** file, you wouldn't need to refer to the full pathname every time you wanted to refer to that directory. You can list multiple directories as long as they are separated by colons (:).
COLUMNS	Sets the number of columns across your display. The default is 80. (Korn shell.)
EDITOR	Sets the default text editor, usually **emacs** or **vi**. Some commands and other applications call an editor. (Korn shell.)

VARIABLE	MEANING
ENV	Establishes the location of the environment file (usually **.kshrc**). (Korn shell.)
HISTSIZE	Sets the history list size. History refers to commands already executed; the list can be referenced on the command line by number. (Korn shell.)
HOME	When you log in to a system, you're immediately placed in your **HOME** directory. When you use the **cd** command with no parameters, you're automatically placed back into that directory.
IFS	Stands for Internal Field Separator. The prompt uses spaces, tabs, and newlines to separate items on a command line. If you were to set the **IFS** to **&,** the prompt would use that symbol to separate items on a command line.
LOGNAME	Stores the current user's login name. (Korn shell.)
MAIL	Designates your mail file, where **mailx** or another mail program automatically sends your incoming mail.
MAILCHECK	Tells the shell how often to check for mail (the default is every 10 minutes), measured in seconds. A setting of **MAILCHECK=3600** checks for mail every hour; a setting of **MAILCHECK=0** checks for mail every time a prompt appears on the screen (not the most efficient use of computing resources).
MAILPATH	Designates multiple mail files.
PATH	Sets the file-search path. If you screw up and mistakenly have the system check for multiple files, you could end up spending a lot of time as the shell searches through a large file system. Since most of your frequently used files are in the same directories, this allows you to tell the system where to look for commands.
PS1	Stands for Primary Shell prompt (the default is **$**). A line like **PS1="Wake up!"** would establish a prompt of **Wake up!**
PS2	Sets the secondary shell prompt (the default is **>**). The secondary prompt is used when a command runs over a single line.
SHELL	Sets the subshell, which is used by commands like **vi** or **ed**.
TERM	Stands for terminal type. For instance, a setting of **TERM=VT100** sets the terminal type for VT100, which is a popular terminal type.

VARIABLE	MEANING
TERMINFO	Stands for terminal information, stored in the **/usr/lib/terminfo** database. (Korn shell.)
TMOUT	Sets the timeout value, which is the period of inactivity (in seconds) before the system logs a user out. (Korn shell.)
TZ	Stands for Time zone, which is referenced by the date command. For instance, if you were located in the Central Time Zone in an area that supports daylight savings time, you'd normally use **TZ=CST6CDT**. (Korn shell.)

The time zone format may be different on your version of UNIX. Check your system documentation.)

C Shell Variables

The C shell dates from the 1970s, when it was originated at the University of California as a more advanced shell. This shell is so named because of its resemblance to the C programming language, although it does make for a nice little pun.

The following is not a full list of shell variables, but merely the most useful and popular ones. Check your documentation or a book listed in the Bibliography for more information on shell variables.

VARIABLE	MEANING
cdpath	Tells the shell where to look for a relative pathname, which allows you to enter shorter command lines. For instance, if you used the following line: **CDPATH=/usr/users/kevin/data** in your **.cshrc** file, you wouldn't need to refer to the full pathname every time you wanted to refer to that directory. You can list multiple directories as long as they are separated by colons (:).
echo	Displays full commands, including shell expansion.
history	Sets the history list size. History refers to commands already executed; the list can be referenced on the command line by number.
HOME	When you log in to a system, you're immediately placed in your **HOME** directory. When you use the **cd** command, you're automatically placed back into that directory.
mail	Designates your mail file, where **mailx** or another mail program automatically sends your incoming mail.

VARIABLE	MEANING
notify	Informs you when a job is completed.
PATH	Sets the file-search path. If you screw up and mistakenly have the system check for multiple files, you could end up spending a lot of time as the shell searches through a large file system. Since most of your frequently used files are in the same directories, this allows you to tell the system where to look for commands.
prompt	Sets the prompt, which informs you that the shell is waiting for a command. The default is %.
savehist	Determines the number of commands to be saved in your **.history** file, which received input thanks to the history command.
shell	This sets the subshell, which is used by commands like **vi** or **ed**.
TERM	Stands for terminal type. For instance, a setting of **TERM=VT100** sets the terminal type for VT100, which is a popular terminal type.
USER	Stores the current user's login name.

Shell Commands and Scripts

When you use a shell, you enter commands at the shell's prompt (usually $ or %). You can enter any of the commands described in this book, as well as a number of shell commands. These commands exist only in a particular shell, such as the **alias** command in the C shell (described in the "C Shell Commands" section later in this chapter).

In addition to entering commands at the prompt, you can also write shell scripts, which are sets of shell commands stored in an ASCII text file. Shell scripts are an easy way to store commonly used sets of UNIX commands. DOS users call shell scripts batch files. In DOS, these files have a **.BAT** extension. In UNIX, though, you are free to name your shell scripts anything you desire (providing you desire a valid UNIX filename, of course).

Shell scripts use both the same commands that you could type in at the shell prompt ($ or %) and some of the complex commands described here. It's usually easier to write a shell script and use it as needed that to reissue the commands whenever you want to do a common task.

You'll find that many of the following commands smack of programming. No, we're not out to make you programmers, but it is useful to know what these commands do, especially if you need to write a short shell script on your own. For more advanced shell scripting, check your documentation or a book listed in the Bibliography.

Comments

It's always wise to describe what a shell script does, so that when you look it up months from now you know why you originally wrote it. To help describe what is going on, you can include comments. A comment in a shell script begins with a # character at the start of the line. Any other text — to the end of the line — is treated as a comment; that is, the shell ignores this text. For example:

```
# This is a comment.
```

Comments apply equally to the Bourne, Korn, and C shells.

Empowering a Shell Script to Run

Most shells accept a special syntax — a comment really — on the first line that names the shell to run. This is important because shell commands differ. C shell scripts may not run under the Korn shell, for example. To specify the shell you want your script run under, you can format the first line as follows:

```
#!/bin/sh
```

The # starts a comment. The #! on the first line alerts the shell that the path of the shell to run follows, in this case **/bin/sh**, the Bourne shell. You can also specify **#!/bin/ksh** for the Korn shell or **#!/bin/csh** for the C shell. The Bash shell usually gets installed in **/usr/local/bin**, making for **#!/usr/local/bin/bash**.

Once you set up the special #! comment on the first line — and it must be on the first line — you can mark the shell script as executable.

You store shell scripts in ASCII text files. Before you can try out a shell script, you must tell UNIX that your ASCII text file really does contain commands. To do this, you can use the **chmod** command:

```
$ chmod +x my_shell_script
```

You need to enable the execute permission on the shell script's file. In the above example, we used **chmod** to enable the execute permission (+**x**) on the file **my_shell_script**.

CROSS-REFERENCE

See Chapter 2 for more on the **chmod** command.

Once you do this, you can execute your shell script by typing in the filename. For example:

```
$ my_shell_script
```

Bourne and Korn Shell Commands

When you're writing shell scripts, you often need to control what happens based on certain conditions. For example, you may want to copy the 1999 report to another directory using the **cp** command. But, if the 1999 report is not done yet (that is, if the file does not exist), you may want to take other action, such as notifying the user that the report is missing. You can use the **echo** command to display a message for the user.

However, you don't want to run both the **echo** command (with an error message) and the **cp** command. To control which command gets executed, you can use the **if-then** command.

If-Then

The Bourne and Korn shells allow you to run a command (or set of many commands) only under certain conditions. The problem is that you must format these conditions in a way that the shell understands. Format your **if-then** commands in the following way:

```
if test expression
   then
     command1
     command2
     command3
     ...
fi
```

11

Basically, **if-then** uses the built-in **test** command (which we cover below) to determine whether or not to run a set of commands. These commands are placed after **then** and before **fi**. (**Fi** stands for if backwards.) You can place any number of commands you need between **then** and **fi**. For example:

```
# Check if 5 is indeed 5.
if test 5 = 5
   then
      echo "5 equals 5"
fi
```

This example tests whether 5 is the same as 5. If so, it echoes (prints out) a statement to that effect.

The Test Command

The **test** command is both a UNIX command and a shell command. **test** returns a true value if the expression you pass to it is true. Otherwise, **test** returns a false value. The shell **if** command uses **test** to determine whether or not to execute the code between **then** and **fi**.

You can use many options with **test** when writing complex shell scripts. Most of these options delve into areas far too advanced for this beginning book. One option that you'll see a lot in shell script files, though, is the cryptic use of square brackets. You can use square brackets, [ ], as shorthand for the **test** command. For example:

```
if [ 5 = 5 ]
   then
      echo "5 still equals 5"
fi
```

For other test options, check your documentation or a book listed in the Bibliography.

If-Then-Else

Sometimes you need to perform a set of commands if the condition in an **if-then** command is not met, as well as if the condition is met. In that case, you can use **if-then-else**, which uses the following format:

```
if test expression
   then
     command1
     command2
     command3
     ...
   else
     command1
     command2
     command3
     ...
fi
```

If the test expression is true, then the shell executes the commands between **then** and **else**. Otherwise, the shell executes the commands between **else** and **fi**. For example:

```
if test 4 = 5
   then
      echo "4 equals 5"
   else
      echo "4 does not equal 5"
fi
```

If you run this, you should see that four does not equal five.

For Loops

The **for** command allows you to write a shell script that loops through a set of values, performing the same commands repeatedly. Most commonly, you want to loop through a set of files and perform the same operation on each file. The **for** command repeats a set of commands over a set of values for a given variable. The **for** command uses the following format:

```
for variable
   in values
   do
```

11

```
        command1
        command2
        command3
        ...
done
```

It often is important to place the **in** statement on its own line.

All commands between **do** and **done** get executed each time through the loop. Each time through the loop, your variable will have one of the values. For example:

```
for filename
   in *.1999
   do
       echo $filename
done
```

The variable *filename* will hold the name of a file ending in .**1999**, such as **jan.1999**, **feb.1999**, and **dec.1999**, each time through the loop.

C Shell Commands

The C shell provides the same basic set of control commands, such as **if-then-else**, as do the Bourne and Korn shells. However, the C shell uses its own syntax, which tends to be confusing at times.

If-Then

Like the Bourne and Korn shells, the C shell provides an **if-then** statement. In the C shell, it has a slightly different format:

```
if (expression) then
     command1
     command2
     command3
     ...
endif
```

For example:

```
if (5 == 5) then
      echo "5 does indeed equal 5"
endif
```

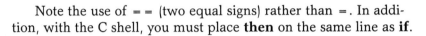

Note the use of == (two equal signs) rather than =. In addition, with the C shell, you must place **then** on the same line as **if**.

If-Then-Else

You can also use an **if-then-else** statement:

```
if (expression) then
     command1
     command2
     command3
     ...
else
     command1
     command2
     command3
     ...
endif
```

For example:

```
if (4 == 5) then
      echo "4 equals 5"
   else
      echo "4 does not equal 5"
endif
```

This example should print out:

```
  does not equal 5
```

11

Foreach

Instead of a command named **for**, the C shell provides a **foreach** command, but the effect is nearly the same:

```
foreach variable (list-of-values)
      command1
      command2
      command3
      ...
end
```

For example:

```
for each filename (*.1999)
       echo $filename
end
```

This example lists all files that end with **.1999**. Each time through the loop, the variable *filename* holds one of the filenames (ending in **.1999**).

Using Alias to Change Identities

In addition to the commands above, the C shell offers the handy **alias** command:

alias *new-name old-command*

For example, if you're more experienced with DOS than UNIX, you may be confused by all the options to the UNIX **ls** command. With alias, you can define your own command named **dir**, which acts more like the DOS **DIR** command:

```
alias dir     ls -alx
```

This command aliases dir for the more complex (and harder to remember) command of **ls -alx**. Thus, when you type in **dir**, the C shell actually executes **ls -alx**; you'll see a long-format directory listing, which is about the closest UNIX equivalent to the DOS **DIR** command. (Of course, this isn't necessary in Linux or FreeBSD, since the **dir** command already summons the **ls** command automatically.)

With alias, you're extending the set of commands offered by UNIX. This is very useful, particularly if you're moving to UNIX from another operating system, like DOS or VMS.

in plain english

12

Window Managers

A *window manager* controls the look and feel of your display if you're running the X Window System, Motif, or the Common Desktop Environment. It controls how and where windows are placed on your screen, what they look like, and how data is input. In addition, a window manager also controls things like icons and mouse actions.

The most popular window manager in the UNIX/X world is the Motif Window Manager, **mwm**. As a commercial offering of the Open Group (formerly from a separate organization called the Open Software Foundation), **mwm** is sold on its own, and it also serves as the basis of the **dtwm** window manager, which is the core of the Common Desktop Environment (CDE). CDE provides the default interface on Sun, Hewlett-Packard, IBM, and other commercial UNIX systems.

Other popular window managers include the Open Look Window Manager (**olwm**), the Tab Window Manager (**twm**), and the **fvwm** window manager that is usually part of Linux. These window managers are free.

The level of user tools differs between **mwm** and **dtwm**. Generally, **dtwm** offers a fuller environment, complete with session and style managers, as well as a full set of user tools (in Chapter 8, anything beginning with **dt** under "Graphical Commands" is part of the **dtwm** command set). A Front Panel centralizes these functions.

Most of the time, a window manager is configured to perform basic tasks in a way that won't attract your attention—you won't be driven to change the defaults or the way the window manager acts. However, if you do want to change the look and feel of your window manager, there's an easy way to make changes. Instead of spending much time on the details of how the **mwm** and **dtwm** window managers work, we will briefly discuss how to configure them.

Command-Line Options

These options, which you specify from the command line, can be invoked when the **dtwm** and **mwm** window managers are launched.

Option	PURPOSE
-display *display*	Specifies a *display* to use upon startup.
-xrm *resourcestring*	Specifies a resource string.
-multiscreen	Manages all screens; this is the default with **dtwm**, and it is usually the default with **mwm**.
-name *name*	Retrieves resources from *name*, as in *name**resource*.
-screens *name* [*name* [...]]	Specifies resource names for screens managed by **dtwm** and **mwm**.

Resources

Resources control the appearance of the window manager and how it interacts with you and application. To change the way **dtwm** or **mwm** behaves, edit the resource settings. These resources are stored in a resource file. Typically, this resource file for the **dtwm** window manager can be found at the following locations:

/usr/dt/app-defaults/$LANG/Dtwm or **$HOME/Dtwm**

Resource information for **mwm** can be found at these locations:

/usr/lib/ X11/app-defaults/Mwm or **$HOME/Mwm**

(For other locations at which you can find these files, see the **mwm** and **dtwm** documentation.)

What will you find in these files? Generally, information regarding files containing bitmaps, fonts, and window-manager-specific resources like menus and behavior specifications. You can control whether or not you want to use an icon box or place icons on the screen. The following types of resources are associated with **mwm** and **dtwm**:

- *Component-appearance resources*, which control menus, frames, icons, and other interface elements. The available resources are listed in Table 12-1.
- *General appearance and behavior resources,* which control how the window manager interact with other applications and applying to all screens and workspaces. The available resources are listed in Table 12-2.
- *Screen-specific appearance and behavior resources,* which are resources applied on a per-screen basis. These are listed in Table 12-3.
- *Client-specific resources,* which are set for a particular client window or class of client windows. These are listed in Table 12-4.
- *Workspace-specific resources,* which apply to a specific workspace. These are listed in Table 12-5, but they apply only to the **dtwm** window manager.

When editing resource files, you can choose to change all values for a given class of resources (such as fonts) or specific resource values. Specific resource values have names that generally start with a lowercase letter. Class resources, which apply to all values of a given class, usually start with an uppercase letter. The more specific settings take precedence over the resource classes.

These names are combined with the name of the window manager; for instance, to set the **background** resource, you'd use **Dtwm*background**. Similarly, to set the keyboard focus to a particular client window, you'd use **Dtwm*keyboardFocusPolicy**. A colon separates the name from the value, for example:

```
Dtwm*keyboardFocusPolicy: pointer
```

This resource command sets the **dtwm** window manager **keyboardFocusPolicy** resource to **pointer**, which means that the keyboard focus will follow the mouse pointer. The alternative value, **explicit**, means that you would need to click in a window to set the keyboard focus before typing.

Table 12-1 *Component-Appearance Resources for Dtwm and Mwm*

NAME	CLASS	VALUE TYPE	SETS...
background	Background	**color**	background color; any valid X value will do.
backgroundPixmap	BackgroundPixmap	**image_file**	the image of the window decoration when the window is not active.
bottomShadowColor	Foreground	**color**	right bevels of the window-manager decoration; any valid X value will do.
bottomShadowPixmap	Foreground	**image_file**	right bevels of the window-manager decoration.
fontList	FontList	**font_name**	font used in the window-manager decoration; the default is fixed.
foreground	Foreground	**color**	foreground color; any X color will do.
saveUnder	SaveUnder	T/F	whether save-unders are used; this is when the contents of windows obscured by the windows are saved. The default is F (false).
topShadowColor	Background	**color**	the top shadow color, on the upper and left bevels.
topShadowPixmap	TopShadowPixmap	**image_file**	the top shadow pixmap on the upper and left bevels.
activeBackground	Background	**color**	the background color of the decoration when the window is active.
activeBackgroundPixmap	BackgroundPixmap	**image_file**	the background pixmap of the decoration when the window is active.

NAME	CLASS	VALUE TYPE	SETS...
activeBottomShadowColor	Foreground	**color**	the bottom shadow color of the decoration when the window is active.
activeBottomShadowPixmap	BottomShadowPixmap	**image_file**	the bottom shadow pixmap of the decoration when the window is active.
activeForeground	Foreground	**color**	the foreground color of the decoration when the window is active.
activeTopShadowColor	Background	**color**	the top shadow color of the decoration when the window is active.
activeTopShadowPixmap	TopShadowPixmap	**image_file**	the top shadow pixmap of the decoration when the window is active.

Table 12-2 *General Appearance and Behavior Resources for Dtwm and Mwm*

NAME	CLASS	VALUE TYPE	SETS...
autoKeyFocus	AutoKeyFocus	T/F	focus when a window with focus is withdrawn from window management or is iconified; the default (T) sets the focus on the previous window with focus.
autoRaiseDelay	AutoRaiseDelay	**millisec**	the time that the window manager will wait before raising a window after it gets keyboard focus in milliseconds.
bitmapDirectory	BitmapDirectory	**directory**	directory containing bitmaps. The default is **/usr/include/X11/bitmaps**.

Continued

Table 12-2 *Continued*

NAME	CLASS	VALUE TYPE	SETS...
bitmapDirectory	BitmapDirectory	**directory**	directory containing bitmaps. The default is **/usr/include/X11/bitmaps**.
clientAutoPlace	ClientAutoPlace	T/F	the position of a window that has no default position; the default is to position a window with the top left corners of the frames offset horizontally and vertically.
colormapFocusPolicy	ColormapFocusPolicy	**value**	the colormap focus policy, one of **explicit** (colormap selection action is done on a client window to set the colormap focus to that window), **pointer** (client window containing the pointer has the colormap focus), or **keyboard** (client window with the keyboard input has the colormap focus).
configFile	ConfigFile	**filename**	the location for the default configuration file; the default for **dtwm** is **$HOME/ dtwmrc**, and the default for **mwm** is **$HOME/.mwmrc**.
deiconifyKeyFocus	DeiconifyKeyFocus	T/F	whether a deiconified window has focus.
doubleClickTime	DoubleClickTime	**num**	the time between clicks in a double-click, in milliseconds.
enableWarp	enableWarp	T/F	the pointer to the center of the selected window during keyboard-controlled resize and move operations if True.
enforceKeyFocus	EnforceKeyFocus	T/F	key focus.

NAME	CLASS	VALUE TYPE	SETS...
frameStyle	FrameStyle	**value**	the frame style: **slab** (the client area appears to be at the same height as the top of the window frame) or **recessed** (where the client area appears lower than the top of the window frame. (**dtwm** only.)
iconAutoPlace	IconAutoPlace	T/F	the placement of an icon, as determined by the iconPlacement setting.
iconClick	IconClick	T/F	whether a system menu is left posted when an icon is clicked.
interactivePlacement	InteractivePlacement	T/F	the initial placement of a window; T lets the user set the placement, while F uses the application configuration defaults.
keyboardFocusPolicy	KeyboardFocusPolicy	**value**	keyboard focus: **explicit** (where the user explicitly chooses a window) or **pointer** (where the pointer determines the window with focus).
lowerOnIconify	LowerOnIconify	T/F	if an icon should be placed on the bottom of the screen (T) or in the same location as the window (F).
marqueeSelect Granularity	MarqueeSelect Granularity	**pixels**	how often changes in the marquee selection are reported to the window manager.
moveThreshold	MoveThreshold	**pixels**	maximum number of pixels before a move operation is initiat-ed; the default is 4.
multiScreen	MultiScreen	T/F	if the window manager should manager all screens (T) or only a single screen (F).
passButtons	PassButtons	T/F	if button-press events are passed to clients after performing a window-manager function.

Continued

12

Table 12-2 *Continued*

NAME	CLASS	VALUE TYPE	SETS...
passSelectButton	PassSelectButton	T/F	if select button-press events are passed to clients after performing a window- manager function.
positionIsFrame	PositionIsFrame	T/F	how window-position information is interpreted: as the position of the window-manager frame (T) or the client area (F).
positionOnScreen	PositionOnScreen	T/F	whether windows should be initially be placed so they are not clipped by the edge of the screen.
quitTimeout	QuitTimeout	**value**	the time (in milliseconds) that the window manager will wait for a client to update the **WM_COMMAND** property after being warned.
raiseKeyFocus	RaiseKeyFocus	T/F	whether a window raised by the **f.normalize_and_ raise** function should receive the 99input focus.
refreshByClearing	RefreshByClearing	T/F	the mechanism for refreshing a screen: T performs **XClearArea**, while F creates a new window and destroys the old one.
rootButtonClick	RootButtonClick	T/F	whether a click on the root window posts the root menu in "sticky" mode. (**dtwm** only.)
screens	Screens	**value**	the resource names to use for managed screens. Each screen can have its own resource name.
showFeedback	ShowFeedback	**value**	whether feedback windows or confirmation dialog windows are displayed.

NAME	CLASS	VALUE TYPE	SETS...
startupKeyFocus	StartupKeyFocus	T/F	whether a window gets keyboard focus when the window is mapped.
useFrontPanels	useFrontPanel	T/F	the display of the front panel (**dtwm** only).
wMenuButtonClick	WMenuButtonClick	T/F	whether a click of the mouse when the pointer is over the window menu button posts and leaves posted the window menu.
wMenuButtonClick2	WMenuButtonClick2	T/F	a double-click on the window menu button does an **f.kill** function.

Table 12-3 *Screen-Specific Appearance and Behavior Resources*

NAME	CLASS	VALUE TYPE	SETS...
buttonBindings	ButtonBindings	**value**	button bindings.
cleanText	CleanText	T/F	the display of window-manager text in client title and feedback windows: T draws with a clear (no stipple) background, while F draws directly on the existing background.
fadeNormalIcon	FadeNormalIcon	T/F	whether an icon is grayed after the window has been normalized.
feedbackGeometry	FeedbackGeometry	**value**	the position of the move and resize feedback window.
frameBorderWidth	FrameBorderWidth	**num**	the size of the border width, in pixels.
iconBoxGeometry	IconBoxGeometry	**value**	the initial position and size of the icon box.

Continued

Table 12-3 *Continued*

NAME	CLASS	VALUE TYPE	SETS...
iconBoxName	IconBoxName	**value**	icon-box resource names.
iconBoxSBDisplay Policy	IconBoxSBDisplay Policy	**string**	the scrollbar policy: **all**, **vertical**, or **horizontal**.
iconBoxTitle	IconBoxTitle	**string**	the title of the icon box.
iconDecoration	IconDecoration	**value**	the general icon decoration.
iconImageMaximum	IconImageMaximum	**wxh**	the maximum size of the icon image.
iconImageMinimum	IconImageMimimum	**wxh**	the minimum size of the icon image
iconPlacement	IconPlacement	-	the icon placement scheme.
iconPlacement Margin	IconPlacement Margin	**num**	the distance between the edge of the screen (in pixels) and the icons placed along the edge of the screen.
keyBindings	KeyBindings	**string**	key bindings.
limitResize	LimitResize	T/F	a user can exceed the maximum window size.
maximumMaximum Size	MaximumMaximum Size	**wxh**	the maximum width and height of a window, in pixels.
moveOpaque	MoveOpaque	T/F	whether the actual window or an ghosted representation of a window is moved.
resizeBorderWidth	ResizeBorderWidth	**num**	the border of a frame border, in pixels.

NAME	CLASS	VALUE TYPE	SETS...
resizeCursors	ResizeCursors	T/F	whether resize cursors are always displayed.
transientDecoration	TransientDecoration	**string**	amount of decoration on transient windows.
transientFunctions	TransientFunctions	**string**	which window-management functions are available to transient (dialog) windows.
useIconBox	UseIconBox	T/F	whether icons should be placed in an icon box.
workspaceCount	WorkspaceCount	**num**	initial number of workspaces that the window manager creates when starting. (**dtwm** only.)

Table 12-4 *Client-Specific Resources for Dtwm and Mwm*

NAME	CLASS	VALUE TYPE	SETS...
clientDecoration	ClientDecoration	**string**	the amount of window frame decoration.
clientFunctions	ClientFunctions	**string**	which **dtwm** functions are appropriate for the client.
focusAutoRaise	FocusAutoRaise	T/F	whether clients are raised when they have the focus.
iconImage	IconImage	**pathname**	icon image for a client.
iconImageBackground	Background	**color**	the color of an icon background.
iconImageBottomShadow Color	Foreground	**color**	the color of an icon bottom shadow.

Continued

Table 12-4 *Continued*

NAME	CLASS	VALUE TYPE	SETS...
iconImageBottomShadow Pixmap	Pixmap	**pixmap**	the pixmap of the bottom shadow of an icon.
iconImageForeground	Foreground	**color**	the color foreground of an icon image.
iconImageTopShadowColor	Background	**color**	the top shadow color of the icon image.
iconImageTopShadowPixmap	TopShadowPixmap	**color**	the top shadow pixmap of the icon image.
matteBackground	Background	**color**	background color of the matte.
matteBottomShadowColor	Foreground	**color**	the bottom shadow color of the matte.
matteBottomShadowPixmap	BottomShadowPixmap	**pixmap**	the bottom shadow pixmap of the matte.
matteForeground	Foreground	**color**	the foreground color of the matte.
matteTopShadowColor	Background	**color**	the top shadow color of the matte.
matteTopShadowPixmap	TopShadowPixmap	**color**	the top shadow pixmap of the matte.
matteWidth	MatteWidth	**value**	the width of the optional matte.
maximumClientSize	MaximumClientSize	**wxh**	either a size specification or a direction that indicates how a client window is to be maximized.
useClientIcon	UseClientIcon	T/F	whether a client-supplied icon should take precedence over a user-supplied icon.

NAME	CLASS	VALUE TYPE	SETS...
usePPosition	UsePPosition	**string**	whether the position in **WM_NORMAL_ HINTS** property is to honored.
windowMenu	WindowMenu	**string**	the name of the menu pane.

Table 12-5 *Workspace-Specific Resources for Dtwm*

NAME	CLASS	VALUE TYPE	SETS...
title	Title	**string**	the workspace name.
ColorSetId	ColorSetId	**num**	the color set for a backdrop.
image	Image	**string**	the image to use as the backdrop.
imageBackground	ImageBackground	**pixel**	the color to use in the background of a backdrop.
imageForeground	ImageForeground	**pixel**	the color to use in the foreground of a backdrop.

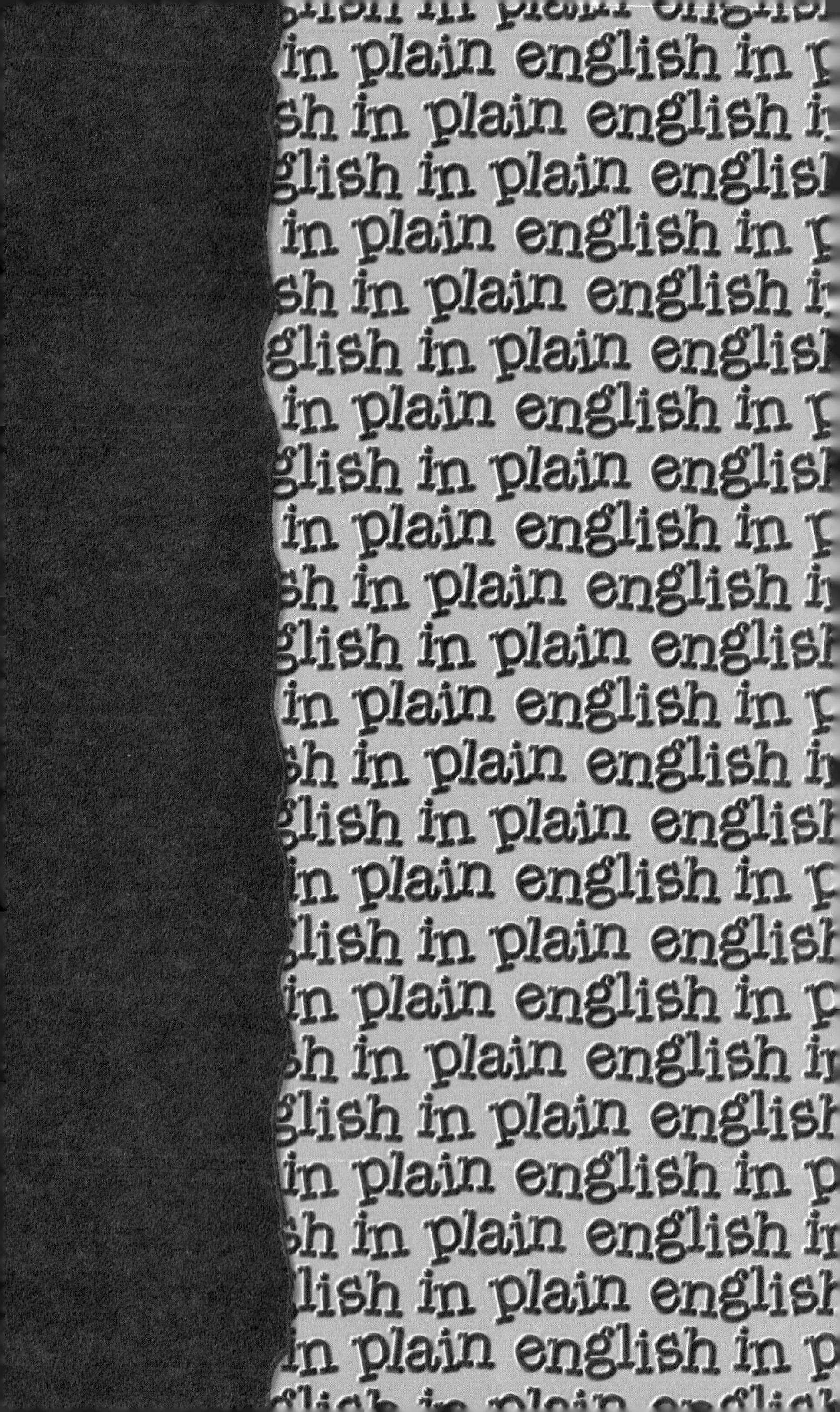
in plain english in
in plain english
in plain
in plain english in
in plain english
in plain
in plain english in
in plain
in plain english in
in plain english
in plain
in plain english in
in plain english
in plain
in plain english in
in plain
in plain english in
in plain english
in plain
in plain english in
in plain english
in plain
in plain english in

Glossary

absolute pathname
The complete name of a file, replete with the total path of directories, indicating the file's location on the directory tree. For instance, the absolute pathname of the file *file1* is **/usr/users/kevin/docs/file1**.

address
Either the name of a specific machine on a network or the name of the entire UNIX system. Both meanings are used in discussions of electronic mail and communications.

aging
Used by the system to determine when passwords or files are old enough to be changed or deleted.

alias
A substitute for a command set up by the user, often a short substitute for a longer, often-used command.

anonymous ftp
A remote login that requires no password; used for downloading files from a remote machine. See **FTP**.

append
To attach text to the end of an existing text file.

application
Software that supplies specific functions to end users; for instance, WordPerfect is a word-processing application.

argument
Used to modify a command on the command line.

ASCII
Stands for American Standard Code for Information Interchange; a standard format used to communicate data between different types of computer. An ASCII file created on a UNIX computer will be readable on other kinds of computers.

awk
A programming language geared to text manipulation.

BSD
(Berkeley Software Distribution) A still-popular version of UNIX, originated at the University of California-Berkeley, especially noted for its advanced networking capabilities. Freeware versions include FreeBSD and NetBSD.

background
When programs are run in this mode, the user can perform other tasks and will be notified when the background program is completed. Background commands are notated with an ampersand (**&**) at the end of the command line.

backup
A archived copy of user-specified files, kept as an insurance policy should the original files be damaged or corrupted. The UNIX operating system uses the **tar** command to create backups.

batch processing
Where the system is given a series of commands (some of which may depend on the output of other commands) and perform these commands without any interaction with the user. Although a throwback to the olden days of computing, much of what can be done in UNIX can be done with batch processing.

bin
Directory that contains most of the standard UNIX programs and utilities.

binary file
A machine-readable format that usually cannot be read directly by other computers.

bitmap
A method of displaying graphics in which the machine maps out specific points (called *pixels*) on a display.

boot

Starting the computer and loading the operating system into memory.

Bourne shell

A commonly used shell (sh) created by Steven Bourne of Bell Labs. The original shell.

buffer

A section of random-access memory (RAM) used to store data temporarily for near-future use.

bug

Errors in software. Sometimes called *unanticipated features*.

C

A programming language created by Dennis Ritchie (Bell Labs) in the 1960s. Most UNIX programming utilizes the C programming language (as well as the C++ language) because most of UNIX is written in C.

C++

An enhanced version of C, written by Bjarne Stroustrup (Bell Labs), that is gaining in popularity in both the general computing world and among UNIX programmers.

C shell

A commonly used shell created by Bill Joy and others at the University of California-Berkeley.

CPU (Central Processing Unit)

The brains of the computer; usually a processor that performs much of the actual work of the computer, including processing data and carrying out instructions.

child process

A process started by a parent process through a fork. Every UNIX process is a child of another process, except for **init**.

client

In a distributed file system, a computer that accesses the files and services on a server. In the X Window System, an application that runs on the local machine (as opposed to the server).

command

An instruction sent to the shell, which interprets the command and acts upon it.

command history

See **history**.

command line
One or more commands, arguments, and options strung together at the prompt to create a command.

command mode
IIn a text editor, the mode in which the user supplies commands for saving and editing files.

command substitution
Using the output of one command as input for a new command.

command-line substitution
When a shell interprets the entire command line, including substitution of values for variables and wildcards.

comments
Text included in script or programming files that is not meant to be acted upon by the computer, but rather used to illuminate commands for someone reading the file.

communications node name
Unique name given to a UNIX system for networking and communications purposes.

compiler
A program that turns source code into programs that can be executed by the computer. For instance, C source-code files must be run through a compiler before being run by the computer as a full program.

compressed file
File that has been shrunk by compression software to 75 percent of its original size, or less.

conditional execution
A construction where one action won't be taken unless another action is performed satisfactorily (if this, then that).

console
Two meanings: A terminal that is the mother of all terminals, displaying all the system error messages; or, more generally, the terminal used by the system administrator.

core dump
A very bad thing. If an error occurs that a program can't deal with, the program will display all the content of the memory before shutting down; this is the core dump.

current directory

Your current location on the file system. The **cd** command is used to change current directories.

cursor

A symbol used to display the current position on a screen. Older terminals use blinking squares; X Window System users can use just about anything, including (our favorite) a Gumby character.

DOS (Disk Operating System)

An operating system designed for personal computers by Microsoft and sold under the MS-DOS and PC-DOS names.

daemon

Despite the title, a good thing. A daemon (pronounced **demon**) is set up to perform a regular, mundane task without any user initialization or supervision.

database management

A structured way of storing information so it can be easily sorted and otherwise managed by the computer.

debugger

A program that provides information about bugs in software.

default

A value or state assumed when no other is supplied.

delimiter

A marker used to distinguish between sections of a command or a database. With UNIX, spaces are used as delimiters between portions of a command line.

destination

As you might expect, the target for a directed command.

dev

Directory containing device files.

device

A physical device attached to the computer system, such as a printer or a modem. UNIX's device drivers allow the system to talk to these devices.

device file

A file that contains a description of the device so the operating system can properly send data to and from the device.

device-independent
Able to perform a task without regard for a specific computer or peripheral. The text processor, **ditroff**, is device-independent because it will work with many different printers.

directory
A grouping of files and other directories; analogous to a folder residing in a file cabinet.

display
The physical part of the computer system used to communicate back and forth with the user.

distributed filesystem
A group of two or more physical computers, containing files and programs, that appears as one contiguous system to the end user. Also refers to the software introduced in System V Release 4 that accomplishes this goal.

distributed processing
A theory of computing that allows resources to be allocated efficiently on a network; for instance, a PC user could use a more powerful workstation on the network for computation-heavy processing.

domain
Best envisioned as a pyramid, a domain is a group that has control over all groups — other domains or no — beneath it.

domain addressing
Electronic-mail addressing scheme that specifies a specific address within a larger domain; if the address name is **reichard@mr.net**, the domain would be **mr.net**.

dot command
Just what the name implies: A command preceded by a dot. Used to tell the shell to execute the commands in a file; also used by **troff** and other text-processing tools to indicate formatting commands.

edit buffer
A section of RAM used to contain a file while you edit the file with a text editor.

editor
A program used to edit ASCII files, such as **ed**, **vi**, and **emacs**.

editing mode
In a text editor, the mode where editing changes (like inserting new text, cutting, pasting, etc.) occur. Also known as **command mode**.

electronic mail
The ability to send and receive mail from different computer systems.

encryption
A method of encoding a file so it's not readable by other users as a security measure.

end-of-file (EOF) character
The character, surprisingly enough, that indicates the end of a file. The combination **Ctrl-D** is the EOF character in UNIX.

environment
The sum of all your exported shell variables, which are set individually by you and either stored in your **.profile** file or set manually by the user as need be.

environment file
Specific to the Korn shell, this file also contains environment settings.

environment variable
An individual shell setting that makes up part of your environment. For instance, you can designate a directory as your HOME directory as an environment variable.

error message
In a nutshell, a message that tells you something is awry.

escape key
Character labeled **Esc** on a keyboard and used for a variety of functions.

etc
Directory containing everything but device files and program files.

executable file
A program file that runs when you type its name on the command line and press Enter.

execute permission
A setting for a executable file that denotes who can run the program.

exit
Quitting a running program; in UNIX, technically you are terminating a process.

export
To make shell variables available to other commands that are executed.

extension
A suffix to a filename that help identify the data contained in the file. A C source-code file usually ends with a **.c** suffix.

field

A vertical column of data in a structured data file, with all the entries of the same type. If we were to create a file containing the names, phone numbers, and salary of every employee, with each employee's phone number contained in the second column, we would call that column a field.

file

A defined set of characters (called *bytes*) referenced by its filename.

file sharing

The mechanisms (RFS and NFS) used to make files on one system available to users on another system.

filename

The obvious: the name given to a file. Files in the same directory cannot have the same filename, but files in different directories may have the same name.

file system

The pyramid-like method used in UNIX to organize files and directories: A root directory (analogous to the top of the pyramid) contains several subdirectories, and these subdirectories in turn may contain further subdirectories. Any directory can hold files. Separate disks and disk partitions are treated as separate file systems that get mounted onto the main UNIX directory hierarchy at locations called mount points.

filling

An action in a text processor where as much text is crammed onto a line as possible.

filter

A type of UNIX program that takes input from one file and provides output to the display or another file based on parameters set up by the user.

foreground

Commands that have the full attention of the system and do not return control to the user until the command is completed. In UNIX, the default is to run commands in the foreground.

fork

When a program starts another program (called a *child process*).

FTP

Process used to connect to any other computer on your network running the **ftp command**; when connected, **ftp** can then be used transfer files to your computer. Can also be used to access files anywhere on the Internet provided you have access to the Internet.

full pathname
The full description of the location of a file on the directory tree, from the root directory down.

function key
A key (usually marked as **F1**, **F2**, etc.) that can be defined by the operating system and/or applications to perform any number of functions. The actions attached to the key usually differ from program to program and operating system to operating system.

gateways
Computers that forward mail to other connected machines.

global
To make changes to all occurrences of a given object; to change every instance of Word to word in a file with emacs would be an example of a global search and replace.

graphical user interface
A metaphoric display of a computer system, with icons, windows and scrollbars. Motif, Open Look, the Macintosh, and Window are all examples of graphical user interfaces.

group
A defined set of users.

header
The beginning area of a file that contains vital statistics about the file. A mail file contains a header that specifies, among other things, the sender of the message and the route it takes.

header file
A C-language file used to include system-specific information. Sometimes called **include** files, as they are specified in a source-code file with the include command.

hidden file
A file beginning with a dot (**.profile**, for example) that is not returned by the **ls** command unless ls is told to return the names of all files in a directory, including hidden files.

hierarchical filesystem
See **filesystem**.

history
A record of previous commands maintained in your computer's memory. Available in the C, **bash**, **tcsh**, and Korn shells.

history substitution
Plucking a command line from a history list and using it again by typing the number assigned to the command. Available in the C, **bash**, **tcsh**, and Korn shells.

home directory
The directory the user is placed in after logging in. This directory is set in the **.profile** file with the **HOME=** command.

hostname
The name of your UNIX system.

icon
A graphical representation of a program or file.

inbox
The storage area for electronic mail that has not been read.

init
The initialization process, which launches when you boot a computer running the UNIX operating system. All processes are children of the init process.

inode
The location of information about files in the file system.

input mode
The mode where a text editor will accept input and includes it in the edited file. The opposite of editing mode.

interactive
Involves a dialogue of sorts between user and computer; the computer does not perform future tasks until given approval by the user. Most UNIX work can be done with the opposite of interactive computing, *batch processing*.

Internet
The umbrella name for a group of computer networks that distribute Web pages, newsgroups, and electronic mail around the world.

Internet address or IP address
The name given to a computer system or single-user workstation that allows it to communicate with other Internet-connected machines.

job
Another name for process or program running.

job control
Changing the status of a job, such as killing it or resuming a suspended job.

job shell

A superset of the Bourne shell (**sh**) devoted to job control.

kernel

The core of the UNIX operating system that interacts directly with the computer.

keyboard

That big thing with keys used to provide input. If you really looked up the definition of **keyboard** in a UNIX tutorial, we strongly advise you take a remedial "Introduction to Computers" class before proceeding with any UNIX usage.

kill buffer

A section of RAM devoted to storage of deleted text, which can then be called back into the text editor for further editing.

Korn shell

The shell (**ksh**) created by David Korn that improved on the older, popular Bourne shell.

language

Instructions translated into commands a computer can understand. Popular languages include C, BASIC, PASCAL, and FORTRAN.

library

A set of commonly used C-language functions.

line editor

A text editor that processes one line at a time, such as **ed**.

link

IInstead of wasting disk space on multiple copies of a commonly used file, one copy of the file is maintained and other filenames are linked to the original file.

local-area network

In the PC world, a group of personal computers connected via cable to a central computer (the server) that distributes applications and files. A UNIX network is also occasionally referred to as a local-area network.

login

The process of establishing a session on the main UNIX system after providing a login name and a password (also called *logging in*, *logon*, or *logging on*).

login name

The truncated, unique name given to all users on a UNIX system.

login shell

A shell launched when you log in. Normally, your login shell is listed in the **/etc/passwd** file. See **shell**.

logname
See **login name**.

logout
The process of quitting a UNIX session, typically by typing **EXIT**, **logout**, or **Ctrl-D**. (Also known as *logging out*, *logoff*, or *logging off*.)

look and feel
The specific arrangement of elements on a screen (scrollbars, title bars, etc.).

loop
A state where commands are to be executed again and again until some condition is met.

macros
Short instructions that are expanded by the shell to mean longer, more explicit commands.

mailbox
The file area used to store electronic-mail messages.

man pages
See **online-manual pages**.

manual macros
Macros used to create formatted online manual pages.

memorandum macros (mm)
Macros used in conjunction with **troff** to create stylized business letters, resumes, and reports.

Meta key
A specified key used in conjunction with other keys to create additional key combinations. On a PC keyboard, the **Alt** key is the **Meta** key; on an older Sun keyboard, the **Alt** key is **not** the **Meta** key.

Motif
Created by the Open Software Foundation and now maintained by the Open Group, Motif is a style guide that defines a particular look and feel for programs. Motif also includes a programming library, window manager, and more. Based on the X Window System.

mount
To make a file system available to users, either locally or remotely.

multiprocessing
To run more than one task or process at a time; one of the great strengths of the UNIX operating system.

multitasking
To run more than one task or process at a time; one of the great strengths of the UNIX operating system.

multiuser
A capability that allows more than one user to be active on the system at once; one of the great strengths of the UNIX operating system.

NFS (Network File System)
Software developed to create a distributed filesystem for use with both UNIX and non-UNIX computers.

networking
Connecting computers via phone line or direct link so they can share data.

newline
Character placed at the end of every line in a text file, usually created by pressing the **Return** (or **Enter**) key.

newsreaders
Software dedicated to reading Usenet newsgroups.

newsfeed
On the Usenet, all the incoming message files from the worldwide newsgroups.

newsgroup
On the Usenet, public discussions of various topics.

noclobber
Condition set where a new file cannot overwrite an existing file with the same line unless the action is approved by the user.

Online-manual page
Technically detailed information about a command, accessed by the **man** command.

Open Look
Created by Sun Microsystems and AT&T, Open Look is a style guide that defines a particular look and feel for programs.

operating system
Software that controls a computer, acts as an interface for a user, and runs applications. UNIX is an operating system.

options
Characters that modify the default behavior of a command.

ordinary file
A text or data file with no special characteristics; the most common file type in the UNIX operating system.

orphan
A process that runs even though its parent process has been killed.

owner
The user with the ability to set permissions for a file.

paging
A memory-management scheme that divides RAM into 4K segments for more efficient shuffling of data to and from RAM and a hard disk.

parent process
A process that generates another process.

parsing
Logically dividing a command so we can divine its meaning.

partition
A section of a hard disk treated as a separate area by the operating system.

password
A unique set of character designed to confirm your status as a legitimate user of a system.

path
A list of directories that the system uses to search for executables.

pathnames
A description of where a file resides in the filesystem. All pathnames flow from the root directory.

permissions
A security tool that determines who can access a file.

pipe
A logical device that allows standard output from one command to be used as standard input for another command.

PostScript
A system-independent page-description language developed by Adobe Systems.

process
Essentially, a program running on the computer.

process identification number (PID)
A unique number assigned to a program so it can be tracked and managed by the operating system and user.

profile
A description of a user's environment variables, stored in the **.profile** file.

program
A set of instructions for the computer to carry out.

prompt
A character used by the shell to indicate that it is waiting for input. In addition, some programs (like **ftp**) supply unique prompts.

RAM (Random-Access Memory)
A physical area of the computer used for short-term storage of data and programs. When a computer is turned off, the data in RAM disappears.

RFS (Remote File System)
Software developed to create a distributed filesystem for use only with the UNIX operating system.

record
A row in a structured data file. If we were to create a file containing the names, phone numbers, and salary of every employee, with each employee's information contained in a single row, we could call that row a record.

redirection
See **standard input and output**.

relational operator
A symbol that sets forth a condition in a programming language, such as C or awk. These conditionals are based on algebraic notation.

relative pathname
The location of a file in relation to another location in the file system.

root directory
The topmost directory in a file system that contains all other directories and subdirectories. Indicated in all pathnames as a slash (/).

root user
See **superuser**.

screen editor
A text editor that allows the user to view a document one screen at a time and edit anywhere on that screen through movement via cursors or mouse.

secondary prompt
A character used by the shell to indicate that additional input is needed before a program can run.

server
In a distributed filesystem, a computer that supplies files and services to other computers. In the X Window System, software that runs on a local machine that links the local machine to other machines.

shell
A program that interprets commands from the user into instructions the computer can understand. Popular shells include the Bourne, Korn, Bash, and C shells.

shell script
A file containing a series of commands for a UNIX shell.

signal
An instruction sent by the operating system to a program, telling it to shut down or otherwise modify its behavior.

SPARCstation
Popular UNIX workstation sold by Sun Microsystems.

standard error
The default location for error messages, usually your screen.

standard input and output
The path the data takes: Input usually comes from your keyboard or another program, while output is usually sent to your screen, to a file, or to a printer. When you specify output to anything but the defaults, you are redirecting the input and output.

state
See **system state**.

status line
A portion of the screen used to provide feedback to the user. Not supported by all UNIX programs.

superuser
The user who can do just about everything possible within the UNIX operating system. Normally the topmost of the privileged users.

swapping
Using the hard disk as a slower form of RAM when there's no RAM available to run programs or store data.

symbolic links
An advanced form of a linked file that allows links between files located on remote file systems.

system administrator
A worker officially assigned to oversee housekeeping details on a UNIX system, including adding new users and scheduling system backups.

system call
Actions available to programs only after communicating with the kernel, such as printing files or saving data to disk.

system name
Name used to identify a UNIX system, usually the version of UNIX used.

system state
The state of the operating system: single user, multiuser, administrative, and more.

TCP/IP (Transmission Control Protocol/Internet Protocol)
Networking protocols used to link UNIX and non-UNIX computers. Serves as the networking basis of the Internet.

terminal
Originally used to describe a dumb machine consisting of little more than a keyboard and a screen that relies on the larger system for its computing power; now used to describe any computer used to communicate with a UNIX system.

text editor
A UNIX program, such as **vi** or **emacs**, used to create ASCII text files.

text-formatting program
A program, such as **troff**, that takes a text file created elsewhere and prepares it with formatting command for output to a printer.

thrashing
A computer slowdown caused when the system is writing extensively to and from its hard disk because all the RAM is in use.

tmp
Directory used by the system for temporary storage of working files.

toggle
Turning features on or off in the C and Korn shells.

UUCP (UNIX-to-UNIX system Copy)
Program that copies files from one system to another via communication on ordinary telephone lines.

UUCP Network
A series of UNIX computers that pass along electronic mail and files all around the world.

UNIX
The greatest operating system in the whole wide world. (We're not prejudiced.) You should be commended for your astute and informed selection of such a great operating system.

Usenet
A loose confederation of computer systems (both UNIX and non-UNIX) that transmits electronic mail and newsgroups.

userid
Number used to represent a user under the hood, but rarely displayed for the user to see and use. See **login name**.

utility
A very specialized program that performs only a few actions.

virtual memory
See **paging**.

wildcards
Special characters within a filename that tells the shell to search for all files with similar filenames: ***r**, for example, would tell the shell to return all files ending with the character **r**.

window manager
X Window program that defines how other programs actually appear and act on the display.

word processor
Software that combines the powers of text editors and text processors into single packages.

workstation
Usually a powerful, networked, single-user computing running the UNIX operating system.

WYSIWYG (what-you-see-is-what-you-get)
A term describing word-processors and electronic-publishing packages that display exactly how a document will look before it is printed.

X terminal
Computer that runs a local X server, but relies on a machine elsewhere on the network for most of its computing power.

X Window System
Graphical windowing system created by MIT and can be described as building blocks for fuller user interfaces, such as Motif or Open Look; is not tied to any particular operating system but has been popularized with the UNIX operating system.

xterm

Popular X Window program that provides a command-line interface to the UNIX operating system.

zombie

Process that is not active, but not yet killed by the parent process. It's a defunct process that remains in the process table.

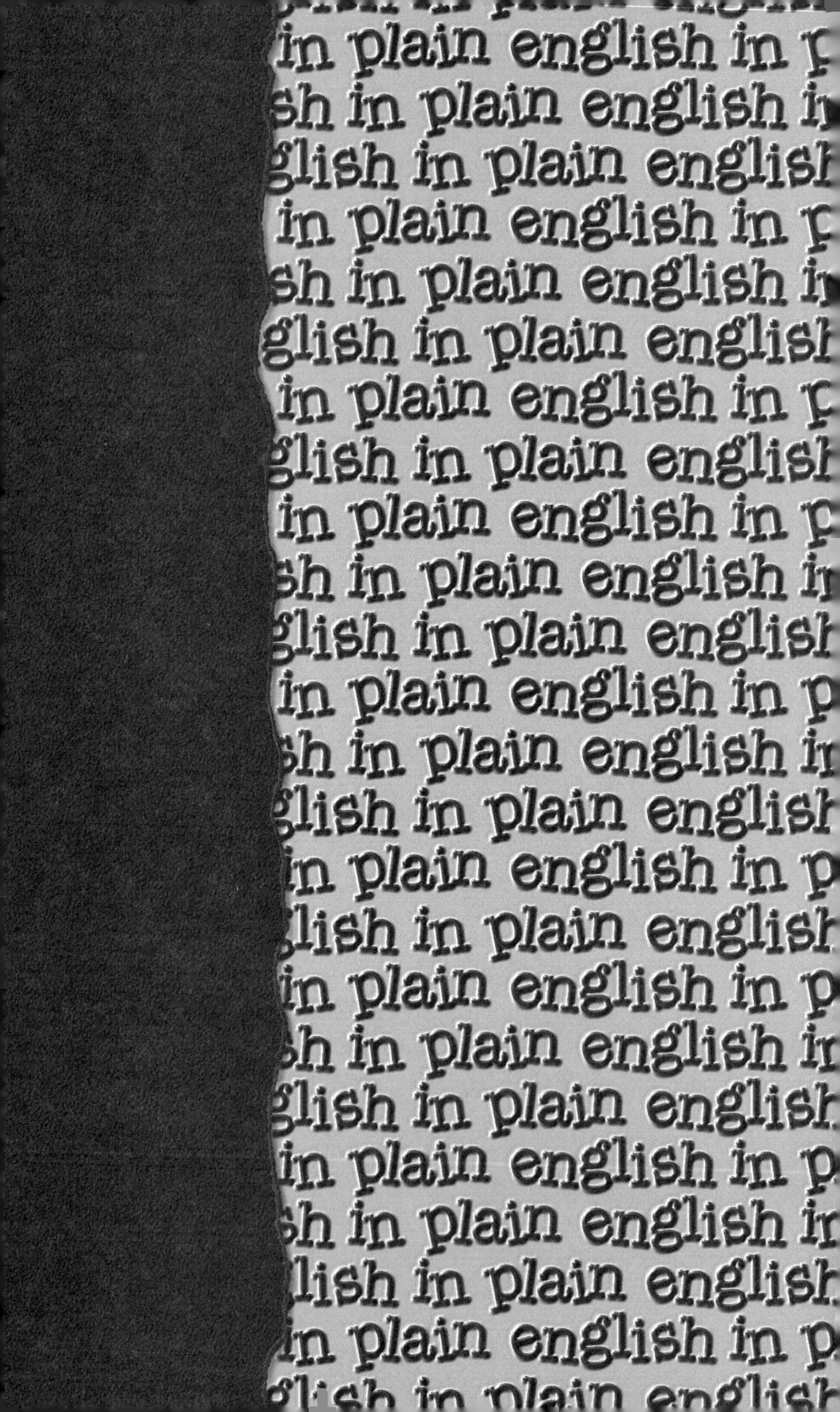
in plain english in plain english in plain english

Bibliography

If you've picked this book out from the shelves of your friendly community bookstore, you've already discovered that a *lot* of UNIX books are on the market. Most of them approach the subject on an advanced level geared to the needs of programmers and system administrators. Other titles are geared for specialized audiences that are just as small, relatively speakng (most UNIX users don't need guides on **sendmail** and Perl, for instance). If you take away those narrowly targeted titles and focus on the ones meant for the larger end-user community, you're left with a much smaller list. Of these, we recommend the following.

General Titles

- **Teach Yourself UNIX**, fourth edition. Kevin Reichard and Eric F. Johnson, IDG Books, 1999. This introduction to the UNIX operating system is designed as a companion to this book. Most of the commands listed in this work are more fully explained in **Teach Yourself UNIX**; the underlying concepts of UNIX are also explained in depth.

- **Unix: The Basics**. Kevin Reichard, IDG Books, 1998. This entry-level text covers the basic principles of UNIX on a level that anyone can understand.
- **Life with UNIX: A Guide for Everyone**. Don Libes and Sandy Ressler, Prentice Hall, 1989. A witty guide to UNIX, more interesting for its account of UNIX's development over the years. It's a little hard to find, but worth the effort.
- **UNIX System V Release 4: An Introduction for New and Experienced Users**. Kenneth Rosen, Richard Rosinski, and James Farber, Osborne McGraw-Hill, 1990. This 1,200-page guide to UNIX is the most thorough documentation of SVR4 in one volume.
- **UNIX in a Nutshell**. Daniel Gilly, O'Reilly & Associates, 1995. More than you ever wanted to learn about UNIX commands.
- **Learning the UNIX Operating System**. Jerry Peek, John Strang, and Grace Todino, O'Reilly & Associates, 1997.
- **Unix for Dummies**. John R. Levine, Margaret Levine Young, IDG Books, 1997.
- **More Unix for Dummies**. John R. Levine, Margaret Levine Young, IDG Books, 1995.
- **Unix for Dummies Quick Reference**. Margaret Levine Young, IDG Books, 1998.

Linux Titles

- **Linux in Plain English**. Patrick Volkerding and Kevin Reichard, MIS:Press, 1997. This book covers the Linux command set in some detail, although in the same general fashion as **UNIX in Plain English**.
- **Linux Configuration and Installation**, fourth edition. Patrick Volkerding, Kevin Reichard, and Eric Foster-Johnson, MIS:Press, 1998. This book covers the installation and configuration of Linux. Slackware Linux is included on an accompanying CD-ROM.

Programming Titles

- **UNIX Programming Tools**, Eric Foster-Johnson, M&T Books, 1997. Covers the commands for programming on UNIX in depth.
- **Advanced Programming in the Unix Environment**, W. Richard Stevens, Addison-Wesley, 1992. Considered to be the Bible of UNIX-programming texts.
- **UNIX Programming for Dummies**. James Edward Keogh, IDG Books, 1996.

Perl

- **Perl Modules**. Eric Foster-Johnson, IDG Books, 1998.
- **Perl Resource Kit: Unix Edition**. David Futato, Nathan Patwardhan, Clay Irving, Larry Wall, O'Reilly & Associates, 1997.
- **Programming Perl**. Larry Wall, Randal L. Schwartz, Tom Christiansen, Stephen Potter, O'Reilly & Associates, 1996.

Security

- **Practical Unix and Internet Security**. Simson Garfinkel and Gene Spafford, O'Reilly & Associates, 1995.

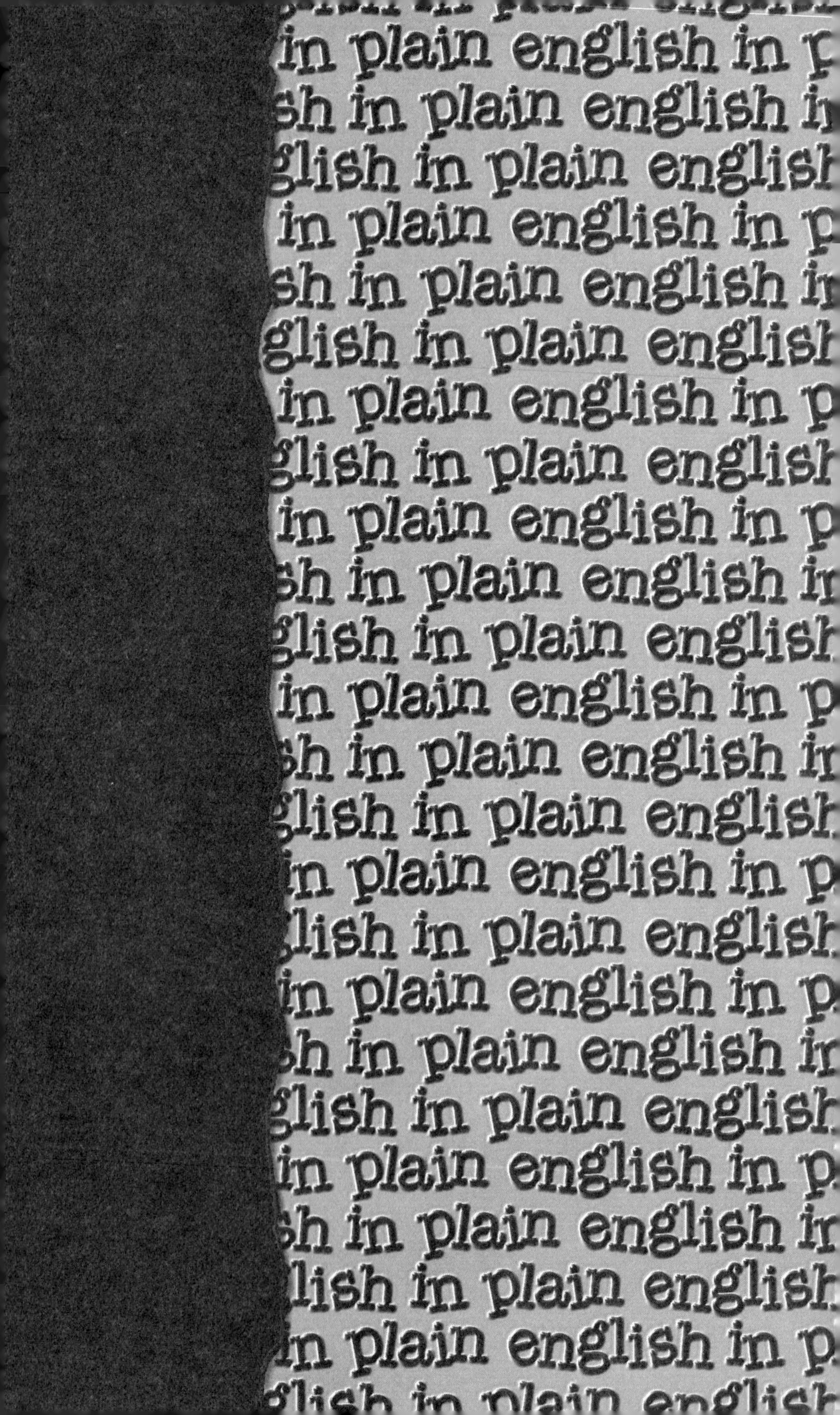
in plain english in p
sh in plain english in
glish in plain english
in plain english in p
sh in plain english in
glish in plain english
in plain english in p
glish in plain english
in plain english in p
sh in plain english in
glish in plain english
in plain english in p
sh in plain english in
glish in plain english
in plain english in p
glish in plain english
in plain english in p
sh in plain english in
glish in plain english
in plain english in p
sh in plain english in
glish in plain english
in plain english in p

Index

G

H

I

Continued

P

U

Continued